WBC GREATEST
FIGHTS OPUS

WBC GREATEST FIGHTS OPUS

OPUS

CONTENTS

TYSON FURY

It is an honour and a privilege to be asked to contribute the Foreword for The Greatest Fights Opus in my position as the WBC's Heavyweight Champion of the World.

To be honest I believe all three fights in my recently-concluded trilogy with Deontay Wilder deserve to be in this Opus and amongst the greatest of fights, which is why I am pleased to see that they are. The most recent fight - the third - is, in my opinion, one of the greatest fights of all time so it is perhaps fitting that I am here today writing this.

I said after that final fight that I did not want to be compared to those who came before me. I believe I am now, without any doubt, the best in my generation but, like you, I grew up watching other boxing greats ply their trade and would never want to disrespect them by making comparisons.

Of course you have the lighter weights and the likes of Sugar Ray Leonard and the four kings of the middleweight and super-middleweight divisions rightly featuring in this Opus, as well as Floyd Mayweather, Oscar De La Hoya, Manny Pacquiao and many others.

My real heroes were, though, my fellow heavyweights from another era. To relive some of the greatest heavyweight bouts of all time - Ali, Frazier, Foreman, Norton, Holmes, Tyson, Lewis - as we do in the Opus is a reminder to all of us of how much we owe them, and what warriors they all were.

We will never really know who was the greatest of them all and neither should we ask. They were all greats and I am happy to now be amongst them.

MAURICIO SULAIMÁN

HE WAS BORN INTO BOXING, KNOWS PERSONALLY ALL THE GREATS OF THE RECENT PAST AND PRESENT, HAS A THOUSAND STORIES TO TELL AND HAS A PASSION UNRIVALED FOR HIS SPORT. THE WBC PRESIDENT IS THE PERFECT FIT FOR THE ENORMOUS JOB HE FACES EACH DAY.

The President of the WBC was born – literally – to play a huge part in boxing. It was in the blood. It was in the family. It was the obvious and only thing to do.

Mauricio Sulaimán followed in the footsteps of his father, José, who was the former President of the world boxing governing body formulated in 1963, since December 5th, 1975, until his death in 2014.

At this point, Mauricio, son of José Sulaimán, was appointed by the Board of Governors of the WBC, for taking over the reins of the Green and Gold, this was completely unexpected, but, in truth, he had been prepared for this role from his earliest memories.

"I can't have been more than three years old and I remember hearing a strange noise downstairs in the house," Mauricio recalled. "I rushed down to discover two huge men talking to my father. One was Muhammad Ali and the other was Don King. The strange noise was Don King's laugh.

"Another time Sugar Ray Leonard had just lost to Roberto Durán and he flew to Mexico to see my father and get the rematch arranged. Sugar Ray was my hero. I remember getting back from school and seeing him sitting there. He smiled at me and showed me his biceps. I recall it as if it was yesterday.

"Then there was the time when I went to a fightto watch another one of my heroes, Carlos Zarate box against a Filipino called Fernando Cabanela. Zarate won and I jumped into the ring. My father went crazy because he thought I'd been lost. I remember gazing up at Zarateas Cabanela came over to congratulate him. A drop of blood fell from his face on to my jacket. I still have that jacket today in my closet. With the blood stain."

The WBC President has a thousand and one stories like these, but it is only possible because his father discovered the sport. "My father was born in a small town in the provinces, but he had friends who were boxers and he went to watch them fight one night," he explained. "He had no ticket so the only way he could pay was to fight in what they called an "appetizer" against another kid. When it was over he reckons he won because he managed to pick up more money thrown into the ring.

"After that, he was hooked. Once he had his nose and jaw broken, however, he got more involved in all aspects of the sport, especially when he moved to Mexico City. He'd tried everything, from ring announcer to publicity to becoming the "go-to guy." He'd already been on the local commission but moved to state and then finally national. The WBC had been created in 1963 but by the time my father became General Secretary he was spending so much time he had little left for running his business, a medical supply company.

"He was about to resign in 1975 at a congress in Tunisia but instead ended up mediating between members arguing with each other and this resulted in one of them announcing that my father would be the new President. He remained in that position until the day he died in 2014."

As a result, Mauricio also fell in love with boxing to the point that he wanted to become a fighter himself. "As a kid, while my friends wanted to be footballers, I just wanted to become a boxer. I'd play fight with myself and ask my father for names so that I could pretend to be fighting between two of them. Then the dream ended very quickly when I was taken to a fight involving another of my heroes, "Mantequilla" Napoles. It was a very bloody fight. Afterwards my father asked if I wanted to see Napoles. I went back to the dressing room and saw him lying down with both his eyes forced shut from punches and both eyebrows split open. That's when I told my father I wanted to be a fireman instead."

The memories keep flooding back for a man who so clearly loves his sport. The Zarate versus Cabanela fight he places in his all-time top three, although he stresses that this is a very personal and subjective choice.

"I think great fights can be defined by a combination of ingredients," he said. "Who are the fighters, what is their stature, where is the fight, what is the atmosphere like, what is the back story, are there two great champions or one superstar and the heir apparent, is it a great comeback story or an unlikely win for the underdog?

"Look at Sugar Ray coming back after four years to beat Marvin Hagler. He'd been such a hero of mine, the way he beat Hearns, the way he came back to avenge his defeat by Durán. I remember my father working hard with the Nevada State Commission to get the fight on after concerns about Ray's detached retina. People accused my father of being a potential murderer by helping Ray go and face the 'monster' that was Hagler. After Ray had won the fight at Caesars Palace my father was the very last person to leave the arena. He had a huge smile of satisfaction on his face."

The other fight that stands out for Mauricio is, by common consent, one of the greatest fights of all time but, once again, he provides a very personal take on the proceedings. "Julio César Chávez against Meldrick Taylor," he recalled. "Two undefeated champions, a unification bout, at the Las Vegas Hilton. I was watching it in my father's studio with 50 friends. Here was Chávez, 66 and 0, being overpowered by a younger, faster undefeated man and then Chávez knocked him down with two seconds to go. When we saw this happen we were jumping and screaming and my brother, Hector, punched an Encyclopedia Britannica with joy, shouting: "This is the moment I needed in my life for inspiration."

"I think the reason why I chose those fights is because I watched them all as a fan, not as the WBC President. Now it's very different. I have extreme responsibilities. I can't and don't have a favorite. I must respect every single boxer who fights under the WBC."

Muhammad Ali, of course, gets a special mention although, once again, Mauricio has two stories which to this day makes him laugh. "Muhammad was upstairs in the family house and wanted to pray. I was only twelve at the time and he asked me to fetch some towels for him. He then asked me which direction was Mecca in. I had no idea.

He then asked where the east was. I pointed and he prayed but later, when I told my mother, she said: "You idiot, that was the west!

"Another time we were at a congress and Muhammad and Mike Tyson were the two main stars, the legend and the current world champion. Muhammad told my father that it was Mike's time, and he should be looked after. My father asked me to take care of Muhammad. When Muhammad said he was hungry I grabbed some food for him. He thought it was delicious until he asked me what the food was, and I replied: "Pork." He spat it out. I didn't know, of course, but was so embarrassed. He put his hand on my shoulder, told me not to worry and prayed."

Tyson is another personal favorite of Mauricio's. "My father and I had and have a deep relationship with Mike," he added. "I first met him properly when he was alone at the bar at a big after fight party and I went up and started to talk to him. From that moment we became great friends. One time he came to Mexico and after days of having to attend meetings with people like my father and Don King he said: "Let's do something different." We arrived at his hotel, he went in surrounded by people and then ran back into the car, catching everyone unawares, and we drove off. We went to a bar and drank tequila until my brother, Hector, joined us and we went on to a disco. There were many couples in there and they all wanted to dance with him. He was so nice to everyone. Another time he climbed halfway up the Angel of Independence statue in Mexico City before attending his own press conference to announce the Razor Ruddock fight while I stood there holding his watch and jewellry."

His happiest memories revolve around his father, though. "After I graduated from school, I eventually became CEO of the family business and I wanted to be involved in the boxing, but my father insisted I stayed at the factory and looked after the business. Then he'd asked me for help. This went on and on and we were fighting with each other many times. One time Chávez was fighting at the Aztec Stadium and my father said I couldn't come. I told him that was it, I would never help him in boxing again. I went anyway, just as a fan. My father was standing in the ring, saw me and beckoned for me to join him with a huge smile. I shouted back: "No, I'm not in boxing anymore." He could not believe it. His smile turned into the saddest face I'd ever seen. I felt so bad I jumped into the ring and hugged my father as Chávez made his ring entrance."

The problem growing up with a father like José Sulaimán was the simple fact that as the WBC President he was often away. "There weren't cell phones, faxes or emails in those days so my father was always travelling in his role with the WBC. He was relentless, always working. He loved his photography, too, so wherever he went he'd take photos and send them back to us.

"Despite being committed so much to his work he was also very caring and loving, humble and kind who loved to hug you all the time. What he taught me was to never look down on anyone, nor look up to them but have the same amount of respect for all of them, and to give everyone the time of day. At the WBC we make a point of answering every single letter, email or call because you can't discriminate. We all began in one place."

He took over his father's role without any intention to do so. "My father fell ill after surgery in California and then passed away. I came back to Mexico and decided that my time as General Secretary at the WBC was over. At my father's burial ceremony thousands of people attending, including famous faces in boxing from all over the world. I told my mother I would be leaving boxing and she told me not to abandon my father's work. At the next Board of Governors, they elected me as President without even asking me if I wanted the job. I accepted it because boxing has been the saving of my family. I feel to this day that I am simply continuing my father's work."

Much has changed in boxing since the early, brutal days and the WBC has very much been at the forefront of this evolution. "Reducing the fights from 15 rounds to 12; social responsibility; changing the day of the weigh-in; putting the care and safety of the boxers as a priority, hence the changes in the gloves, ropes, the ring; the clean boxing program to ensure all our fighters are not taking any banned substances, however difficult it may have been on occasions; and much more. I am very proud of all these achievements."

What of the future for a sport that is continually challenged? "There are always new challenges and there always will be," Mauricio answered. "Amateur boxing at the Olympics is a concern now that AIBA has been expelled by the IOC. The new trend of influencers,

YouTubers and former champions setting up exhibition fights which are unauthorized and need to be better regulated. The changes to the boxing platforms.

"In ten years' time I hope there will be one world champion per weight division and that WBC shows will be staged all around the world on a daily basis with WBC merchandise available in every corner of the world. Most of all, I hope we continue to produce the greatest of fights."

The greatest? That is what this Opus is all about. For Mauricio Sulaimán the definition of this is simple."It is a moment in boxing or life that will live for eternity."

There have been plenty of these moments in the history of the WBC.

25 FEBRUARY 1964

LISTON
VS CLAY

WORLD HEAVYWEIGHT CHAMPIONSHIP
CONVENTION HALL, MIAMI BEACH, FLORIDA, U.S.A.

TALE OF THE TAPE

CHARLES L. LISTON	NAME	CASSIUS CLAY
THE BIG BEAR / SONNY	NICKNAME	THE LOUISVILLE LIP
SAND SLOUGH, ARKANSAS, U.S.A.	BIRTHPLACE	LOUISVILLE, KENTUCKY, U.S.A.
33	AGE	22
35—1—0	PRE-FIGHT RECORD	19—0—0
25	KO'S	15
6'1"	HEIGHT	6'3"
218 LBS	WEIGHT	210 LBS
84"	REACH	79"
ORTHODOX	STANCE	ORTHODOX

CONTROVERSIAL UNDERDOG

*IT WAS BEAUTY AGAINST THE BEAST, AND NOBODY
BELIEVED THE BEAST COULD GET BEAT. CASSIUS
CLAY HAD OTHER IDEAS AS THE LEGEND WAS BORN.*

Liston versus Clay one has gone down as one of the most controversial fights in the history of boxing. The build-up saw a young, brash Clay (as he was called then) come into the fight on a record of 19-0 but given, with odds of 7-1 against in a two-horse race, next to no chance by the pundits, press or fellow fighters against the world champion many saw as one of the hardest-hitting ever and virtually unbeatable.

Yet there were a few chinks in Liston's so-called impenetrable armor. For a start nobody knew for sure his age, and rumor suggested he was much older than the 32 years old he stated. He suffered from bursitis in his shoulder, took cortisone as a result, and with three, first-round knockouts in his previous three fights, had less than six minutes ring experience in the past 35 months.

Moreover Liston trained lightly, not taking Clay to be a serious threat whilst Clay, for all his public utterances mocking his more experienced opponent, studied hours and hours of tapes of Liston's fights and detected how the defending champion telegraphed his punches with eye movement.

Certainly neither boxer were popular at the time. One respected American writer said: "180 million Americans will be rooting for a double knockout."

At the weigh-in Clay resorted to almost crazed antics and had to be calmed down by his entourage. He shouted: "You're scared, chump," to Liston but admitted later: "I won't lie, I was scared. It frightened me knowing how hard he hit. But I didn't have no choice but to go out and fight."

The fear soon left him after his superior speed and movement forced numerous lunges and missed punches from Liston in the early stages of the fight. In the third Clay's incessant jabs caused bruising under Liston's right eye, and a cut under his left that would require eight stitches. As they walked back to their corners Clay shouted: "You big sucko, I got you now."

At the end of the fourth Clay was seconds away from being disqualified by referee Barney Felix after his eyes were burning up amid claims of foul play. Later it appeared lotion used on Liston's cut splashed into Clay's eyes during the round. It took Clay all of the fifth to recover, a round in which he mainly evaded a tiring Liston, but in the sixth he dominated the champion.

Bouncing up and down on the soles of his feet Clay was up and ready for the start of the seventh but opposite him Liston remained stuck to his stool. Moments later he spat his mouthguard out on to the canvas and declared: "That's it." Afterwards some suggested Liston's injured shoulder was all but paralyzed from the fight.

It made no difference to Clay. He had just pulled off one of the all-time upsets in boxing and shouted to anyone who cared to listen: "I'm the Greatest" and "I shook up the world."

Indeed he did. It would begin a remarkable career - perhaps the most remarkable in boxing - and pave the way for a rematch exactly one year later

"LOOK AT ME. NOT A MARK ON ME. I COULD NEVER BE AN UNDERDOG. I'M TOO GREAT. HAIL THE CHAMPION!... EAT YOUR WORDS, I'M THE GREATEST!... I SHOOK UP THE WORLD."

CASSIUS CLAY

21 MAY 1966

ALI vs COOPER II

WORLD HEAVYWEIGHT CHAMPIONSHIP
ARSENAL STADIUM, HIGHBURY, LONDON, ENGLAND, U.K.

TALE OF THE TAPE

MUHAMMAD ALI	NAME	HENRY COOPER
THE GREATEST	NICKNAME	OUR HENRY
LOUISVILLE, KENTUCKY, U.S.A.	BIRTHPLACE	BELLINGHAM, LONDON, U.K.
24	AGE	32
23—0—0	PRE-FIGHT RECORD	33—11—1
18	KO'S	23
6'3"	HEIGHT	6'1.5"
202 LBS	WEIGHT	188 LBS
78"	REACH	75"
ORTHODOX	STANCE	ORTHODOX

BLOOD-SOAKED REMATCH

A FAMOUS REMATCH AFTER THE FAMOUS ORIGINAL, BUT CLAY
HAD BECOME ALI AND HAD LEARNED TOO MUCH FROM THE
FIRST FIGHT AGAINST A BLOODIED AND BRAVE ENGLISHMAN.

The context of this much-anticipated clash made this second meeting between the now Muhammad Ali and Britain's Henry Cooper a sporting event of enormous interest. Back in 1963 the then Cassius Clay came to London for the first time and was floored by Cooper's famed left hook in the 4th round in front of a live, open air audience of 35,000 at Wembley Stadium. Saved by the knockdown occurring seconds before the end of the round, and the cushioning of the ropes, a disorientated Clay staggered to his corner. In what went down in boxing folklore Clay's glove had been split - some say purposefully to allow more time for him to recover - and in the following round the fight was stopped after a cut saw Cooper bleeding profusely enough for the referee to step in.

Even in defeat Cooper became a national celebrity overnight and by the time the rematch took place three years later Clay had become Ali and was world champion, on the back of his shock win over Sonny Liston and subsequent defenses against Liston, Floyd Patterson and George Chuvalo.

As a result of all this 46,000 packed into the home stadium of Arsenal Football Club at Highbury in London in the hope that they would see their local hero be crowned the new world champion, a new record for a live audience at a British boxing event and one that would last until 2007 when Joe Calzaghe fought Mikkel Kessler. One of the earlier experiments with Pay Per View also resulted in 16 cinemas screening the fight in the UK grossing $1.5M (nearly $12M today with inflation). It was recorded and aired later on the BBC to a 21M audience and broadcast live back in America to 20M viewers via satellite.

Prior to the first fight Clay had delivered his customary mocking comments about his opponent, but afterwards was full of respect for the brave British fighter. Nonetheless, with contrasting records of 23 and 0 compared to 33 and 11, Ali returned to London as the firm favorite.

The champ's intelligence soon became apparent. Cooper may not have had the best record but Ali found him awkward in their first match, and equally as awkward in their second. The difference was he had a plan which he followed to the tee. Gripping Cooper when close, and then jumping out of the Cooper reach when separated, appeared to be a much safer policy, but it was still a tight affair that saw Ali complain openly to the referee as Cooper cut off the ring landing a flurry of punches to the kidney.

It might have gone down as an epic, and maybe even an upset of enormous proportions, but Cooper's one weakness - his penchant for being cut - reared its ugly head again in the 6th round. Ali caught his plucky opponent with a quick right hander that sliced open the British fighter's left eyebrow and blood began to gush from the open wound. Knowing his time was almost up Cooper attempted to finish it but was hit by an Ali counter-attack that gave the referee no option but to inspect the Cooper wound and end the fight.

"He's a quick learner," Cooper said afterwards. "Whenever I got close to him he held me. It was like being in a vice."

Ali was uncharacteristically respectful afterwards, too, stating that he had never faced a braver man nor a more difficult opponent. He would, as time would pass, face stiffer challenges than this.

"HE WAS ABOVE ANY HEAVYWEIGHT. HE DID THINGS THAT NOBODY ELSE COULD DO."

HENRY COOPER

22 JANUARY 1973

FRAZIER vs
FOREMAN

WORLD HEAVYWEIGHT CHAMPIONSHIP
INDEPENDENCE PARK, KINGSTON, JAMAICA

TALE OF THE TAPE

JOE FRAZIER	NAME	GEORGE FOREMAN
SMOKIN' JOE	NICKNAME	BIG GEORGE
BEAUFORT, SOUTH CAROLINA, U.S.A.	BIRTHPLACE	MARSHALL, TEXAS, U.S.A.
29	AGE	24
29–0–0	PRE-FIGHT RECORD	37–0–0
25	KO'S	34
5'11"	HEIGHT	6'3"
214 LBS	WEIGHT	217.5 LBS
72.9"	REACH	78.3"
ORTHODOX	STANCE	ORTHODOX

THE SUNSHINE SHOWDOWN

THIS WAS THE FIGHT WHEN GEORGE FOREMAN REALLY ANNOUNCED HIMSELF ON THE WORLD STAGE. NOBODY HAD EVER DONE OR WOULD EVER REPEAT THE BEATING HE HANDED OUT TO 'SMOKIN' JOE'.

Dubbed as 'The Sunshine Showdown' because of its Jamaican venue, this heavyweight clash of heavyweights saw two of the all-time greats get it on with one of the most devastating conclusions. Joe Frazier was the undisputed champion of the world after beating Muhammad Ali in their first encounter and then successfully overseeing two defenses of his title. Entering his 30th professional fight he had never tasted defeat.

Neither had his powerful opponent, however, who was taller, heavier and younger. George Foreman had dismissed 37 heavyweights facing him in just four years, 18 by a clean knockout and a further 15 by Technical Knockout.

His power and punching prowess had catapulted him to being the number one contender but he was up against a man who had one of the biggest hearts in boxing.

It was a contrast in size and style but promised to be a compelling battle. In reality it was anything but.

Inside two minutes of the first round Foreman had the champion on the canvas after a series of punches that culminated in a brutal right uppercut. Stunned, Frazier rose to his feet but sank to his knees again with 17 seconds remaining of the round after being caught full on with a left uppercut. Amazingly, there was still time for Frazier to go down for a third time in the first round when a combination from Foreman resulted in the smaller man on his back staring up to the heavens.

During the break there was consternation in the large crowd and in the ringside press. Foreman's punching was already well-known but nobody expected such an opening round against a man who had traded blows with Ali for 15 rounds and emerged the victor just three fights previously.

Frazier had already revealed his refusal-to-quit mentality by three times rising from the floor but surely there was no way back from this? Indeed, there was not.

Moments into the second round Foreman had his man down again following a vicious overhand right. Frazier had barely got to his feet and been allowed to continue when he was back down again for a fifth time.

Still the fight continued, but not for long. After one minute, 35 seconds of the second round a powerful right dropped the defending champion for an astonishing sixth time. Angelo Dundee, Ali's trainer who was at ringside on a scouting mission, had seen enough, shouting at the referee to stop the bout.

His wishes were met. Referee Arthur Mercante Sr agreed and brought proceedings to an abrupt halt.

Frazier would never be world champion again and Foreman would later be part of one of the greatest fights of all time and upsets when he faced Ali in the 'Rumble in the Jungle'. The pair managed a rematch in 1976 and although Frazier was more competitive, Foreman would still send him crashing down twice before it would end with a Technical Knockout in the fifth round. "People often talk about how Joe Frazier was knocked down six times in that fight," Foreman would say later. "But the amazing thing is he got up six times. I'd never seen anything like it. He was the toughest fighter of my era."

"PEOPLE OFTEN TALK ABOUT HOW JOE FRAZIER WAS KNOCKED DOWN SIX TIMES IN THAT FIGHT, BUT THE AMAZING THING IS, HE GOT UP SIX TIMES. I'D NEVER SEEN ANYTHING LIKE IT. I WAS THINKING TO MYSELF, IF THEY DON'T HURRY UP AND STOP THIS FIGHT, THEN HE'S GONNA GET ME."

GEORGE FOREMAN

8 MARCH 1971

FRAZIER
VS ALI

WORLD HEAVYWEIGHT CHAMPIONSHIP
MADISON SQUARE GARDEN, NEW YORK CITY, NEW YORK, U.S.A.

TALE OF THE TAPE

JOE FRAZIER	NAME	MUHAMMAD ALI
SMOKIN' JOE	NICKNAME	THE GREATEST
BEAUFORT, SOUTH CAROLINA, U.S.A.	BIRTHPLACE	LOUISVILLE, KENTUCKY, U.S.A.
27	AGE	29
26—0—0	PRE-FIGHT RECORD	31—0—0
23	KO'S	25
5'11.5"	HEIGHT	6'3"
205 LBS	WEIGHT	215 LBS
73"	REACH	78"
ORTHODOX	STANCE	ORTHODOX

FIGHT OF THE CENTURY

THE FORMER WORLD CHAMPION, STRIPPED OF HIS TITLE AND UNBEATEN, AGAINST THE NEW WORLD CHAMPION. THIS WOULD GO DOWN AS AN EPIC AND A CLASSIC START TO THE MOST FAMOUS BOXING TRILOGY OF THE LOT.

The build up to what was dubbed the 'Fight of the Century' made this first ever encounter between two unbeaten heavyweights fighting for the world championships compelling. Ali had been stripped of his title in 1967 for refusing to fight in the Vietnam War and, with his license returned as opinion had wavered had secured two unconvincing wins before facing a man recognized by the boxing authorities as world heavyweight champion with two major belts to his name. It became a match between Ali, representing the left, anti-war establishment and Frazier, on the side of the conservative, pro-war faction.

As a result the iconic Madison Square Garden was, with a crowd of 20,455, so sold out that Frank Sinatra, in a desperate attempt to be ringside, took photos for Life Magazine. Hollywood superstar Burt Lancaster, meanwhile, would serve as the color commentator for the closed circuit TV broadcast. Both fighters would be paid $2.5M while the fight was screened to 50 countries in 12 different languages to a global audience of 300 million.

Ali seemed to forget how Frazier had spoken in his defense during his enforced exile, goading the champion by referring to him as "Uncle Tom" and "the white man's champion."

If he wanted to rile his opponent he succeeded. "He betrayed my friendship," Frazier responded. "I sat down and I said to myself: "I'm gonna kill him." Simple as that. I'm gonna kill him."

The clash would live up to all expectations. Ali dominated in the first two rounds with his jabs but Frazier hit back in the next two with his pounding left hook and body shots. Ali, clearly ring-rusty after his long lay-off appeared tired after the sixth round and almost went down in the eighth after a crunching left hook found his jaw. In the 11th he did after receiving another left hook and then slipping on water in Frazier's corner, placing both hands and his right knee on the canvas. The experienced referee, Arthur Mercante Sr, shouted "no knockdown" and waved for the fight to continue.

Many at ringside had it fairly even up to this point but for the remaining four rounds Frazier took control. Mercante would later say: "They both threw some of the best punches I've ever seen." The problem for Ali was that it was Frazier who repeatedly found his target as the bout reached its denouement. Finally, in the 15th and last round, Frazier sent Ali crashing to the canvas after another jolting left hook. This time there was no debate about it. This was the only the third time Ali had ever been knocked down and it confirmed what those packed into the Garden already knew. He rose to his feet and lasted until the final bell but Frazier had done more than enough to win and inflict Ali's first professional defeat.

For once Ali had nothing to say as Frazier screamed in the ring: "I kicked your ass."

Later he refused to publicly admit defeat, saying it had been a white man's conspiracy, but Frazier would enjoy what turned out to be his greatest victory in the ring.

It would prove to be one of the most intense and epic rivalries in the history of boxing to be played out over a trilogy of fights that have entered the annals of sport, and it was Frazier who took first blood.

"I ALWAYS KNEW WHO THE CHAMPION WAS."

JOE FRAZIER

6 APRIL 1987

HAGLER vs
LEONARD

WORLD MIDDLEWEIGHT CHAMPIONSHIP
CAESARS PALACE, LAS VEGAS, NEVADA, U.S.A.

TALE OF THE TAPE

MARVIN HAGLER	NAME	RAY LEONARD
MARVELOUS	NICKNAME	SUGAR
NEWARK, NEW JERSEY, U.S.A.	BIRTHPLACE	WILMINGTON, NORTH CAROLINA, U.S.A.
32	AGE	30
62—2—2	PRE-FIGHT RECORD	37—0—1
52	KO'S	24
5'9.5"	HEIGHT	5'10"
159 LBS	WEIGHT	158 LBS
75"	REACH	74"
SOUTHPAW	STANCE	ORTHODOX

THE SUPER FIGHT

THOUGHT TO BE LEONARD'S GREATEST CHALLENGE AFTER EMERGING
FROM RETIREMENT TO TAKE ON THE SEEMINGLY UNBEATABLE HAGLER.
ANOTHER FIGHT AND RESULT TO GO DOWN IN BOXING FOLKLORE.

In truth both these giants of boxing were past their best, but it did not seem to matter one iota to the sport, to the fans and to the high-rollers that invaded Las Vegas to watch this still mouth-watering battle billed as 'The Super Fight' in an open air arena constructed outside Caesars Palace.

On the face of it Hagler was the overwhelming favorite. Leonard had fought once in the preceding five years, having retired first in 1982 and then again in 1984 after what he felt was a below-standard win over Kevin Howard. He'd also had surgery on a detached retina and was moving up a weight to middleweight, the division Hagler had reigned supremely in since 1980. But Leonard knew what he was doing from the moment he was at ringside one year earlier and encouraged enough observing Hagler struggle to see off John Mugabi to challenge him to a showdown.

In fact he was even prepared to take a million dollars less than Hagler, at a still sensational $11M, and even less in the extras, but under three conditions that would prove to be crucial.

First, the ring would be 22 foot by 22 foot, larger than usual. Second the gloves would weigh ten ounces, not the usual eight. And third, the fight would be 12 rounds long, not 15.

All three terms were designed to be in Leonard's favor, with more space to evade Hagler's dangerous attacks, heavier gloves to help negate Hagler's power, and less time for Leonard to be subjected to his opponent's punches.

"I know exactly what it takes to beat this man," he announced just prior to the fight. It turned out he did, but only just.

The fight would prove to be as controversial as the interest in it. Hagler began with an orthodox stance, rather than his usual southpaw. It was a decision that would cost him, crucially, the first two rounds. At the start of the third round he switched to southpaw but from that point onwards needed to play catch-up.

In what proved to be the classic fighter (Hagler) versus boxer (Leonard) encounter, Hagler was consistently the aggressor, whilst Leonard would dance and dodge, landing a punch then stepping back, before hitting out with a flurry of punches in the final minute in an attempt to steal the round. In the process Leonard would land 306 of his 629 punches (49%) to Hagler's 291 out of 792 (37%). There was little doubt that Leonard edged the first six rounds in this cat and mouse affair, and Hagler the second half. Finally, in the 12th and last round, Hagler had his opponent on the ropes as they went toe-to-toe, but the defending champion could not close it out and Leonard danced his way out of the corner accompanied by the cheers of the crowd.

The final decision caused a fair degree of consternation. Two of the judges had it at 115-113 (7 rounds to 5) in each boxer's favor, but the third judge, Jojo Guerra, gave it to Leonard by 118-110 (10 rounds to 2). In what was seen to be an incredibly tight affair, that final scorecard has been debated ever since.

It would prove to be Hagler's last fight. He demanded a rematch but by the time Leonard granted it, three years later, he was long retired. As for Sugar Ray, this unlikely win made him the tenth boxer in his sport's history to win world titles at three different weights.

"EVEN THOUGH THE OUTCOME WASN'T THE WAY IT SHOULD HAVE BEEN, PUBLICLY I STILL FEEL IN MY HEART I WON THE FIGHT."

MARVIN HAGLER

12

15 SEPTEMBER 2018

ÁLVAREZ *vs*
GOLOVKIN II

WORLD MIDDLEWEIGHT CHAMPIONSHIP
T-MOBILE ARENA, LAS VEGAS, NEVADA, U.S.A.

TALE OF THE TAPE

SAUL ÁLVAREZ	NAME	GENNADIY GOLOVKIN
CANELO	NICKNAME	GGG
GUADALAJARA, JALISCO, MEXICO	BIRTHPLACE	KARAGANDA, KAZAKHSTAN
28	AGE	36
49—1—2	PRE-FIGHT RECORD	38—0—1
34	KO'S	34
5'8"	HEIGHT	5'10.5"
159 LBS	WEIGHT	160 LBS
70.5"	REACH	70"
ORTHODOX	STANCE	ORTHODOX

SUPREMACY II

TAKE TWO AND ANOTHER ENTHRALLING FIGHT WITH NOTHING BETWEEN THEM ONCE AGAIN AT THE END. THERE WAS A WINNER AND A LOSER THIS TIME, HOWEVER, AND A RESULT WHICH WAS FAR FROM UNIVERSALLY AGREED.

The world's top two middleweights would meet again following their controversial draw the previous September at the same venue. If ever there was the case for a rematch this second meeting between the defending champion, Golovkin, and the heir to his throne, 'Canelo', was it, and once again the fans would not be disappointed.

It should have taken place in May but for a doping suspension meted out to the Mexican.

This only served to grow the tension between the pair, with 'Canelo' noticeably aggressive at the weigh in.

He took this aggression into the fight, too, where he was far more offensive in his tactics early on compared to their first meeting.

After a cautious first round from both fighters 'Canelo' took early control, taking the next two rounds with his power punches that, surprisingly gained him the edge over the more powerful man from Kazakhstan.

Although Golovkin tried to employ his renowned jab Álvarez mainly eluded it and countered with a series of hard-hitting body blows. Indeed, the final fight stats showed 46 landed body blows from the Mexican challenger and just six from Golovkin.

The champion stepped it up in rounds four and five, landing more punches than his opponent, but 'Canelo' replied with interest in the next three rounds, buoyed by the largely Latin fans making up most of the 22,000 packed inside the T-Mobile Arena.

Golovkin was staring at his first professional defeat at this point, but 'Canelo' was beginning to tire and the champion remained strong. Rounds nine to eleven went to the man from Kazakhstan as his incredible fitness came to the fore.

The tenth round would prove especially difficult for Álvarez. Twice he was visibly hurt and by the end a large cut had appeared above his right eye.

Golovkin was not unmarked either, sporting a cut above his right eye and a large swelling below it.

As the two warriors rose from their stools for the final round both realized the fight was still up for grabs. All three judges had 'Canelo' 105-104 ahead.

Both fighters went for it to try and finish it off. 'Canelo' had earlier predicted that he would knock Golovkin out. This was something no professional boxer had ever achieved, of course, and not even the Mexican could fulfill this prophecy.

The final round turned into a slugfest. Many felt Golovkin had edged it but two out of the three judges saw it the other way.

In doing so it meant that when the final bell tolled Álvarez was judged the winner by a split decision: 115-113, 115-113, 114-114.

If just one of the other two judges had given that final round to Golovkin the fight would have ended up a second, successive draw.

The beaten champion was far from happy with the verdict and stormed out of the ring to receive some stitches for his eye wound.

Later he was a little more collected in his thoughts. "The victory belongs to 'Canelo', according to the judges" he said. "I thought it was a very good fight for the fans and very exciting. I also thought I fought better than he did."

Álvarez was understandably the happier of the two. "I feel satisfied because it was difficult, but I gave a great fight," he explained. "It was a great victory for Mexico. I am a great fighter and I showed it tonight."

Indeed he did although, in the time-honored tradition of boxing, it still left many debating whether it had been the correct result.

"WE HAD A GREAT FIGHT, THE ONE WE EXPECTED THE FIRST TIME AROUND. I HAD IT CLOSE GOING INTO THE 12TH ROUND. WE HAD GOOD JUDGES WHO SAW IT FROM DIFFERENT ANGLES — I CAN'T COMPLAIN ABOUT THE DECISION. 'CANELO' FOUGHT A GREAT FIGHT."

ABEL SANCHEZ

28 SEPTEMBER 1976

ALI vs
NORTON III

WORLD HEAVYWEIGHT CHAMPIONSHIP
YANKEE STADIUM, BRONX, NEW YORK, U.S.A.

TALE OF THE TAPE

MUHAMMAD ALI	NAME	KEN NORTON
THE GREATEST	NICKNAME	THE BLACK HERCULES / THE JAW BREAKER / THE FIGHTING MARINE
LOUISVILLE, KENTUCKY, U.S.A.	BIRTHPLACE	JACKSONVILLE, ILLINOIS, U.S.A.
34	AGE	33
52—2—0	PRE-FIGHT RECORD	37—3—0
37	KO'S	30
6'3"	HEIGHT	6'3"
221 LBS	WEIGHT	218 LBS
78"	REACH	80"
ORTHODOX	STANCE	ORTHODOX

GREATEST VS JAW BREAKER

BY HIS OWN ADMISSION MUHAMMAD ALI FOUND KEN NORTON TO BE HIS
TOUGHEST OPPONENT AND THIS WAS PROVED FOR THE THIRD TIME IN THEIR
TRILOGY AS A FADING ALI SCRAPED THROUGH AGAINST RINGSIDE OPINION.

The last fight ever to be staged at the old Yankee Stadium proved to be one of the most controversial in the history of boxing's heavyweight division and a result that, to this day, rages heated debate.

It would be the third and final meeting in the trilogy between Muhammad Ali and Ken Norton, a man who in another era could have dominated his division had he not found himself competing against Ali, Foreman and Frazier. Norton had won the first bout, just, in a tight, points decision, in a fight where Ali had his jaw broken in the first round but went the distance. At the time it proved to be a tremendous upset. Ali, determined to salvage his name and career won the rematch just six months later, although many observers had it either too tight to call or Norton shading it.

A further three years would pass before they concluded unfinished business, and in that time Ali had beaten both Foreman in the 'Rumble in the Jungle' and Frazier in that bruising 'Thrilla in Manilla'. He was probably the most famous human on the planet, but the intervening three years had worn him down and it would be plain to see during this final encounter that the defending champion was a shadow of his former self.

Still, the interest was such that Ali received the richest payday in history at the time, a cool $6M. Beforehand he was his usual confident self. "I'll knock the sucker out inside five rounds," he predicted. On the evidence of the first two fights not even Ali could have believed this, not least because he found Norton's unorthodox style - jabs from below and crossing his hands in defense - difficult to master.

Thus it would be the same again in this third encounter. In what was a closely-fought tussle Ali failed to land his punches, appeared sluggish and tired in the ring, and to all at ringside appeared to be behind as the 15th and final round approached.

It was then that Norton - or rather his corner - made their only mistake. But it would prove to be crucial. Referee Arthur Mercante takes up the story. It all went down to the last round," reported the sought-after adjudicator. "I went to Ali's corner and Dundee was screaming at him to fight like hell. I went to Norton's corner and they were telling him he had the fight won and to just move."

So whilst Norton tried to stay out of trouble Ali fought as his life and career rested on the next three minutes, dominating the first two to an extent that when the split decision came in Ali, somehow, had sneaked home with a close, unanimous decision.

The stats begged to differ. Ali landed 199 of his 709 punches (28 %) whereas Norton succeeded with 286 of his 635 punches (45 %).

"I won at least nine or ten rounds," an embittered Norton said afterwards.

A month later Ali made an astonishing admission. "Kenny's style is too difficult for me," he said. "I cannot beat him and I sure don't want to fight him again. I honestly thought he beat me in the Yankee Stadium, but the judges gave it to me and I am grateful to them."

In later years they would become close friends. But Ken Norton went to his grave convinced he had won all three of the famed trilogy.

"I WAS TOLD BY MY TRAINER, AT THE TIME WHICH WAS BILL SLAYTON, THAT I WAS AHEAD ON POINTS. HE SAID DON'T GO OUT AND GET CUT, DON'T GO OUT AND GET HURT, JUST GO OUT AND CONTROL THE ROUND AND WATCH YOURSELF AND BE CAREFUL. I WENT OUT AND THOUGHT I DID ENOUGH TO HAVE A DRAW IN THAT ROUND."

KEN NORTON

15 FEBRUARY 1978

ALI vs SPINKS

WORLD HEAVYWEIGHT CHAMPIONSHIP
HILTON HOTEL, LAS VEGAS, NEVADA, U.S.A.

TALE OF THE TAPE

MUHAMMAD ALI	NAME	LEON SPINKS
THE GREATEST	NICKNAME	NEON LEON
LOUISVILLE, KENTUCKY, U.S.A.	BIRTHPLACE	ST. LOUIS, MISSOURI, U.S.A.
36	AGE	25
55—2—0	PRE-FIGHT RECORD	6—0—1
37	KO'S	5
6'3"	HEIGHT	6'1"
224 LBS	WEIGHT	197 LBS
78"	REACH	76"
ORTHODOX	STANCE	ORTHODOX

UPSET OF THE YEAR

IT WOULD GO DOWN AS ONE OF THE GREATEST SHOCKS IN THE HISTORY OF BOXING AND YET ANOTHER EXAMPLE OF HOW TAKING AN OPPONENT LIGHTLY IN THE HEAVYWEIGHT DIVISION CAN SPELL DISASTER.

On the face of it this should have been a mis-match. Muhammad Ali, 'The Greatest', against the most inexperienced world title challenger ever with just seven professional bouts under his belt. No wonder the bookmakers had him down as the 10-1 underdog. And no wonder the purses reflected this imbalance. Ali earned $3.5M whereas Spinks a 'mere' $320,000.

But dig a little deeper and one of the all-time shocks in the history of boxing is easier to explain. It was not just that Ali was 36, but that in the previous few years he had experienced wars in the ring with Joe Frazier, Ken Norton and Earnie Shavers.

He needed an easy fight and believed he had secured one with the man who won the 1976 Olympic light-heavyweight gold medal. Such was his disinterest in the fight that he trained lightly and could not even be bothered to utter his customary pre-fight insults and predictions.

On the night both fighters played their respective roles. Ali entered to the sound of 'Land of Hope and Glory' while his challenger applauded his hero.

But as soon as the fight began the roles were immediately reversed. Ali resorted to his 'rope-a-dope' tactics that had served him so well four years previously against George Foreman in the 'Rumble in the Jungle'. It worked then but it had not worked so well subsequently and against the younger, fitter, honed Spinks the somewhat fleshy Ali became target practice.

As a result Spinks dominated his illustrious opponent virtually from start to finish in terms of aggression, accuracy and punches. Nobody in the whole of Ali's career had landed anything close to the 419 punches Spinks managed during this shock reversal.

Realizing that he was in trouble Ali rallied to produce a big tenth round. He knew that Spinks had never fought more than ten rounds in his career whilst Ali had gone the full 15 rounds on ten occasions.

But Ali was old, tired and beaten up, whilst Spinks was young, fitter and hungrier, and Ali's brief glimmer of a revival faded. What also went against him was that the referee, Davey Pearl, refused to allow Ali to get away with his usual, and illegal, tactic, of holding. It gave him no recovery time and Spinks the freedom to hit his target.

The 15th and last round was a classic as Ali threw everything he had left in his arsenal at Spinks but it was the huge underdog who closed out the round, and the fight, well enough to be crowned the new undisputed world heavyweight champion.

It still took a split decision, which surprised everyone at the time, and meant that Spinks became the first challenger to win the heavyweight crown since James Braddock achieved this feat against Max Baer in 1935.

"I'm the latest but he's the greatest," pronounced a still admiring Spinks afterwards.

"I let him rob my home when I was out to lunch," a philosophical Ali responded. "Winning the championship two times is rough. Only me and Floyd Patterson have done it. If I win it a third time I think I'll establish a record that won't be broken in a thousand years." This is precisely what would happen seven months later in the rematch.

"I WAS VERY SERIOUS DURING THE FIGHT... HE KEPT SAYING THINGS TO ME, TRYING TO MAKE ME MAD, BUT ALL HE DID WAS MAKE ME LAUGH. IT WAS LIKE HE WAS TELLING ME JOKES. ONE TIME HE CALLED ME A DIRTY NAME. I SAID, 'OH, ALI, HOW COULD YOU SAY SUCH A THING?' CAN YOU IMAGINE YOUR IDOL CALLING YOU A DIRTY NAME?"

KEN NORTON

26 MARCH 1996

BRUNO vs
TYSON II

WORLD HEAVYWEIGHT CHAMPIONSHIP
MGM GRAND GARDEN ARENA, LAS VEGAS, NEVADA, U.S.A.

TALE OF THE TAPE

FRANK BRUNO	NAME	MIKE TYSON
TRUE BRIT	NICKNAME	IRON MIKE
LONDON, ENGLAND, U.K.	BIRTHPLACE	BROOKLYN, NEW YORK, U.S.A.
34	AGE	29
40—4—0	PRE-FIGHT RECORD	43—1—0
38	KO'S	37
6'3"	HEIGHT	5'10"
247 LBS	WEIGHT	220 LBS
82"	REACH	71"
ORTHODOX	STANCE	ORTHODOX

THE CHAMPIONSHIP - PART 1

THE REMATCH WAS AS BRUTAL AS ITS PREDECESSOR AS THE NEWLY-CROWNED BRITISH WORLD CHAMPION FOUND THE HUNGRY AMERICAN TOO HOT TO HANDLE AS ONE CAREER ENDED AND ANOTHER REBORN.

It took Frank Bruno almost all of his professional career to finally achieve his dream of becoming world champion. Three times previously he had challenged and lost, including to Mike Tyson in his pomp in 1989 in five, bruising rounds. Eventually, in a triumph of perseverance, the popular British heavyweight reached his goal in his fourth attempt, beating Oliver McCall to become the WBC's new champion of the world.

Unfortunately for Bruno, his first defense of the title would be against a brooding Tyson, two wins into his comeback after a three year absence. Promoter Don King had already arranged for the winner of the McCall-Bruno bout to defend their title next against still the biggest name in boxing, and that is why big Frank found himself in Las Vegas hoping that time away from the ring had diluted Tyson's desire and power.

On both counts this would prove not to be the case. In fact, unusually for a title fight featuring a champion and a challenger, it was the challenger who was firm favorite to win, and the challenger who took home $30M compared to Bruno's moderate $5M.

From the first bell Tyson took the fight to Bruno, and at no point eased off. The American unlashed a series of booming overhand right-handers that had Bruno in immediate trouble and all the British fighter could do was to grapple with his smaller, lighter opponent in the hope of delaying what soon became the inevitable. In the final 30 seconds of the first round they went toe-to-toe, exchanging punches as another Tyson right staggered Bruno, leaving a cut just above his left eyebrow.

Round two was a repeat of the first, with Tyson hunting down his opponent while Bruno threw a few punches in defense but mainly tried to hold on to his adversary to slow him and the beating down. It made little difference. Tyson's low-crouch stance meant that he could get under Bruno's armory and connect almost at will.

It all came to a brutal end less than a minute into the third round. Tyson dodged a Bruno jab and then unleashed a furious, 13-punch combination, starting with a right hand to the champion's body and ending with a left hook that saw Bruno lifted off his feet before crashing into the ropes, sitting on the first strand absorbing the blow. Referee Mills Lane had seen more than enough and waved Tyson back to his corner to end the proceedings and award the fight to the challenger via a Technical knockout.

If there was any doubt concerning Tyson's ability to return as dangerous as he was before his imprisonment, this night answered it. Bruno would retire following advice that if he continued an eye injury could blind him, whilst Tyson went on to claim the WBA crown in his next fight.

As for his second encounter with Bruno? Tyson got straight to the point. "I hit him like a mule," he declared. Frank Bruno would vouch for that.

2 SEPTEMBER 1995

MCCALL
VS BRUNO

WORLD HEAVYWEIGHT CHAMPIONSHIP
WEMBLEY STADIUM, LONDON, ENGLAND, U.K.

TALE OF THE TAPE

OLIVER MCCALL	NAME	FRANK BRUNO
THE ATOMIC BULL	NICKNAME	TRUE BRIT
CHICAGO, ILLINOIS, U.S.A.	BIRTHPLACE	LONDON, ENGLAND, U.K.
30	AGE	33
26—5—0	PRE-FIGHT RECORD	39—4—0
18	KO'S	38
6'2"	HEIGHT	6'3"
235 LBS	WEIGHT	248 LBS
82"	REACH	82"
ORTHODOX	STANCE	ORTHODOX

THE EMPIRE STRIKES BACK

AFTER THREE FAILED WORLD TITLE ATTEMPTS REDEMPTION FINALLY
CAME TO THE BRITISH NATIONAL TREASURE AS HE PROVED
PERSISTENCE AND DETERMINATION PREVAILS IN THE END.

The little-known Oliver McCall came into this fight as the WBC heavyweight world champion after upsetting all the odds by taking the title off Lennox Lewis the year before. Against him stood the sixth-ranked heavyweight in the WBC division, and a man fast running out of time. On three occasions Frank Bruno had challenged for the world title - against Tim Witherspoon back in 1986, Mike Tyson in 1989 and Lewis in 1993 - and three times he had failed.

Even in defeat Bruno had become a firm favorite in British households, a national institution, and a man who simply refused to believe that he did not deserve to be a world champion during a chaotic time for the heavyweight division in the 1990s.

Most observers felt that this fight would be his last, and best, opportunity.

Bruno was accompanied on his ring walk by the British middleweight Nigel Benn, who had just dispatched his opponent on the undercard, in front of 30,000 partisan fans at a chilly Wembley Stadium. He was then made to wait 15 minutes until the defending champion finally appeared.

The pair had been regular sparring partners eight years previously and Bruno remembered how McCall did not take well to body shots. For the first few rounds it was all Bruno, peppering the American with left jabs and shots to the body. In return McCall produced little until the 5th round when he finally landed a meaningful punch. By then

Bruno had leapt into a healthy lead and although McCall rallied in the 7th and 8th rounds, Bruno hit back in the 9th to regain the momentum.

It was obvious to all that the champion required a knockout if he were to retain his title. Time was running out for McCall but he also knew how Bruno had a history of running out of gas, as his late defeats to Witherspoon and also James 'Bonecrusher' Smith proved.

Bruno, however, had learned from these painful defeats. The final two rounds were one-sided, with McCall throwing everything he could at the British fighter. Bruno looked out on his feet and may well not have survived a 13th round.

He did not need to. Working hard with his left-right to keep McCall at bay the local hero held on for the required final moments before the bell rang and was told that, by unanimous decision, he was the new world champion.

"It's down in history that I'm the new heavyweight world champion," an exhausted and emotional Bruno declared afterwards. "I want to show people that through hard work and perseverance you can get what you want out of life. That last round was very tough. He came at me like a madman. All I could do was survive and survive I did."

His reign would prove short-lived. Five months later, under contractual obligation, he would fight Mike Tyson. An eye injury meant that retirement would follow.

But Bruno had achieved his goal of joining the pantheon of heavyweight world champions, and there had never been a more popular nor deserving champion in Britain than big Frank.

"IF I NEVER WALK AGAIN, GET RUN OVER OR GET SHOT, IT'S DOWN IN HISTORY THAT I'M HEAVYWEIGHT CHAMPION. I DON'T WAN'T TO GET COCKY, BUT BELIEVE ME THIS BELT IS A NICE THING."

FRANK BRUNO

2 MAY 2015

MAYWEATHER
VS PACQUIAO

WORLD WELTERWEIGHT CHAMPIONSHIP
MGM GRAND GARDEN ARENA, LAS VEGAS, NEVADA, U.S.A.

TALE OF THE TAPE

FLOYD MAYWEATHER	NAME	MANNY PACQUIAO
MONEY	NICKNAME	PAC-MAN
GRAND RAPIDS, MICHIGAN, U.S.A.	BIRTHPLACE	KIBAWE, BUKIDNON, PHILIPPINES
38	AGE	37
47—0—0	PRE-FIGHT RECORD	57—5—2
26	KO'S	38
5'8"	HEIGHT	5'5.5"
146 LBS	WEIGHT	145 LBS
72"	REACH	67"
ORTHODOX	STANCE	SOUTHPAW

THE FIGHT OF THE CENTURY

A FIGHT BETWEEN TWO OF THE ALL-TIME GREATS WAS PROBABLY FIVE YEARS LATER THAN THE BOXING WORLD WANTED BUT IT WOULD BE MAYWEATHER WHO WOULD CONTINUE HIS INVINCIBLE JOURNEY.

Billed as 'The Fight of the Century', this battle between two of the biggest superstars of any division in the history of boxing was a long time in the making. A good seven years earlier discussions had begun and continued, off and on, as both fighters continued to collect new world titles in different divisions for fun, and as these talks kept stalling so the demand rose until, by 2015, it had reached fever pitch. No wonder some of the biggest global celebrities assembled at the MGM Grand Garden Arena to witness one of the most anticipated fights in the history of the sport. These included Beyoncé and Jay Z, Andre Agassi and Steffi Graf, Clint Eastwood, Robert De Niro, Denzel Washington, Donald Trump, Leonardo DiCaprio, Michael Jordan, Lewis Hamilton and many more. Jamie Foxx sang the star-spangled banner whilst Justin Bieber was part of Mayweather's entourage whilst Jimmy Kimmel went with Pacquiao.

With a specially-made, emerald-encrusted, $1M belt created by the WBC, individual earnings of $100M for the two star fighters and even referee, Kenny Bayless, being paid a record $25,000 to officiate, boxing had never seen anything quite like this. Meanwhile Las Vegas was booming, and the international airport was forced to close temporarily in order to let in all the arriving private jets.

It would be impossible to live up to such enormous hype in the ring, especially as both fighters would be so wary and respectful of each other. Mayweather, one of the smartest exponents in the sport's history, was unusually aggressive at the beginning, gaining an early lead with his body shots and hitting his target under the Filipino's right side. In the third round a low blow made Pacquiao react angrily and in the fourth he upped the tempo throwing punches at a rapid pace, including a big left hander. It would be, according to the judges, the first round he would win, which meant Mayweather held a handy lead. This would be maintained as 3-1 became 4-2 in the eyes of two of the judges, and then 6-4, although the third had 'Money' Mayweather 8-2 up.

Pacquiao became more aggressive as the fight approached its end, but made little headway against the American who proved a difficult target to hit whilst continuing to score points with his trademark counters. In the 12th and final round Pacquiao again attempted to make the telling blow but Mayweather avoided any trouble with ease, dancing around the ring and picking his illustrious opponent off enough to win the round and confirm that he had won the day. All three judges agreed, with two having Mayweather down as the winner by 116-112 and one 118-110.

"Manny had his moments," Mayweather admitted afterwards. "He's a really smart fighter. I had to take my time. I knew he is competitive and extremely dangerous."

Pacquiao was unhappy. "I thought I won the fight," he insisted. "I thought I caught him more times than he caught me."

The stats begged to differ, with Mayweather landing 67 more punches than Pacquaio.

Yet, even in victory and defeat, neither star's glow diminished. Pacquiao still holds the record for the most divisions secured as a world champion and Mayweather would end his career with the unparalleled stat of 50 fights and 50 wins.

"MANNY PACQUIAO IS A HELL OF A FIGHTER. I TAKE MY HAT OFF TO HIM, I SEE WHY HE'S ONE OF THE GUYS THAT ARE AT THE PINNACLE OF THE SPORT OF BOXING."

FLOYD MAYWEATHER

29 SEPTEMBER 2001

HOPKINS vs
TRINIDAD

WORLD MIDDLEWEIGHT CHAMPIONSHIP
MADISON SQUARE GARDEN, NEW YORK, NEW YORK, U.S.A.

TALE OF THE TAPE

BERNARD HOPKINS	NAME	FÉLIX TRINIDAD
THE EXECUTIONER	NICKNAME	TITO
PHILADELPHIA, PENNSYLVANIA, U.S.A.	BIRTHPLACE	CUPEY ALTO, PUERTO RICO
36	AGE	28
39—2—1	PRE-FIGHT RECORD	40—0—0
28	KO'S	33
6'1"	HEIGHT	5'11"
157 LBS	WEIGHT	158.5 LBS
75"	REACH	72.5"
ORTHODOX	STANCE	ORTHODOX

AND THEN THERE WAS ONE

A HIGHLY EMOTIONAL NIGHT WOULD END WITH CONFIRMATION OF ONE MAN'S PLACE IN BOXING HISTORY AND DEFEAT AND THE END OF ANOTHER MAN'S STELLAR CAREER.

It was billed as 'And There Was One', for the very simple reason. In a meeting between the WBC/IBF World Middleweight champion and the WBA equivalent to unify all three titles, something had to give. Hopkins had made 12 defenses of his title whilst Trinidad had dominated the welterweight division, including a win over Oscar De La Hoya, moved up into super-welterweight and now found himself looking to see off all challengers at middleweight. Promoter Don King decided to set up a mini tournament which pitched Hopkins against Keith Holmes and Trinidad against William Joppy. When both came through it meant a showdown in the final at Madison Square Garden.

Initially meant for September 15th the bout was postponed by a fortnight following the terrorist attacks in New York on September 11th, meaning the night was emotionally-charged. Tension had already been created when Hopkins threw the Puerto Rican flag to the floor first in New York and then, dangerously, in San Juan at separate promotional conferences.

On the night he would enter the ring wearing his customary executioner's mask whilst Trinidad emerged wrapped in the colors of his homeland. He was unbeaten in 40 bouts compared to two defeats blemishing his opponent's record, but had moved up two weight divisions in relatively short time to face a man who felt he had not acquired the recognition he deserved. Hopkins saw this as his defining fight, the moment when he would join the greats.

"I WAS NAIVE ENOUGH, AT THAT MOMENT, TO FAVOR TRINIDAD VERY HEAVILY AND FEEL AS THOUGH HE WAS POTENTIALLY TOO DYNAMIC AND TOO GOOD AN OFFENSIVE FIGHTER FOR BERNARD TO BEAT HIM."

JIM LAMPLEY

For the first two rounds both were cautious, sizing each other up and moving around the ring in safety. Hopkins would land the first big punch right at the end of the second round, a sign of how the fight would eventually pan out. His jab started to tell and although both would hit the target with crunching blows in the third and fourth rounds Hopkins was clearly moving ahead.

His strategy on the night was unexpected and certainly threw Trinidad. Hopkins had made a name for himself as a brawler. But on this night he danced and moved and out-boxed his illustrious opponent.

Trinidad enjoyed his first outright winning round in the sixth but by the tenth he realized he was so far behind on points that a knockdown would be required. In going after Hopkins and failing to land any meaningful blows he only exposed himself to telling counter-attacks, including one which left the Puerta Rican stunned in the final seconds. By the 11th he looked a spent force as the American started to pick him off at will. In the interval Trinidad appeared to slump on his chair devoid of any energy. Opposite him, in contrast, was a smiling Hopkins. Both knew the score.

It would all come to a resounding end in the 12th and final round. Midway through it Hopkins unleashed a crunching right hander flush on Trinidad's chin. It was doubtful whether he would have raised his shattered body from the canvas or not before referee Steve Smoger could finish the count Trinidad's father, Felix Sr, entered the ring and told Smoger to stop the fight. At that point all three judges had Hopkins comfortably ahead in any case.

The American, and now the first undisputed middleweight world champion for six years since Marvin Hagler, fell to his knees in celebration and prayer. He would go on to defend his title six more times before coming unstuck against Jermain Taylor. In 2011 he became the oldest world champion in boxing history at 46 when he took the WBC's light-heavyweight crown.

Trinidad, in contrast, would retire a fight later and, although he attempted several comebacks, never reached such heady heights again.

"BERNARD JUST HAD ANSWERS FOR EVERYTHING THAT TITO HAD, I RECALL SPECIFICALLY IN THE MIDDLE ROUNDS, TITO LANDED A CRISP, CLEAN, SIGNATURE RIGHT-HAND FLUSH. BERNARD GRUNTED AND CONTINUED PRESSING THE ACTION, AND I COULD SEE THE DEMEANOR OF TITO, "I HIT THIS GUY WITH EVERYTHING, AND HE'S STILL HERE."

STEVE SMOGER

11 FEBRUARY 1990

TYSON *vs*

DOUGLAS

WORLD MIDDLEWEIGHT CHAMPIONSHIP
TOKYO DOME, TOKYO, JAPAN

TALE OF THE TAPE

MIKE TYSON	NAME	JAMES DOUGLAS
IRON MIKE	NICKNAME	BUSTER
BROOKLYN, NEW YORK, U.S.A.	BIRTHPLACE	COLUMBUS, OHIO, U.S.A.
23	AGE	29
37–0–0	PRE-FIGHT RECORD	28–4–1
33	KO'S	18
5'10"	HEIGHT	6'4"
210 LBS	WEIGHT	231 LBS
71"	REACH	83"
ORTHODOX	STANCE	ORTHODOX

TYSON IS BACK

ANOTHER OF THE ALL-TIME UPSETS BETWEEN A
MAN WHO WAS DEEMED UNBEATABLE AGAINST
AN OPPONENT GIVEN ZERO CHANCE OF WINNING.

To say that few gave James 'Buster' Douglas any chance at all - despite it being a two-horse race - is something of an understatement. His odds said it all. At 42-1 against Douglas was viewed as nothing more than a warm-up for the undisputed heavyweight champion of the world, boasting an unblemished professional record after 37 fights, before he took on Evander Holyfield. Up to this point Mike Tyson had created an aura of vicious invincibility. No wonder all the casinos bar The Mirage refused to offer odds.

Tyson's issues were beginning to mount up. His manager, Bill Cayton, and his promoter, Don King, were arguing over the contractual agreements whilst he had just dismissed his long-term trainer, Kevin Rooney. But in his previous fight he had demolished Carl Williams in 93 seconds. No challenger had taken him beyond the 5th round since 1987.

Douglas came into this fight on the back of six, straight wins but his mother had died 23 days prior to the fight and he contracted the flu the day before he entered the ring.

Despite all this it was Douglas who started the better, using his 12-inch reach advantage to jab away at his opponent and prevent him from attacking from the inside. Whatever Tyson managed to do he was met with a flurry of punches. Douglas landed a sharp uppercut at the end of the second round and after a lacklustre third round from the firm favorite Tyson's corner man, Jay Bright, was heard to shout: "Don't just stand there and look at him, you've gotta work."

Instead Douglas continued to dominate into the middle rounds, wobbling the champion with a chopping right hander that caused Tyson's left eye to swell up.Surprisingly, Tyson's new corner team had chosen not to bring an 'endswell' (small piece of metal used to cool bruising) or an ice pack. Instead resorting to filling a rubber glove with iced water to press on his expanding wound.

In the last ten seconds of the eighth round, against the run of play, a big right uppercut from the unbeaten fighter saw Douglas hit the floor and spark subsequent controversy. The referee, Octavio Meyran, beganhis count two beats after the knockdown timekeeper. The challenger rose to his feet on nine, although later Tyson and Don King would argue it was a 'long count' and Douglas should have lost there and then. The bell would ring moments later, potentially saving Douglas who responded by pounding the canvas with his glove in frustration.

Tyson emerged from his corner knowing that he needed to do more and launched an aggressive attack on Douglas. This was fought off and a four-punch counter not only closed Tyson's damaged eye completely had Tyson barely surviving the round.

Few at ringside could believe what was unfolding. The champion, the seemingly unbeatable who had dismissed all before him with almost contempt, was in trouble and moments into the tenth Douglas moved in for the kill, finding his target with a searing right upper cut that snapped Tyson's head upwards. Still reeling he was then subjected to four punches in quick succession to the head that saw him down for the first time in his career. As the iconic pictures showed, he fumbled around for his mouthpiece on the canvas before lodging it crookedly in his mouth as he tried and failed to make the count.

King lodged an appeal immediately afterwards after the so-called 'long count' but after four days of arguments and deliberation Douglas was declared the new, undisputed champion of the world. "How did I do it?" he asked afterwards. "Because of my mother. God bless her."

It would go down as one of the all-time upsets in boxing, if not sport. Douglas would lose to Holyfield in his next fight. Tyson became world champion again later in his career but his aura would never be quite the same again.

27 NOVEMBER 2004

MORALES vs
BARRERA III

WORLD SUPER FEATHERWEIGHT CHAMPIONSHIP
MGM GRAND GARDEN ARENA, LAS VEGAS, NEVADA, U.S.A.

TALE OF THE TAPE

ERIK MORALES	NAME	MARCO ANTONIO BARRERA
EL TERRIBLE (THE TERRIBLE)	NICKNAME	BABY-FACED ASSASSIN
TIJUANA, BAJA CALIFORNIA, MEXICO	BIRTHPLACE	MEXICO CITY, DISTRITO FEDERAL, MEXICO
28	AGE	30
47—1—0	PRE-FIGHT RECORD	58—4—0
31	KO'S	39
5'8"	HEIGHT	5'6"
130 LBS	WEIGHT	129.5 LBS
72"	REACH	70"
ORTHODOX	STANCE	ORTHODOX

ONCE AND FOR ALL

THE CULMINATION OF ONE OF THE GREATEST TRILOGIES IN BOXING HISTORY BETWEEN TWO FELLOW COUNTRYMEN WHOSE BRAGGING RIGHTS OVER EACH OTHER WERE SETTLED ONCE AND FOR ALL ON THIS NIGHT.

Boxing likes to hype up its fights, creating a rivalry and sometimes even an enmity to gain more interest. In the case of this all-Mexican battle, the third and last installment in what has gone down as one of the great trilogies in the sport, there was no need. The score stood at one win each, with Morales edging a split decision in their first bout and Barrera answering back with a unanimous verdict in the second, inflicting his opponent's first professional defeat in the process. But it wasn't just their history in the ring that made these two bitter and genuine rivals.

Some put it down to their different backgrounds. Morales was a working-class street kid hailing from the ghettos of Tijuana, whereas the better-educated Barrera came from a middle-class, big city background from the nation's capital. There had been an altercation between the pair of them at a football match and an exchange of blows before the second fight.

The third and final meeting was billed 'Once and For All' and it was very personal. Despite Barrera's triumph in their last fight Morales was seen to be the favorite for a very obvious reason. Barrera had stepped up to super featherweight for the first time in his career to take him on, giving size, reach and weight on the night.

Perhaps because of this he came out of the traps far the better of the two, beating Morales to the punch and proving far more accurate to the head and body. He managed, seemingly at will, to get inside the defending 130 lbs champion where he was at his most dangerous, and where he also avoided the longer range punching of the taller Morales. After six rounds Barrera had won five and Morales just could not seem to get his jab going.

Realizing his plight Morales finally stepped it up in rounds seven and eight, using a chopping right hand to some effect, but Barrera rallied back in the next two to ward off any meaningful comeback and resume control of the fight.

Morales knew, as the bell for the 11th round sounded, that only a knockout could win the day. Thus followed one of the greatest rounds, widely accepted to this day. Barrera's corner recognized the situation and screamed at their man to bring the fight to his larger opponent rather than sit back. And so they stood, toe-to-toe, refusing to defend as they traded blows. Morales had his moments but Barrera edged it with left hooks to the face and ribs. The 12th and final round was similar, albeit at a lesser level than the high-octane drama that had preceded it and, at the end of it, there was little complaint when two judges gave their verdicts in Barrera's favor by two rounds and one round, and the third judge made it out to be a draw.

Morales was crestfallen while Barrera enjoyed the moment, sticking two fingers up at his beaten foe and shouting 'dos' (two) to signify his two victories over his fellow Mexican. "It's the most rewarding fight of my career," he said afterwards. "I did this fight to show all fans that this is what boxing is about."

Latterly, and somewhat belatedly, the two men would become friends, recognizing as they mellowed that both deserved equal respect for their stellar careers.

"HE CAME FORWARD
AND HE FOUGHT
HARD AND OF THE 70
OPPONENTS I FOUGHT
HE HIT THE HARDEST
AND HE WAS THE BEST."

MARCO ANTONIO BARRERA

13 MARCH 1999

HOLYFIELD
VS LEWIS

WORLD HEAVYWEIGHT CHAMPIONSHIP
MADISON SQUARE GARDEN, NEW YORK CITY, NEW YORK, U.S.A.

TALE OF THE TAPE

EVANDER HOLYFIELD	NAME	LENNOX LEWIS
THE REAL DEAL	NICKNAME	THE LION
ATMORE, ALABAMA, U.S.A.	BIRTHPLACE	LONDON, ENGLAND, U.K.
36	AGE	34
36–3–0	PRE-FIGHT RECORD	34–1–0
25	KO'S	27
6'2.5"	HEIGHT	6'5"
215 LBS	WEIGHT	246 LBS
77.5"	REACH	84"
ORTHODOX	STANCE	ORTHODOX

UNDISPUTED

ONE OF THE MOST HOTLY DISPUTED AND CONTROVERSIAL DRAWS
IN HEAVYWEIGHT HISTORY BETWEEN TWO OF THE GREATS WHO
BOTH CLAIMED VICTORY BUT HAD TO SETTLE FOR A DRAW.

In the chaotic years of the 1990s in boxing's heavyweight divisions world titles were swapped almost at will as the likes of Michael Moorer, Oliver McCall, Bruce Seldon, Riddick Bowe and Mike Tyson all shone and dimmed. Lennox Lewis had won, lost and then regained his own heavyweight title, whilst Evander Holyfield had emerged from wins with, amongst others, Tyson and Moorer. When the two came together at the Garden it was for the undisputed heavyweight title of the world, last held by Bowe back in 1992, with Holyfield the WBA and IBF champ and Lewis holding the WBC version. Holyfield would earn $20M for his efforts, double his opponent's fee.

Prior to the fight Lewis had made the astute move of appointing the legendary trainer, Emmanuel Seward who, among other fighters, had previously trained Holyfield. It seemed to have worked.

Uncharacteristically for the normally reserved Holyfield he had declared on the eve of the encounter that he would knock Lewis out in the third round.

Perhaps this inspired Lewis because it was the British-born fighter who started much the better, keeping Holyfield off balance with his long, left jab and producing combinations at will.

In the 2nd round Lewis landed 42 of his 87 punches compared to a meager 8 out of 24 from Holyfield.

Reminded of his prediction Holyfield made a fight of it in the 3rd round only for Lewis to win the next two comfortably. In the 6th he dropped his gloves to his sides allowing Holyfield to find his elusive target with a right-left combination, but the WBC champion struck back again in the next round, shaking Holyfield with a strong left jab and later having him on the ropes.

At this stage Lewis appeared to be winning by five rounds after seven, but then eased off to allow the WBA champion to win the next four rounds in succession.

As the two gladiators left their corners for the 12th and final round, Lewis still held the edge but, to make sure, he finished the fight the stronger of the pair to claim the round and, so it seemed, the night.

Then came the results and one of the most hotly-disputed decisions in the history of boxing. One judge gave it to Lewis 116-113, but another awarded Holyfield the fight 115-113 whilst the third saw it as a draw.

The stats begged to differ, with Lewis landing 348 punches to Holyfield's 130.

He stood with his cornermen in disbelief.

"I won the fight," he declared afterwards. "It was my time to shine. I'm the undisputed heavyweight champion and the whole world knows it. He should give me his two belts because he knows they're mine."

Holyfield somehow managed to differ in his view. "I feel like the champ," he said. "I can't fight and score. People around the ring are not the judges."

The post-fight reaction was sympathetic towards Lewis. His enraged manager, Frank Maloney, called for the UK Prime Minister, Tony Blair, to break off relations with the US.

The sanctioning bodies felt they had no other option but to install a rematch eight months later. It would go the distance again but this time Lewis would win by a unanimous verdict.

9 OCTOBER 1993

BENN vs
EUBANK II

WORLD SUPER MIDDLEWEIGHT CHAMPIONSHIP
OLD TRAFFORD, MANCHESTER, ENGLAND, U.K.

TALE OF THE TAPE

NIGEL BENN	NAME	CHRIS EUBANK
DARK DESTROYER	NICKNAME	SIMPLY THE BEST
ESSEX, ENGLAND, U.K.	BIRTHPLACE	LONDON, ENGLAND, U.K.
29	AGE	27
37−2−0	PRE-FIGHT RECORD	35−0−1
32	KO'S	18
5'9.5"	HEIGHT	5'10"
167 LBS	WEIGHT	168 LBS
72.8"	REACH	72.8"
ORTHODOX	STANCE	ORTHODOX

JUDGEMENT DAY

THE SECOND FIGHT OF AN EPIC BATTLE BETWEEN TWO BRITISH WORLD CHAMPIONS WITH GENUINE ENMITY TOWARDS EACH OTHER, WITH A RESULT NEITHER WANTED AFTER A FIGHT THAT WAS ONE OF THE GREATEST IN A BRITISH RING.

They called it 'Judgement Day' and it would be one of the most hotly-anticipated, all-British encounters in the history of boxing. Three years earlier Chris Eubank ended Nigel Benn's unbeaten record and took his WBO Middleweight title off him with a stoppage in the ninth round after a brutal fight that could quite easily have gone either way.

Before that fight their rivalry and dislike of each other was apparent and genuine. Three years on and this had not diminished. Both had moved up a weight and both were world champions, Benn holding the WBC belt and Eubank the WBO version. A unification fight was in much demand and veteran promoter Don King managed to arrange it, with a clause in the contract that made both winner and loser join his stable afterwards.

Benn, so desperate to avenge his only defeat at the time by his opponent, even put up the £10,000 sanctioning fee to the WBO to ensure that both titles were on the line.

The venue was Old Trafford, Manchester United's famous stadium, and 42,000 packed inside on a chilly October evening to witness a second, savage meeting between two of the most controversial figures in the sport. No wonder ITV, the British terrestrial channel, enjoyed a live audience figure of 16.5 million viewers, whilst an estimated half a billion watched worldwide.

Their ring entrances could not have been more different. Eubank, all preening and posing, ended it with his customary vault over the ropes. His corner team had the affront to have the words "WBO and WBC Champion emblazoned on their jackets. Benn, all anger and menace, stormed into the ring covered by a hood denoting his 'Dark Destroyer' nickname.

It was Benn who would start the quicker of the two, as if he wanted to end it quickly and emphatically. Eubank withstood the early pressure and then decided to strut around the ring for the first 40 seconds of the first interval before eventually returning to his corner stool.

The theme would continue, with Benn gaining the upper hand in the first four rounds, landing numerous blows and sending his opponent into the ropes. Eubank would hit back in the 5th with a bone-crunching left hook and a flurry of punches but even after Benn was docked a point in the 6th for hitting low the WBC champion had gained a healthy lead.

The problem for Benn was that whilst he tired into the later rounds so Eubank bounced back, especially in the final three rounds. This was one of the Hove fighter's main strengths, the ability to maintain his fitness and power deep into fights. His corner team realized this, shouting out to their fighter: "He's more tired than you" and it was clear for all to see that Eubank finished the stronger of the pair.

As the final bell rang both held their arms aloft in the belief they had done enough to take both world titles. The judges, at least as a collective, saw it differently, with one going for Benn 115-113, another for Eubank, 114-113 and the third deciding the two could not be divided. The feeling ringside was that Benn had probably edged it but it was close enough for a draw to not be considered incorrect.

Benn begged to differ, storming out of the ring in anger when he heard the decision announced whilst Eubank remained appearing, to some, a little relieved. As an extra twist to this unexpected result Don King failed to land either fighter having omitted to include the outcome of a draw in his contract.

Despite interest and big money offerings for a third battle between the two it never materialized. But the two times they fought would not be forgotten. Boxing News described both fights as 'titanic clashes'. Barry McGuigan, the popular, former world featherweight champion, described it as thus. "There was real antipathy and ill will there," he said. "But what fights. What fights."

"EVEN THOUGH THE REFEREE TOOK AWAY A POINT FROM HIM FOR HITTING ME LOW, HIM HAVING BEEN WARNED OF SUCH, HE STILL DID ENOUGH TO WIN THE FIGHT."

CHRIS EUBANK

25 FEBRUARY 1995

BENN VS MCCLELLAN

WORLD MIDDLEWEIGHT CHAMPIONSHIP
LONDON ARENA, LONDON, ENGLAND, U.K.

TALE OF THE TAPE

	NAME	
NIGEL BENN	**NAME**	GERALD MCCLELLAN
THE DARK DESTROYER	**NICKNAME**	THE G-MAN
LONDON, ENGLAND, U.K.	**BIRTHPLACE**	FREEPORT, ILLINOIS, U.S.A.
31	**AGE**	27
39–2–1	**PRE-FIGHT RECORD**	31–2–0
32	**KO'S**	29
5'9.5"	**HEIGHT**	6'0"
168 LBS	**WEIGHT**	165 LBS
73"	**REACH**	74"
ORTHODOX	**STANCE**	ORTHODOX

SUDDEN IMPACT

BOXING BRUTALITY FROM START TO A PREMATURE FINISH WITH A FIGHT THAT WILL BE LONG REMEMBERED AND, SADLY, A TRAGIC ENDING.

It was promoted as 'Sudden Impact' but the impact this fight would have on the sport of boxing would last much longer than what turned out to be a brutal and fateful February night in London.

Nigel Benn was the heavier weight world champion and had the advantage of fighting in his home town of London in front of a partisan crowd of 12,500 at a packed London Arena.

But McClellan strode to the ring as the favorite based on his brutal record that saw 14 straight knockouts in his previous 14 fights, ten inside the first round. In fact his last three world title defenses had lasted in total 3 minutes and 20 seconds.

No wonder he spoke so confidently prior to the night. "I can't see anything less than a vicious knockout," he said. His words would prove to be sadly prophetic.

The fight started as it would continue. Inside 35 seconds of the first round Benn found himself sent flying through the ropes by a McClellan attack, The 'G-Man' was used to ending his fights early and clearly expected a repeat result.

The Londoner may have been the underdog but he had proven the size of his heart many times before and he revealed it once again by bouncing back strongly in the second round, realizing that he had to take the fight to the American or be overwhelmed.

This is the fashion in which the fight would continue, back and forth, cut and thrust, with neither man taking a backward step. Midway onwards Benn began to take control but this advantage disappeared when McClellan knocked him down for a second time in the eighth round.

In the ninth a visibly tiring Benn was throwing bombs which were largely missing his opponent. One such pile-driver was sent with such force that the effort forced Benn to topple over and accidentally head butt McClellan, an impact that appeared to affect the American's physical well-being.

It would reach a dramatic and, subsequently, tragic denouement one round later. McClellan had never fought further than eight rounds in his career. This was unchartered territory for the middleweight champion and he was clearly feeling it. Midway through the round a Benn right hand forced him to drop to one knee. Rising at the count of seven he was down again on the same knee moments later after another right hander. This time he stayed on his knee until counted out.

It was seen at first to be a bizarre ending to a vicious fight but as McClellan walked back to his corner he collapsed and his head was placed in a neck brace.

Benn would collapse minutes later back in his dressing room but that was through exhaustion. Both were taken to the same London hospital but whilst the Englishman would recover his beaten American foe would be operated on to have a blood clot removed, and would subsequently be blind, deaf and wheelchair-ridden.

It was and is a reminder that whilst this was a very rare worse case scenario in boxing, it has its dangers and few if any in sport are braver than the two who face each other in a ring.

Benn was deeply affected by the outcome and also full of praise and respect for McClellan. "I came out of that fight with a damaged nose, a damaged jaw and I was urinating blood," he said. "I was in bed for three days afterwards. That shows you how powerful a champion that man was."

"MY HEART GOES OUT TO GERALD MCCLELLAN AND HIS FAMILY. IT WAS A FIERCE AND FAIR FIGHT, BUT NO ONE COULD IMAGINE THAT SUCH A GREAT SPORTING SPECTACLE COULD END SO SADLY."

NIGEL BENN

10

07 MAY 2005

CORRALES
VS CASTILLO

WORLD LIGHTWEIGHT CHAMPIONSHIP
MANDALAY BAY RESORT & CASINO, LAS VEGAS, NEVADA, U.S.A.

TALE OF THE TAPE

DIEGO CORRALES	NAME	JOSÉ LUIS CASTILLO
CHICO	NICKNAME	EL TEMIBLE
SACRAMENTO, CALIFORNIA, U.S.A.	BIRTHPLACE	EMPALME, MEXICO
27	AGE	31
39—2—0	PRE-FIGHT RECORD	52—6—1
32	KO'S	46
5'10.5"	HEIGHT	5'8"
135 LBS	WEIGHT	135 LBS
70"	REACH	69"
ORTHODOX	STANCE	ORTHODOX

MONSTROUS COMEBACK

IT WOULD PROVE TO BE A CLASSIC FIGHT WITH A BRUTAL ENDING WHERE, ONCE AGAIN, THE YOUNGER MAN WOULD PREVAIL JUST SECONDS FROM DEFEAT, BUT IT WOULD ULTIMATELY END IN TRAGEDY.

This unification fight between two lightweight world champions would be voted Fight of the Year for 2005 after a brutal encounter that quite could easily have swung either way. Diego Corrales, an American born to Colombian and Mexican parents, had won 32 of his 39 victories by knockout on his way to world titles in two weight divisions.

Castillo, the older man by three years, was born and bred Mexican and had dismissed 46 opponents in his 52 wins by knockout. Recognized as one of the best lightweights of his era he had won world titles in this weight on two separate occasions. Something would have to give.

Once the fight had got underway both advanced towards each other in the center of the ring and began trading punches. Joe Goossen, Corrales' trainer, had advised his man to copy Castillo's style and fight inside his man.

It resulted in a like for like as both men set out their stall and went toe-to-toe from the off. By the 4th round Castillo had suffered a cut above his left eye and by the 7th Corrales sported welts below both his eyes, whilst his left eye had swollen almost shut.

The tenth round would become one of the most memorable three minutes in modern boxing history. Deep into the round Castillo dropped his younger opponent with a punch full on the chin. Corrales spat his mouthguard out and rose on the count of

"I DON'T REMEMBER ANYTHING ABOUT THE FIGHT OR ANY SPECIFIC ROUNDS. ALL I REMEMBER WAS THAT LAST ROUND WHEN I WENT ON THIS EMOTIONAL ROLLERCOASTER."

TODD DUBOFF

eight. Moments later he was down again. The American managed to beat the count on nine but was deducted a point by referee Tony Weeks for excessive spitting of his mouthguard.

Ringsiders would have placed heavy odds on Castillo moving in for the kill but instead he was met by a punch he described later as "a perfect right hand." Out of nowhere the Mexican was in big trouble. Corrales had him trapped on the ropes and, realizing that he was on the verge of snatching victory from the jaws of defeat, landed a series of hard blows on his stricken opponent. Referee Weeks had no option but to stop the fight when Castillo appeared to have momentarily lost consciousness whilst still on his feet.

There was little time for celebration or commiseration as both men were taken straight to hospital. "The beating Diego got from Castillo's body punches was unbelievable," his trainer, Goossen, admitted later. "They took a urine sample and it looked like a bottle of tomato juice."

Corrales had stated before the fight that he would go to hell before losing this fight.

It seemed like he had.

There would be no happy ending for the unified champion. This would be the last fight he ever won.

In the rematch, just five months later, he was stopped by Castillo in the 4th round in a non title bout after the Mexican failed to make the weight. He then lost his title to Cuban-American Joel Casamajor and the next fight against Ghanaian Joshua Clottey. He was then due to fight Castillo for a third time but the Mexican again failed to make the weight and this time the fight was canceled.

Two years to the day of his famous win over Castillo tragedy stuck. Corrales died in a motorcycle accident in Las Vegas at the age of 29. Castillo would continue fighting knowing that he provided Corrales with his greatest feat in boxing.

"TO ME IT WAS A GREAT HONOR TO FIGHT HIM. I AM GLAD THAT WE FOUGHT THE KIND OF FIGHT THAT EVERYONE LIKED, AND THAT IS WHY I WANT TO FIGHT THE BEST. GUYS I COME TO FIGHT ARE GUYS THAT REALLY WANT TO DO THEIR BEST OUT THERE, AND THAT IS WHAT I LIKE TO DO."

JOSÉ LUIS CASTILLO

"THE FIRST TIME I WATCHED IT, WAS SAY SOMETHING LIKE "WOW." IT WAS SHOCK, TO SEE SOME OF THE SHOTS THAT I TOOK AND SOME OF THE SHOTS THAT HE TOOK. I FINALLY SAW HOW BRUTAL AND HOW EXHAUSTING OF A FIGHT IT WAS, TO BE INVOLVED IN. THE SECOND TIME I WATCHED IT WAS LIKE MORE OF THE, WOW, I REALLY WENT THROUGH THAT?."

DIEGO CORRALES

22 APRIL 2001

LEWIS vs RAHMAN

**WORLD HEAVYWEIGHT CHAMPIONSHIP
CARNIVAL CITY CASINO, BRAKPAN, SOUTH AFRICA**

TALE OF THE TAPE

LENNOX LEWIS	NAME	HASIM RAHMAN
THE LION	NICKNAME	THE ROCK
LONDON, ENGLAND, U.K.	BIRTHPLACE	BALTIMORE, MARYLAND, U.S.A.
35	AGE	28
38—1—1	PRE-FIGHT RECORD	34—2—0
29	KO'S	28
6'5"	HEIGHT	6'2.5"
253.5 LBS	WEIGHT	238 LBS
84"	REACH	82"
ORTHODOX	STANCE	ORTHODOX

THUNDER IN AFRICA

ANOTHER HUGE, UNEXPECTED HEAVYWEIGHT UPSET THAT PROVED IN THE HEAVYWEIGHT DIVISION, MORE THAN ANY OTHER, A BIG PUNCH CAN WIN ANY FIGHT NO MATTER WHO THE OPPONENT.

It should have been a mis-match. Lennox Lewis entered the 15th defense of his WBC World Heavyweight crown on an unbeaten run for six and a half years against a man who the bookmakers offered odds of 20-1 against. It would turn out, however, to be one of the greatest shocks in heavyweight history.

Lewis would accept later that he failed to take Rahman seriously. His eye was on the bigger prize of a showdown with Mike Tyson. The fight, named 'Thunder in Africa', would take place at a South African venue 5,200 feet above sea level on the high veldt. The American arrived in Brakpan four weeks prior to the fight to acclimatize. Lewis, in contrast, arrived just 12 days before, preferring to train in Las Vegas (at 2,000 feet above sea level), dividing his time between the gym and filming his cameo role in the movie, 'Ocean's Eleven'.

It soon became clear, after the fight began at 5.30am local time to marry in with US prime time, that Lewis had underestimated both the conditions, his lack of preparation and the hunger of his opponent, faced with an unexpected opportunity to become the undisputed world champion.

The first four rounds were closer than anyone expected, with Rahman clipping Lewis in the second and responding to a rare attack from the champion with a big right hander in the third. In the fourth the man from Baltimore upped the tempo, becoming much more the aggressor and throwing 60 punches to 33 from Lewis. Both landed 20 and Lewis edged the round, as he had edged the fight but in the 5th it all went horribly wrong for the Londoner.

Changing his tactics Lewis appeared to want to end the proceedings there and then, throwing more punches and sizing Rahman up before delivering the final, telling blow. Instead the underdog managed to jab the champion into a corner and when Lewis momentarily dropped both hands to his side, smiling in the process, Rahman unleashed a ferocious right hander that dropped his opponent to the canvas. There was no way back from here and a blinking Lewis was counted out.

"No Lewis-Tyson, no Lewis-Tyson," Rahman shouted as he danced around the ring.

Later, a little calmer, he expanded. "I came up with one punch," he said. "One punch. I told you I was confident. Not one time since the fight was made was I nervous. He came out and tried to dictate the fight but I wouldn't let him."

A stunned Lewis was honest in his appraisal afterwards. "I can't believe that," he admitted. "I felt fine in there. I was going about my work nice and comfortably and there was no way Hashim Rahman could beat me. This is what happens in heavyweight boxing. He hit me with a good shot. He threw a big right hand and caught me right on the chin."

Rahman probably knew lightning would not strike twice, which is why he attempted to dodge a second fight. It would end up in court before a judge's ruling favored Lewis with his rematch clause. Seven months later they would meet again and a Lewis, intent on avenging his unexpected defeat, knocked Rahman out in four.

It was back to business as usual, but it failed to erase the sheer shock of what had taken place on the high veldt.

8 JUNE 2002

LEWIS
VS TYSON

WORLD HEAVYWEIGHT CHAMPIONSHIP
PYRAMID ARENA, MEMPHIS, TENNESSEE, U.S.A.

TALE OF THE TAPE

LENNOX LEWIS	NAME	MIKE TYSON
THE LION	NICKNAME	IRON MIKE
LONDON, ENGLAND, U.K.	BIRTHPLACE	BROOKLYN, NEW YORK, U.S.A.
36	AGE	35
39—2—1	PRE-FIGHT RECORD	49—3—0
30	KO'S	43
6'5"	HEIGHT	5'10"
249.25 LBS	WEIGHT	234 LBS
84"	REACH	71"
ORTHODOX	STANCE	ORTHODOX

LEWIS — TYSON: IS ON

A DEFINING FIGHT FOR BOTH HEAVYWEIGHT SUPERSTARS AS ONE WOULD RETIRE ONE FIGHT LATER HAPPY TO HAVE INCLUDED THIS ON HIS CV, AND THE OTHER THREE FIGHTS LATER REALIZING HIS TIME HAD COME AND GONE.

Their previous records plus an unsavory press conference brawl the previous January in New York meant enormous interest had been created prior to these two giants of boxing finally meeting. Initially set for April in Las Vegas the Nevada boxing commission refused to grant Tyson a license after the brawl, a decision replicated by several other states until Memphis came in for the fight.

Such was the concern over their previous history that referee Eddie Cotton handed out instructions to the fighters in the sanctuary of their own dressing rooms rather than in the center of the ring. As a result there would be no touching of gloves.

No wonder the likes of Samuel L Jackson, Denzel Washington, Tom Cruise, Clint Eastwood, Donald Trump, Michael Jordan and Morgan Freeman were all ringside at the Pyramid Arena to witness this spectacle. It had been a long time in the making and neither were in their prime anymore.

If they were expecting a tight, ferocious battle then they would be disappointed because Lewis, the man with most of the heavyweight belts to his name, would dominate this fight after a first round that Tyson, seemingly in a hurry, had won.

The British fighter was twice warned in the second round by referee Eddie Cotton for holding onto Tyson after Lewis realized the tactic would nullify the challenger's aggressive, forward advances, also enabling him to land some powerful uppercuts that saw the American stagger back.

In the third round Tyson headbutted his opponent but Lewis responded by cutting him above the right eye, and in the 4th Tyson went down after receiving a brutal combination only for the referee to not only judge it as a slip but to then deduct a point from Lewis for pushing.

Cotton would stop the fight in the fifth to talk to Lewis about pushing but Tyson's face was swelling up fast and by the end of the sixth both his eyes were cut and blood was appearing from both his nose and mouth.

Now Lewis, the pre-fight 2-1 favorite, was in complete control. His sharp, left jabs, stinging uppercuts and overhead rights were piling into Tyson who appeared to have little to offer back. Indeed in the 7th Round Lewis landed 31 punches compared to a pitiful four from Tyson. He held a healthy lead on all three judges' scorecards.

The end was nigh and it came with 47 seconds remaining of the eighth round when Tyson, trying vainly to hit back, was sent sprawling to the canvas by an overhand right hander that caught him full on the side of his face. He made little effort to rise from his prostrate position and was counted out.

"This is my defining fight," an exhilarated Lewis declared afterwards. "It's the one the world wanted to see. Mike at the age of 19 ruled the world but, like a fine wine, I came along later and I'm the ruling man."

A much-changed Tyson from the angry, out-of-control fighter beforehand, was magnanimous in defeat. "I am happy for him." he said. "He knows I love him and I hope he gives me the chance to fight him one more time."

It would never happen. Lewis would fight one more time and retire. Tyson would follow suit three fights later after losing on successive times.

"HE'S COMING FOR ME? HE'S CRAZY. DOESN'T HE REALIZE I'M COMING FOR HIM?"

LENNOX LEWIS

13 NOVEMBER 1992

HOLYFIELD
VS BOWE

WORLD HEAVYWEIGHT CHAMPIONSHIP
THOMAS & MACK CENTER, LAS VEGAS, NEVADA, U.S.A.

TALE OF THE TAPE

EVANDER HOLYFIELD	NAME	RIDDICK BOWE
THE REAL DEAL	NICKNAME	BIG DADDY
ATMORE, ALABAMA, U.S.A.	BIRTHPLACE	BROOKLYN, NEW YORK, U.S.A.
30	AGE	25
28—0—0	PRE-FIGHT RECORD	31—0—0
22	KO'S	27
6'2.5"	HEIGHT	6'5"
205 LBS	WEIGHT	235 LBS
77.5"	REACH	81"
ORTHODOX	STANCE	ORTHODOX

EQUAL DETERMINATION

THE FIRST FIGHT AND THE BEST OF THEIR TRILOGY WOULD SEE
A FIRST DEFEAT FOR THE CHAMPION AND THE EMERGENCE OF
A NEW, ALBEIT BRIEF, FORCE IN HEAVYWEIGHT BOXING.

The first meeting in what would become a trilogy gave Evander Holyfield the opportunity to legitimize his two year standing as the undisputed heavyweight champion of the world. The problem was in those two years since beating an out of shape Buster Douglas - a man who had over-celebrated after his shock win over Mike Tyson - Holyfield had seen off two famous but old veterans of the ring, George Foreman and Larry Holmes, and a journeyman called Bert Cooper, who had the champ down in the third round. It had not, to say the least, been convincing.

Now, however, he was facing a younger, bigger, taller, heavier and stronger fighter, also unbeaten, and with a three inch reach advantage. He may have been narrow favorite but it was clear if Bowe was on song then Holyfield would need to dig into his famous reserves and big heart to withstand the challenge.

Thus 'The Real Deal' met 'Big Daddy' in Nevada for what would go down as one of the great heavyweight clashes in the history of the sport, a fight recognized by all as the best of their trilogy.

Although Holyfield started well Bowe began to dictate the pace, a fighter surprisingly quick with both his feet and hands for a man of his size. Trained by Eddie Futch, one of the greatest trainers there has ever been, and a man who taught the likes of Joe Frazier and Larry Holmes in their pomp, Bowe also possessed a more than solid chin. Holyfield had his moments but Bowe threw and landed more punches and this began to tell. The end of fight stats revealed Bowe landed 53% of his 248 punches compared to Holyfield's 39% of his 161.

After nine rounds Bowe held a healthy lead but had never ventured more than ten rounds in his entire career before.

The tenth would go down in history as one of the stand out rounds of all time. It would later be voted 'Round of the Year' by The Ring magazine. Bowe rocked the champion with a series of combinations, getting the better of toe-to-toe brawls to send Holyfield wobbling backwards. It seemed as if the end was nigh. Holyfield looked set to drop at any moment. Instead, and to the astonishment of all at ringside, Holyfield mustered up all his powers of determination to bounce back from the brink of oblivion to end the round the stronger and with Bowe on the defense. As the bell was sounded Bowe gave his opponent a little tap on the waist with his glove. It was a nice touch, a show of respect from a man who had seen Holyfield take everything he could throw at him and still survive.

The round would take its toll on a now exhausted champion, however. In the 11th round a right hook followed by a right hander to the side of the head finally sent Holyfield down. He rose to his feet and, knowing only a knockout could save him, finished the fight aggressively.

It made little difference. The three judges were unanimous in their verdict. Riddick Bowe had inflicted Holyfield's first defeat and was the new, undisputed champion of the world.

One month later Bowe vacated his WBC title after refusing to meet Lennox Lewis, the number one contender, due to disagreement over the purse split. He would meet Holyfield twice more, losing to him on a majority decision in 1993 and then winning two years later after stopping an aging Holyfield in the eighth round.

But it would be this first fight that would remain long in the memory banks.

"EVANDER WAS SMART, HE WAS A THINKER, HE WAS IN GREAT SHAPE, HE HAD ALL THE ATTRIBUTES TO MAKE HIM A GREAT CHAMPION. THAT'S WHY HE AND I FOUGHT AGAINST EACH OTHER SO HARD."

RIDDICK BOWE

11 JUNE 1982

HOLMES VS COONEY

WORLD HEAVYWEIGHT CHAMPIONSHIP
CAESARS PALACE, LAS VEGAS, NEVADA, U.S.A.

TALE OF THE TAPE

LARRY HOLMES	NAME	GERRY COONEY
THE EASTON ASSASSIN	NICKNAME	GENTLEMAN / GREAT WHITE HOPE
CUTHBERT, GEORGIA, U.S.A.	BIRTHPLACE	MANHATTAN, NEW YORK, U.S.A.
32	AGE	26
39—0—0	PRE-FIGHT RECORD	25—0—0
29	KO'S	21
6'3"	HEIGHT	6'6"
213 LBS	WEIGHT	226 LBS
81"	REACH	81"
ORTHODOX	STANCE	ORTHODOX

THE PRIDE AND GLORY

A FIGHT THAT UNDERLINED THE GREATNESS OF AN UNDERVALUED HEAVYWEIGHT CHAMPION AND A DEFEAT THAT IMPACTED ON THE CHARISMATIC CHALLENGER'S LIFE.

It was one of the most highly-anticipated fights of the early 1980s between one of the true greats in the history of the heavyweight division and a contender with frightening potential. Larry Holmes had been the world champion for four years when he faced a man dubbed the 'Great White Hope', a nickname that helped fan the flames of the racial undertones surrounding this clash. Cooney had only been a pro since 1977 but in that time he had made alarmingly quick progress and came to Vegas unbeaten after 29 bouts. His last had made the world take notice, dismissing Ken Norton inside 54 seconds of the first round at Madison Square Garden. Known for his left hook and imposing size he represented an enormous threat to the champion.

Holmes, though, had seen off all challengers, defending his title 11 times with ten knock outs. This, coupled with Cooney's still relative inexperience at this level, made the defending world champion the 8-5 favorite, but it was the Irish-American who enjoyed all the pre-bout hype, featuring on the covers of both Time and Sports Illustrated magazines, the former alongside actor Sylvester Stallone who was enjoying fame as his alter ego, Rocky Balboa.

'Sly' was joined by the likes of Joe DiMaggio, Wayne Gretzky and Jack Nicholson on the night as almost 30,000 packed into the outside arena in the Caesars parking lot.

There had been much bad mouthing before the fight during one of the most high-profile promotional tours, especially between the rival management teams, but when the boxers finally touched gloves in the ring Holmes leant over and said: "Let's have a good fight."

They kept this promise. Holmes dropped the challenger in the 2nd round and the signs were that for all Cooney's threat it may not last long. Instead he bounced back, visibly hurting the champion in the fourth with one of his trademark body shots. Rounds five to eight saw the two men going toe-to-toe, trading punches whilst standing in the center of the ring. By the ninth, however, Cooney was beginning to tire. He had, after all, fought for just 54 seconds in a year, after his team held off other fights through fear of missing out on a big pay day with Holmes. Referee Mills Lane deducted a point for a low blow and, moments later, a second point for the same offence. Almost criminally, Cooney then lost a third point in the 11th for a repeat low blow.

At this point in the proceedings all three judges would have had him ahead if it were not for those lost three points.

It would all prove immaterial. Cooney began to run out of gas and in the 13th it would all come to an abrupt end. He began to take some heavy punishment from his more experienced opponent. A cut appeared above his left eye. Blood began to pour from his nose. Midway through the round a powerful cross shot from Holmes landed flush on Cooney's left cheek. His legs buckled as he staggered back onto the ropes close to his own corner. Holmes moved in to finish the job but referee Lane decided to give Cooney a standing count as he clutched onto the top rope to keep himself upright. During the count his trainer, Victor Valle, had seen enough, entered the ring and threw in the towel.

"I'm sorry, I'm sorry," Cooney said, apologizing to his legion of fans. "I tried with all my heart."

It would be his first defeat, a result that rocked him and affected the rest of a career that promised so much, but eventually failed to match the hype.

Holmes, in contrast, would remain champion a further three years. In later life he and Cooney became close friends.

28 JANUARY 1968

TORRES *vs*
CHIONOI

WORLD FLYWEIGHT CHAMPIONSHIP
EL TOREO DE CUATRO CAMINOS, MEXICO CITY, DISTRITO FEDERAL, MEXICO

TALE OF THE TAPE

EFREN TORRES	NAME	CHARTCHAI CHIONOI
EL ALACRAN (THE SCORPION)	NICKNAME	MARCIANO OF ORIENTAL (LITTLE MARCIANO OF ASIA)
LA PALMA, MICHOACÁN DE OCAMPO, MEXICO	BIRTHPLACE	BANGKOK, THAILAND
24	AGE	27
53—4—1	PRE-FIGHT RECORD	46—10—2
35	KO'S	30
5'3"	HEIGHT	5'5"
112 LBS	WEIGHT	110 LBS
64.5"	REACH	65.5"
ORTHODOX	STANCE	ORTHODOX

BLOOD-DRENCHED SPECTACLE

A BRUTAL FIGHT BETWEEN TWO BRAVE MEN PREPARED TO PUT THEIR BODIES ON THE LINE AND CROSS IT, WITH ONE OF THE BLOODIEST ENDINGS IN THE HISTORY OF THE SPORT.

This was a fight that has remained in the memories of anyone present at ringside or who caught it on television, a meeting between two incredibly gutsy fighters who created one of the most blood-drenched spectacles boxing has ever seen.

Chionoi had been the WBC's world flyweight champion for two years when he stepped into the lion's den of taking on Torres in the Mexican's capital city. The expectation of a good fight was huge, but nobody quite foresaw what was about to unfold.

The initial signs were good for Torres. It was evident that he was the more technically-gifted fighter of the two but as early as the second round he decided to mix it up more with the experienced Thai champion.

This was a bad move. Torres not only hit the canvas but also had a cut open up above his left eye. From that point onwards Chionoi targeted the injury with chopping right handers.

Undeterred Torres varied his attacks, finding both head and body whereas, in comparison, the champion seemed to focus wholly on the challenger's cut.

In the fourth round the Mexican made the Thai's knees buckle. In the sixth he had him in trouble again. Torres knew his profusely bleeding eye injury spelled big trouble and seemed intent on finishing the fight before his eye finished him.

In the seventh Chionoi was caught again and was lucky, as he stumbled back, that the ropes beside his own corner helped him recover his balance. It was the message the champion needed. From that point he started to jab much more and avoid trading blows with the hungry Mexican.

The blood was now becoming an issue. Torres was covered in his own blood as the cut opened up more. Hampered and half-blinded he knew the fight was running away from him and launched a spirited attack in the tenth that resulted in Chionoi's eye swelling up dramatically.

By now the corner men were wiping a floor sticky with blood clean after every round. Although Torres was by far in a worse condition both men's eye injuries meant that they were fighting each other practically one-eyed. Incredibly, neither seemed too concerned about their state, instead taking the fight to each other.

The fight was evenly-matched, with perhaps Torres enjoying a slender lead, but a left hook, right cross combination from Chionoi in the 12th opened up his opponent's eye even more and the Mexican continued to fight with his own blood now splattered all over his torso, shoulders, legs and, of course, his face.

These were different times, of course, and it was not unusual to see blood in the ring, but even by the standards of the late 60's, the state of Torres was a sight few would ever forget. Even the ringside fans and press were being hit by the Mexican's red juices.

In the 13th the ringside doctor had seen enough. Deep, dark, dried blood had now covered the Mexican's right eye and celebrated referee Arthur Mercante called a halt to the violent proceedings.

"It was a fantastic fight," Mercante reported afterwards. "I had Torres ahead 7-4 with two rounds tied when I had to call it."

Torres required 15 stitches to close the cut and the victorious champion was quick to praise his defeated foe. "He's the toughest man I've ever fought," Chionoi said. "He's definitely the second best flyweight in the world."

The pair would meet twice more inside the next two years, Torres winning the second encounter and the WBC world title, only to lose it to Chinoi in the deciding bout in 1970.

Both were excellent fights but it was their first, bloody encounter that is talked about in the boxing gyms of Mexico City.

9

MORALES vs BARRERA

WORLD SUPER BANTAMWEIGHT CHAMPIONSHIP
MANDALAY BAY RESORT & CASINO, LAS VEGAS, NEVADA, U.S.A.

TALE OF THE TAPE

ERIK MORALES	NAME	MARCO ANTONIO BARRERA
EL TERRIBLE (THE TERRIBLE)	NICKNAME	BABY-FACED ASSASSIN
TIJUANA, BAJA CALIFORNIA, MEXICO	BIRTHPLACE	MEXICO CITY, DISTRITO FEDERAL, MEXICO
23	AGE	26
35—0—0	PRE-FIGHT RECORD	49—2—0
28	KO'S	36
5'8"	HEIGHT	5'6"
121 LBS	WEIGHT	129.5 LBS
72"	REACH	70"
ORTHODOX	STANCE	ORTHODOX

CHAMPION VS CHAMPION

IT HAS GONE DOWN AS ONE OF THE ALL-TIME GREAT FIGHTS AND SET UP ONE OF THE ALL-TIME GREAT BOXING TRILOGIES. AND AFTER 12 PULSATING ROUNDS THERE WAS NOTHING IN IT.

It was always likely that the long-awaited clash between these two world super bantamweight champions could produce a classic but, as it turned out, it was the beginning of a trilogy of epics, with perhaps their first meeting edging it as the best of the lot.

In one corner you had the older, grittier Marco Antonio Barrera, who had reclaimed his world title in 1998 after losing twice to Junior Jones, his only two losses. This would be his third defense of a title he also bossed in the mid-90's. He was known throughout boxing as the 'Baby-Faced Assassin'.

In the other the taller, somewhat slimmer and younger Erik Morales, unbeaten so far in a run of victories that included Jones. 'El Terrible' and Barrera had traded insults in the run up to the fight, as only two passionate, competitive Mexican fighters can.

The stage was thus set in Las Vegas but few predicted quite what a fight it would be. Morales, making his ninth defense, was seen as the slight favorite, but everybody knew that Barrera would not give an inch.

They would not be disappointed, Barrera would win the first two rounds, his level of intensity and his trademark left hooks to the body edging them over Morales who responded with his usually lethal right hand.

Towards the end of the first round Morales was cautioned for landing a low blow. Barrera refused to accept his apology by touching gloves.

In the fourth Morales landed a huge right hander but, in his excitement, slipped to the floor as he tried to take advantage of this punch.

It set the scene for the fifth and most memorable round. Both would hurt each other with shots, with Barrera beginning the round the better before Morales took the initiative with 20 punches without reply. Barrera responded with a huge right hander that caught his younger opponent full in the face and then refused to apologize after landing a blow on Morales after the referee had called for a break.

It was that type of fight, and that kind of round. Later round five would be voted the Round of the Year by Ring Magazine.

It seemed as if all the exertions of the previous round had taken their tollmore on the older fighter, with Morales winning the sixth. But from this point onwards a pattern began where Barrera would start well, then Morales would take over before the WBO Champion would finish the stronger.

Thus Barrera ended round eight with three big punches that all found their target, and then round nine by stunning Morales with a late rally. In the tenth Barrera's legs were beginning to look weak, but he still managed to almost drop 'El Terrible' with just a few seconds remaining. And by the end of the 11th Barrera was sporting a cut below his left eye after Morales had landed a series of big rights.

The pair finally touched gloves at the start of the 12th and final round, a grudging recognition that they had earned each other's respect. Knowing that the fight was too close to call both disregarded their defense and stood in the middle of the ring trading blows.

With 30 seconds remaining Morales slipped to the floor and was incensed when referee, Mitch Halpern, recorded it as a knockdown and delivered a standing count. With blood now seeping out from below his right eye an angry Morales finished the stronger in the final flurry of punches and, as the final bell rang, the packed auditorium inside the Mandalay Bay Resort roared their approval.

It was desperately close, as the stats would support. Morales threw 319 punches to Barrera's 299, 290 power punches to 272 and landed 29 jabs to 27 from Barrera.

Perhaps because of this Morales would be announced as the winner on a split decision, with two judges rewarding the fight to him by 115-112 and 114-113, with the third going with Barrera, 114-113.

"People wanted a great fight and we gave it to them," said Morales afterwards.

But it was not the end, far from it. After such a close-fought slugfest boxing demanded more. Morales and Barrera would duly deliver. Twice!

"MORALES IS DEFINITELY THE TOUGHEST OPPONENT I HAVE FACED, BECAUSE IT ALMOST SEEMED WHENEVER I HIT HIM IT WOULDN'T HURT HIM. HE'S A GUY WHO WOULD CONSTANTLY GIVE ME PRESSURE, AND HE HIT REALLY, REALLY HARD."

MARCO ANTONIO BARRERA

09 JUNE 1978

HOLMES vs NORTON

WORLD HEAVYWEIGHT CHAMPIONSHIP
CAESARS PALACE, LAS VEGAS, NEVADA, U.S.A.

TALE OF THE TAPE

LARRY HOLMES	NAME	KEN NORTON
THE EASTON ASSASSIN	NICKNAME	THE BLACK HERCULES / THE JAW BREAKER / THE FIGHTING MARINE
CUTHBERT, GEORGIA, U.S.A.	BIRTHPLACE	JACKSONVILLE, ILLINOIS, U.S.A.
28	AGE	34
27—0—0	PRE-FIGHT RECORD	40—4—0
19	KO'S	32
6'3"	HEIGHT	6'3"
209 LBS	WEIGHT	220 LBS
81"	REACH	80"
ORTHODOX	STANCE	ORTHODOX

BAD BLOOD

IT WAS THE BEGINNING OF A LONG REIGN FOR LARRY HOLMES AND THE END OF AN ERA FOR KEN NORTON, AS THE OLD GAVE WAY TO THE NEW, BUT NOT WITHOUT ONE HELL OF A FIGHT FIRST.

Larry Holmes perhaps never quite received the recognition he deserved. He was, after all, the third-longest reigning world heavyweight champion in the history of boxing but his problem was that he was sandwiched between the great era of heavyweights spearheaded by Muhammad Ali and the new breed headed by Mike Tyson.

Against the big-hitting Ken Norton, who more than stood his own against the greats of the 1970s, Holmes made everyone stand up and notice after what was, arguably, his greatest performance.

Norton was the WBC's heavyweight champion after defeating Jimmy Young in an eliminator. He should have fought Leon Spinks for the title but Spinks went for a rematch after his shock win over Ali and was stripped of a title that was thus awarded to Norton.

Although few knew at the time Holmes injured his left arm five days before the fight after a stray elbow from his sparring partner. His trainer, Richie Giachetti, informed the press Holmes had stopped training because he was too sharp.

Norton made his tactics clear. "Holmes claims he throws a hundred punches a round," explained the defending champion. "So if I can make him throw 150 a round I've done my job. I'll make him work harder than he wants to work."

And this is precisely what happened. Norton barely threw a meaningful punch, instead tying himself up in defense and allowing Holmes to indeed do all the work. It was a dangerously calculating ploy because after five rounds Holmes had won four.

As he prepared to rise from his stool for the sixth round Norton turned to his corner and said: "Now it's my turn."

That round Norton turned aggressor, shaking Holmes with a right to the head. In the seventh he hurt the challenger with a right to the body followed by a hard left to the head. Midway through this round he also caught Holmes on his left bicep, a punch more painful than he knew due to Holmes' secret injury.

As he predicted Norton came storming back into this fight, winning five of the next six rounds. And, although Holmes rallied in the 13th, winning the round after twice staggering Norton with a couple of heavy right handers, the champion hit back in the 14th with two big blows followed, right at the end, with six unanswered punches to the head and body.

Neither could barely lift themselves for the 15th round. All three judges up to this point had both fighters winning seven rounds each. Norton started the round the stronger, finding his target with overhand rights. Blood began to flow profusely from Holmes' lip that was split in the eighth round. It would later require 11 stitches. Holmes managed a four punch rally but Norton was on him again.

Midway through the round, however, Holmes showed the size of his heart. Going toe-to-toe with Norton he began to dominate. Defense was almost forgotten as both fighters swung their arms in what became a brawl, but it was Holmes who came out on top. With seconds remaining he staggered Norton with a big right, a punch that might just have won him the fight and the world title.

The judges scorecards came in. One went 143-42 to Norton but, crucially, two decided 143-142 Holmes. And so began the comparatively long reign of Larry Holmes whilst Norton, the only heavyweight champion in boxing history never to actually win a world title fight, would retire five fights later.

"The way we were trading in the 15th I knew I was gonna get hit so I didn't pay it no mind," Holmes reflected afterwards. "I had to stay in there and show the people that I had the fight in me. Norton fought like hell and I had to match him. I'm proud because I won the heavyweight championship of the world from a great fighter. Nobody thought I could do it. Norton beat Ali - he broke his jaw - so everyone picked against me. I went out and showed them what Larry Holmes was made of."

Indeed he did and, for the next seven years, no fight proved harder for the new champion.

"I THOUGHT I WON THE NORTON FIGHT BY MORE THAN ONE POINT BUT THEY STILL GAVE ME THE NEWS I WANTED TO HEAR, I WAS THE NEW HEAVYWEIGHT CHAMPION OF THE WORLD. I DON'T CARE IF I WIN BY ONE POINT OR 10 POINTS."

LARRY HOLMES

28 JUNE 1991

TYSON vs
RUDDOCK II

WORLD HEAVYWEIGHT CHAMPIONSHIP
THE MIRAGE HOTEL & CASINO, LAS VEGAS, NEVADA, U.S.A.

TALE OF THE TAPE

MIKE TYSON	NAME	DONOVAN RUDDOCK
IRON MIKE	NICKNAME	RAZOR
BROOKLYN, NEW YORK, U.S.A.	BIRTHPLACE	ST. CATHERINE PARISH, JAMAICA
24	AGE	27
40—1—0	PRE-FIGHT RECORD	25—2—1
36	KO'S	18
5'11.5"	HEIGHT	6'3"
216 LBS	WEIGHT	238 LBS
71"	REACH	82"
ORTHODOX	STANCE	ORTHODOX

THE REMATCH

*ILL-DISCIPLINED, WITH GENUINE ILL-FEELING AND NO LACK OF
DRAMA, FEW EXPECTED IT TO GO THE DISTANCE AND YET IT WOULD
BECOME A HEAVYWEIGHT CLASH FEW WOULD EVER FORGET.*

This classic was dubbed 'The rematch' following the first encounter,
just three months previously, had ended in controversy when the fight
was stopped in the 7th after Tyson had landed a six punch combination.
Referee Richard Steele believed Ruddock was in trouble despite the
fact that he was on his feet and appeared unperturbed.

Under the circumstances a rematch at the same venue- albeit with
a different referee - was the only way to satisfy an outraged Ruddock
camp who had been disagreeing with their Tyson counterparts ever
since.

It also served to underline the two fighters' mutual dislike for
each other, something they made clear in their feisty pre-match press
conferences.

There was much to play for here. Tyson was honing in on a return
to the world title following his shock defeat to Buster Douglas whilst
'Razor' Ruddock had impressed despite losing last time out and
was eyeing up a potential shot at the world title himself. The winner
would become the mandatory challenger to undisputed heavyweight
champion Evander Holyfield.

Few, if any, expected it to go the distance and, judging by the way
Tyson began the evening, neither did 'Iron Mike'. Inside the last few
seconds of the first round the American had his big opponent in
trouble with a huge right hander. Fired up he also landed two more
blows after the bell had sounded. Ruddock responded but missed

with his counter. It would be a taste of what would prove to be an ill-disciplined and ill-tempered bout.

In the second round Tyson carried on from where he left off, landing another strong right hander in the first few seconds and then, a little later, a three punch combination which included one below the belt.

Referee Mills Lane would utter a warning to Tyson on what would prove to be a busy night for the man trying to keep these two fighters on the right side of the boxing law. Close to the bell Tyson's big weapon on the night, his right hander, knocked Ruddock down to the canvas. The Canadian jumped up almost immediately, as if to confirm that he had been unhurt.

The truth was somewhat different. After the fight it was confirmed that his jaw had been broken by the force of Tyson's haymaker.

Amazingly, the third round went to Ruddock but he found himself back on the floor again in round four after being on the receiving end of a vicious right hook, thus emulating the first fight when he was twice decked by Tyson inside four rounds.

Ruddock leapt to his feet again, showing enormous powers of recovery and heart to withstand such an onslaught and, before the round was over, Tyson received his first point deduction for another low blow.

Despite this Tyson was by some distance ahead at this stage but Ruddock, just as he did in their first encounter, rallied to win the next few rounds. Indeed, in the sixth, a fierce counter from the Canadian resulted in Tyson's mouthpiece flying across the ring. In the eighth it would be Razor's turn to be deducted a point, this time for striking out after the bell, but Tyson was to lose two more points in the ninth and tenth for a low blow and then a late punch respectively.

When both fighters landed further low blows almost simultaneously in the 11th referee Lane let his feelings be known. Deciding not to deduct any further points he instead shouted: "Knock that shit off."

The twelfth and final round was brutal. Tyson believed he could finish it and dominated the final three minutes with an all-out attack but somehow, unlike so many before him, Ruddock survived.

It was some achievement to go the distance with 'Iron Mike' but that last round finished Ruddock off. His left eye was now swollen shut to add to his broken jaw.

Tyson, too, was not unscathed. Later his camp would reveal he had suffered from a perforated eardrum.

The judges were unanimous in their decision, with one awarding Tyson the fight by 113-109 and the other two, 114-108. The margin of victory would have been so much more had it not been for those three deducted points.

Both would eventually go on to fight for world titles - in Tyson's case with success, but only after a three-year spell in prison - but most observers in the sport believed that neither fighter would ever quite regain the same level of intensity and power as witnessed in this spellbinding second encounter in the desert.

16 SEPTEMBER 2017

ÁLVAREZ vs
GOLOVKIN

WORLD MIDDLEWEIGHT CHAMPIONSHIP
T-MOBILE ARENA, LAS VEGAS, NEVADA, U.S.A.

TALE OF THE TAPE

SAUL ÁLVAREZ	NAME	GENNADY GOLOVKIN
CANELO	NICKNAME	GGG
JALISCO, MEXICO	BIRTHPLACE	KARAGANDA, KAZAKHSTAN
29	AGE	24
49—1—1	PRE-FIGHT RECORD	37—0—0
34	KO'S	33
5'9"	HEIGHT	5'10.5"
160 LBS	WEIGHT	160 LBS
66.5"	REACH	78.3"
ORTHODOX	STANCE	ORTHODOX

SUPREMACY

IT WAS TOUGH TO CALL BEFORE THE FIGHT AND, AS IT TURNED OUT, A TOUGH CALL AFTERWARDS, BUT WHAT BEFELL IN BETWEEN WAS A NO-HOLDS-BARRED SLUGFEST BETWEEN TWO OF THE GREATEST BOXERS IN ANY DIVISION IN THE WORLD.

Talks began for this much-anticipated encounter as early as 2015 but it would take another two years to get it on, by which stage both Álvarez and Golovkin were considered as strong contenders to be the number one, pound for pound boxer in the world.

In 2016 Álvarez vacated his WBC middleweight title after knocking out Amir Khan. The belt was thus handed over to Golovkin. Finally, in May 2017, Álvarez saw off Julio César Chávez Jr and promptly announced in the ring that his clash with the big-hitting Kazakh was set for September at the same venue in Las Vegas. "Golovkin, you are next, my friend," Álvarez said as his rival clambered into the ring to join him. "I've never feared anyone. When I was born, fear was gone."

The respect between the pair was palpable. "I'm ready," Golovkin responded. "Everyone is excited for September. 'Canelo' looked very good tonight and 100% he will be the biggest challenge of my career."

Unsurprisingly the T-Mobile was sold out as over 22,000 fight fans packed into the arena to watch a bout entitled 'Supremacy'. Both boxers quickly found their feet as the fight began even if they were also quite clearly checking each other out. It was an interesting contrast in styles. 'Canelo' was all about speed and footwork, Golovkin - as befitting a man with 33 knockouts in his 37 straight wins - power, especially his jab in the early rounds.

Golovkin would edge the first two rounds, although he struggled with his opponent's elusiveness, only for 'Canelo' to hit back in the third with a left uppercut to the chin.

Yet it only really began to take off between the rounds of four to eight. That is when the barrage from the intimidating Kazakh began, and the impressive defense and counter-attacking from the Mexican responded.

These rounds took a reoccurring theme. 'Canelo' would start the stronger and attack before tiring and allowing 'Triple G' to take over and, so ringside observers felt, do enough to win the rounds. In the fourth, for example, Golovkin ended the round with 'Canelo' on the ropes taking a series of ab-crunching body blows.

The unbeaten champion stepped it up in rounds seven, eight and nine. It is arguable that nobody else could have lasted the onslaught that Golovkin produced but 'Canelo'. The Mexican not only showed the size of his heart but also the size of his brain, digging deep to first survive and then out-box the Kazakh as they headed for home. By the end he was even out-punching him, too.

As dominant as Golovkin had been in his career his pre-fight prediction was correct. 'Canelo', no mug with 34 knockouts out of his 49 wins, could fight fire with fire and the final third of the fight turned into a toe-to-toe slugfest, with neither boxer willingly taking a backward step.

In the tenth 'Canelo' hit the target with a monstrous right hander. Golovkin had never gone down in 350 amateur fights and his entire professional career but he staggered first back and then to his left before his fighting instincts kicked in and he fought back.

As the final bell rang after twelve, hard-fought rounds, the crowd roared their appreciation and both fighters, their faces bruised and swollen, raised their hands in victory.

At ringside and across the global TV audience fans wondered just how they managed to take everything they threw at each other, a testament to both men on the night.

In the end neither won, at least not officially. One judge had it 115-113 Golovkin, a second a 114-114 draw, but a third, Adalaide Byrd, somehow scored it 118-110 'Canelo'. The fight was declared a controversial draw leaving pretty much everyone - even 'Canelo's' promoter Oscar De La Hoya - wondering just quite how the Mexican had 'won' by such a large margin with one of the judges.

The stats suggested a closely-fought win for the Kazakh. He landed 218 of his 703 punches compared to 'Canelo's' 169 out of 505 but, crucially, out-punched the challenger in ten of the twelve rounds.

Golovkin was surprisingly philosophical afterwards, despite seeing his perfect record blemished. "The scoring is not my fault," he said. "I put pressure on him in every round. I still have all the belts. I am still the champion."

'Canelo', in time-honored tradition, begged to differ."I think I was superior," he insisted. "I won seven or eight rounds. I was able to counter punch and make Gennady wobble at least three times. I feel frustrated by the draw."

It would mean, of course, a rematch, one year later and a second, epic encounter considered superior even than their first meeting.

"I'M GENNADY GOLOVKIN UNTIL I WALK INTO THE RING. THEN I TURN INTO TRIPLE G. I'M OLD SCHOOL, THERE SHOULD ONLY BE ONE CHAMPION."

GENNADY GOLOVKIN

3 NOVEMBER 2007

CALZAGHE
VS KESSLER

WORLD SUPER MIDDLEWEIGHT CHAMPIONSHIP
MILLENNIUM STADIUM, CARDIFF, WALES, U.K.

TALE OF THE TAPE

JOE CALZAGHE	NAME	MIKKEL KESSLER
PRIDE OF WALES	NICKNAME	VIKING WARRIOR
LONDON, ENGLAND, U.K.	BIRTHPLACE	COPENHAGEN, DENMARK
35	AGE	28
43—0—0	PRE-FIGHT RECORD	39—0—0
33	KO'S	29
5'11"	HEIGHT	6'1"
166 LBS	WEIGHT	168 LBS
73"	REACH	74"
SOUTHPAW	STANCE	ORTHODOX

PRIDE VS WARRIOR

THIS WAS THE NIGHT WHEN JOE CALZAGHE FINALLY GAINED THE RECOGNITION FOR EVERYTHING HE HAD ACHIEVED IN BOXING AFTER PRODUCING A MASTERCLASS IN FRONT OF A RECORD-BREAKING INDOOR CROWD VIRTUALLY ALL SHOUTING FOR HIM.

For a man who had been world champion for nine years and been unbeaten in a 43-fight professional career Joe Calzaghe was surprisingly under-valued in the highest echelons of world boxing. A win over Jeff Lacy to temporarily claim the IBF title improved his stock but it would be this unification bout against the hard-hitting Dane that finally gave the Welshman the recognition he deserved.

Talks, as ever, had been ongoing for a while. It prompted Kessler, also unbeaten after 39 bouts, to complain that Calzaghe was more interested in fighting big names in the light-heavyweight division such as Bernard Hopkins and Roy Jones Jr. Nonetheless, the fight was finally agreed for Cardiff, just a few miles from Calzaghe's South Wales home town, and on the line was unification of all the super middleweight belts.

What took place that night under the closed roof of the Millennium Stadium turned out to be a boxing masterpiece by the considerably older man, although it took a while for the Welshman to find his stride.

The fight began in the early hours due to the demands of US TV. Calzaghe would admit later that he tried too hard in the first few rounds, buoyed by a hugely partisan home crowd of 50,150, the vast majority on his side. This would be a new European record for an indoor boxing event.

If the first two rounds were even Kessler took the third, courtesy of two, separate right uppercuts. From that point onwards Calzaghe took over, upping his work rate noticeably and proving too fast and too elusive for the Dane taken aback by the speed and quantity of punches raining down on him.

It was not as if Kessler failed to find his target from time to time. He did, but in doing so he discovered what a strong chin his opponent possessed. Add Calzaghe's better defense, his assortment of hard punches and his superior energy and it soon became obvious that the home boy would have the better night.

In the eighth round Calzaghe hurt the Dane with a fierce body shot and it soon became apparent that Kessler was at a loss about how to counter this. "His punches weren't particularly hard," he insisted afterwards. "But it was confusing when he hit you twenty times."

By the 12th it was obvious that Kessler could only win via a knockout, a tall order against the unbeaten champion. He hunted for Calzaghe but came up against a boxer too smart to be caught in a late trap.

The judges' scores read 117-111, 116-112 and 116-112, all in favor of the Welshman who had just inflicted a first defeat in Kessler's career and, in doing so, recorded the fourth highest sequence of word title defenses, at 21, in the history of boxing. The stats simply backed up Calzaghe's superiority. He threw a staggering 1,010 punches compared to 585 from Kessler, no mean number in itself.

The victory finally made the boxing world sit up and take serious notice of a man who entered the pantheon of British greats after this night in Cardiff.

Kessler was magnanimous in defeat. "He stopped me boxing," he admitted afterwards. "When I put him under pressure I thought I'd be OK, but he has such a good chin. I have to give him that."

Now there was no more debate. Calzaghe had elevated himself to the top three in the world's pound for pound best boxers. "I could tell Kessler was convinced he would win the fight," he said. "Why wouldn't he have been? He was the young champ, I was the old man. "So for me this is my crowning moment. After all the years of struggle and injury to win the four belts and *The Ring* magazine title is great."

He would go on to fight Hopkins and Jones Jr, defeating them both before hanging up his gloves with an unbeaten record of 46 wins and 0 defeats, cementing his name in boxing history in the process.

"I WAS COOL, CALM AND COLLECTED, I BELIEVED WINNING WAS MY DESTINY."

JOE CALZAGHE

5 MAY 2007

DE LA HOYA VS MAYWEATHER

WORLD LIGHT MIDDLEWEIGHT CHAMPIONSHIP
MGM GRAND GARDEN ARENA, LAS VEGAS, NEVADA, U.S.A.

TALE OF THE TAPE

OSCAR DE LA HOYA	NAME	FLOYD MAYWEATHER
GOLDEN BOY	NICKNAME	PRETTY BOY
MONTEBELLO, CALIFORNIA, U.S.A.	BIRTHPLACE	GRAND RAPIDS, MICHIGAN, U.S.A.
34	AGE	30
38—4—0	PRE-FIGHT RECORD	37—0—0
30	KO'S	24
5'10.5"	HEIGHT	5'8"
154 LBS	WEIGHT	150 LBS
73"	REACH	72"
ORTHODOX	STANCE	ORTHODOX

THE WORLD AWAITS

A CLASH BETWEEN TWO OF THE BIGGEST NAMES EVER IN BOXING, BUT WHILST THIS WAS THE BEGINNING OF THE END FOR DE LA HOYA IT WAS THE TURNING POINT IN GLOBAL RECOGNITION OF MAYWEATHER'S GREATNESS.

It was dubbed 'The World Awaits' and, considering it pitted a six division world champion against an undefeated four division world champion, a 'Super Fight' to boot. No wonder the likes of Jack Nicholson, Leonardo DiCaprio and Jennifer Lopez were at ringside outside at the MGM Garden Arena to see this one pan out.

The build-up had been extremely public thanks, in no small measure, to an HBO series called 24/7 following both fighters as they prepared to meet. Moreover, there had been a sub-plot. Mayweather's estranged father, Floyd Sr, was talking with De La Hoya to be his trainer against his own son. Negotiations would breakdown over the agreed financial package and Floyd Sr would reunite with his son, but with no official role because Mayweather's choice of trainer was his uncle, former world champion Roger. This resulted in his father leaving the camp because of this decision and comments made by brother and son during the HBO series against him.

As if this was not enough Mayweather wasted no time in goading De La Hoya. At a promotional event on the Hollywood Boulevard, for example, he asked one of his entourage to "bring Oscar up." Up came a chicken wearing a fake gold medal (a nod to De La Hoya's 1992 Olympic gold medal) and a sign saying 'Golden Girl' - De La Hoya's Golden Boy Promotions were promoting the fight. "I'm the villain in boxing, but I'm damn good," Mayweather announced.

Finally the American showed particular nerve in entering the ring wearing shorts in the green, red and white colors of the Mexican flag and wearing a sombrero in front of what was estimated to be a 90 % pro-De La Hoya audience.

Small wonder it became the most lucrative boxing in history at the time, generating $130M in revenue. De La Hoya would receive a cool $52M, also the biggest payday in boxing back then, and Mayweather $25M.

Although De La Hoya was the slight favorite the reality was he had lost twice in his previous four fights and had only fought three times in the last 32 months. He was nearing the end of his career and was ring rusty as he approached what would be his first defense of the WBC's world light-middleweight title.

It was therefore not a surprise that he started the fight as the aggressor, perhaps hoping to get to Mayweather before any later round tiredness kicked in. He tried to turn it into a brawl, cornering Mayweather on the ropes and attempting to land a flurry of punches onto the challenger's body but instead got caught by 'Pretty Boy's' counter-attacks.

It was a classic encounter between an aggressor and a defensive specialist and from the fifth round onwards an even fight began to shift Mayweather's way as he scored points consistently against a tiring De La Hoya.

The stats concerning punches at the end of the fight reveals just how Mayweather would go on to win. De La Hoya threw 587 punches to Mayweather's 481, but landed with 122 compared to 207. It was even more in Mayweather's favor when it came to the power punches, with De La Hoya landing 82 of his 341 whilst Mayweather, incredibly, scored 57% with 138 out of 241.

With these tactics, speed, accuracy, defensive and counter-punching he would win four of the remaining five rounds to see him home, although it remained extraordinarily tight right up to the final minute of the final round when, at last, both fighters stood toe-to-toe and swapped punches.

After a split decision the judges went 115-113 and 116-112 Mayweather, to 115-113 De La Hoya. Judge Jerry Roth scored the last round to Mayweather, the only judge to do so. Had he gone with De La Hoya his final score would have been a draw and the fight would also have been declared a draw.

No matter, Mayweather was the victor and, in doing so, he solidified his place in boxing history as arguably the supreme defense specialist. It was his 38th straight win in his professional career on his way to achieving an unbeaten record of 50 wins before he retired in 2017.

"I landed the harder, crisper punches," De La Hoya insisted afterwards. "I was pressing the fight. If I hadn't there wouldn't have been a fight. I'm the champion and you have to do more than that to beat a champion."

Mayweather was unconcerned by his beaten foe's comments.

"It was a masterpiece of boxing," he declared. "I showed you why I am the best fighter of this era."

21 JUNE 2003

LEWIS vs KLITSCHKO

WORLD HEAVYWEIGHT CHAMPIONSHIP
STAPLES CENTER, LOS ANGELES, CALIFORNIA, U.S.A.

TALE OF THE TAPE

LENNOX LEWIS	NAME	VITALI KLITSCHKO
THE LION	NICKNAME	DR. IRONFIST
LONDON, ENGLAND, U.K.	BIRTHPLACE	BELOVODSKOE, KYRGYZSTAN
37	AGE	31
40—2—1	PRE-FIGHT RECORD	32—1—0
31	KO'S	31
5'10"	HEIGHT	5'7"
146 LBS	WEIGHT	146 LBS
83.8"	REACH	77.9"
ORTHODOX	STANCE	ORTHODOX

BATTLE OF THE TITANS

EVEN IN VICTORY IT WOULD PROVE TO BE THE END OF AN ERA FOR LENNOX LEWIS AND IN DEFEAT FOR KLITSCHKO, A PERFORMANCE THAT MADE THE BOXING WORLD SIT UP AND TAKE NOTICE.

Billed as the 'Battle of the Titans' this encounter between two huge heavyweights took a while to happen due to the champion, Lewis, taking a year out following his knockout of Mike Tyson and initial negotiations then breaking down. The British world champion was then set to take on Kirk Johnson until the challenger pulled out with an injury and Klitschko, the fierce Ukrainian who packed a notorious punch, stepped up to the plate. As denoting a champion who the bookmakers had as 4-1 favorite, Lewis received $7M to appear at the Staples Center, as opposed to the $1.4M that came Klitschko's way, but it was the challenger who started the fight better as the aggressor, landing big shots to the British fighter's head to take the first two rounds. Two hard rights in particular staggered Lewis and opened up a small cut under his left eye.

Sensing the danger his veteran trainer, the celebrated Emmanuel Seward, ordered his man to adopt more aggressive tactics and inside the first ten seconds of the third round a strong right hander caused a deep cut above Klitschko's left eye.

Although Lewis would take the round, and his opponent's vision was subsequently impaired as a result of the severe wound, Klitschko would counter strongly to win the 4th round as they traded blows. In the 5th, as the Ukrainian's cut worsened, Lewis landed four consecutive punches whilst holding the challenger in a clinch, the legality of which would be hotly debated later.

It was clear, as medics examined Klitschko's eye, that the fight would not last the distance and in the 6th round, with his face half-covered by his own blood, he received a huge uppercut that simply made the injury worse.

In between the 6th and 7th rounds the ringside physician, Dr Paul Wallace, had seen enough and advised for the fight to be stopped. As the wounds were inflicted by Lewis' punches the fight was awarded tothe defending champion by way of a TKO.

At the time of the stoppage the judges had Klitschko ahead by four rounds to two.

He was suitably furious afterwards. "I did not want the fight to stop," he said. "My strategy was working. I knew his conditioning was not good."

In reality, despite his lead, Klitschko could not have continued. He would later receive 60 stitches to treat four cuts on his face and one in his mouth.

It was a point Lewis seized upon. "I was getting to him," he insisted. "Look at his face. It was only a matter of time. The ref saved his face."

It would prove to be Lewis' last defense, though. His age had caught up with him and Lewis knew a likely re-match with Klitschko could end badly. He would retire shortly afterwards and later admitted that this was his toughest fight. Klitschko would go on to beat Corrie Sanders to claim the WBC title and, post-retirement, would become Mayor of Kiev back in his home country.

And both knew, deep down, that the champion had got lucky when Klitschko's wound ended the affair.

"RIGHT NOW, I FEEL LIKE THE PEOPLE'S CHAMPION. I DID NOT WANT THEM TO STOP THE FIGHT. MY STRATEGY WAS TO TAKE IT INTO THE SEVENTH AND EIGHTH ROUNDS. MY STRATEGY WAS WORKING. I KNEW HIS CONDITIONING WAS NOT GOOD."

VITALI KLITSCHKO

18 SEPTEMBER 2004

HOPKINS vs
DE LA HOYA

WORLD MIDDLEWEIGHT CHAMPIONSHIP
MGM GRAND GARDEN ARENA, LAS VEGAS, NEVADA, U.S.A.

TALE OF THE TAPE

	NAME	
BERNARD HOPKINS	NAME	OSCAR DE LA HOYA
THE EXECUTIONER	NICKNAME	GOLDEN BOY
PHILADELPHIA, PENNSYLVANIA, U.S.A.	BIRTHPLACE	MONTEBELLO, CALIFORNIA, U.S.A.
39	AGE	31
44–2–1	PRE-FIGHT RECORD	37–3–0
31	KO'S	29
6'1"	HEIGHT	5'10"
156 LBS	WEIGHT	155 LBS
75"	REACH	73"
ORTHODOX	STANCE	ORTHODOX

IT'S HISTORY

TWO HOUSEHOLD BOXING NAMES, TWO LEGENDS OF THE SPORT, BUT A NATURAL MIDDLEWEIGHT SHOULD ALWAYS BEAT A NATURAL LIGHT-MIDDLEWEIGHT AND IT TOOK ONE, DEVASTATING PUNCH TO PROVE IT.

On paper this was a clash between two of the all-time greats in boxing history. In reality it was a huge call by Oscar De La Hoya, despite being eight years younger than his renowned opponent.

Having started out as a super featherweight most argued that De La Hoya's natural weight was light-middleweight whereas there was little doubt middleweight was the perfect division for Hopkins, a man who had not been beaten in eleven years.

However De La Hoya, after losing his world light middleweight titles to Shane Mosley, decided to move up a weight to set up this monster clash against a man as legendary as himself.

First, both had to get past Robert Allen and Felix Sturm in a double header on the same night in June. Hopkins dispatched Allen with ease but De La Hoya fighting for the first time at middleweight, scraped home against Sturm, winning unanimously but only by 115-113 on all three judges scorecards. In doing so he claimed the WBO world middleweight title, his eighth world title now in six, separate weight divisions.

A catchweight of 157lbs was agreed for the big clash, a weight limit that did not adhere to the traditional weight limits of the division. This was in recognition of De La Hoya, the Hispanic hero from East Los Angeles, moving up a weight and having fought just once as a result. Despite him being the underdog for the first time in his whole fighting career - the bookmakers had Hopkins down as 2-1 favorite - De La

Hoya would still earn a cool $32M for this fight, a career high until he met Floyd Mayweather later. Hopkins would take home a 'mere' $10 M for his part, another best pay packet in a distinguished career.

He would hold a considerable height advantage over De La Hoya, although the new middleweight held a slight reach advantage despite this.

For the first half of the fight both boxers revealed an inordinate amount of respect for each other, coupled with the desire not to be caught. It was a cagey, tactical game of defense, interspersed with the occasional attack and flurry.

The judges had it dead even at the halfway stage. The stats backed this up with De La Hoya having thrown just eight more punches than Hopkins and landing just one more after six rounds of action.

This was the cue for Hopkins to step up the attacks as De La Hoya began to tire. By the end of the eighth round two of the judges had Hopkins ahead 79-73 and 78-74, although the third seemed to think De La Hoya was edging it by 77-75.

It would not matter. Almost exactly halfway through the ninth round Hopkins struck his opponent with a devastating left hook into the liver. De La Hoya crumpled into an agonized heap on the canvas, in clear and obvious pain from the blow. Although he made an attempt to rise from the deck he was in too much discomfort to do so and was counted out.

It was the first knockout loss in his stellar career and, conversely, the last time Hopkins would win by a knockout. As the referee waved his arms and the bell sounded to signify the fight was over De La Hoya pounded the canvas with his fists in frustration. "I'm a better fighter than I showed out there," he insisted afterwards.

Wisely he returned to light-middleweight, winning back the world title in his next fight before losing it to Floyd Mayweather.

Hopkins would go on to fight many more times, including winning back a world light-heavyweight title at the age of 48, but he had just produced his last great display in seeing off the great Oscar De La Hoya.

"I GIVE HIM A LOT OF CREDIT, HE DIDN'T RUN AND HE CAME TO BOX."

BERNARD HOPKINS

28 SEPTEMBER 1979

HOLMES VS SHAVERS II

WORLD WELTERWEIGHT CHAMPIONSHIP
CAESARS PALACE, LAS VEGAS, NEVADA, U.S.A.

TALE OF THE TAPE

LARRY HOLMES	NAME	EARNIE SHAVERS
EASTON ASSASSIN	NICKNAME	BLACK DESTROYER
CUTHBERT, GEORGIA, U.S.A.	BIRTHPLACE	GARLAND, ALABAMA, U.S.A.
29	AGE	31
31—0—0	PRE-FIGHT RECORD	59—7—1
22	KO'S	57
6'3"	HEIGHT	6'0"
210 LBS	WEIGHT	233 LBS
81"	REACH	79"
ORTHODOX	STANCE	ORTHODOX

PUNCHER'S CHANCE

IT WAS THE DAY LARRY HOLMES FINALLY EMERGED FROM THE SHADOW OF MUHAMMAD ALI, BUT ONLY AFTER RECEIVING ONE OF THE MOST THUNDEROUS PUNCHES OF ALL TIME.

Up to this point Larry Holmes had not received the recognition he deserved for being the heavyweight world champion, mainly because Muhammad Ali had still been fighting and had just announced his retirement. He had already fought and beaten Shavers the year before in the fight before he claimed the WBC world title after defeating Ken Norton, but it had been a one-sided affair against a lack-luster Shavers.

The challenger was recognized to be one of the destructive punchers of all time, famously shaking Ali to the core en route to losing against 'The Greatest'. And when he bounced back from that first defeat to Holmes by knocking Norton out inside two minutes of the first round the world of boxing was reminded that Shavers could never be written off.

Holmes would enter the Shavers rematch on the back of an unimpressive victory over Mike Weaver and knew he had to step it up in what would be his fourth defense of his hard-earned world title.

Shavers, who insisted he was not in shape and had managerial problems on the eve of his first fight with Holmes, knew the score. "It's my best shot at the world title, and maybe my last," he admitted. No wonder he had the word 'Holmes' emblazoned on the headguards of all his sparring partners.

On a night described by promoter Don King as the "Greatest Boxing Show on Earth," partly because the likes of Sugar Ray Leonard, Roberto Durán and Wilfred Gomez were all on the card as well - the two heavyweights produced a moment in the fight that has been talked about ever since.

At first it all seemed to be going to plan for the champion. For six rounds Holmes worked behind his powerful jab, opening up Shavers with the occasional combination and avoiding at any cost a booming cross shot from the challenger. From the third round Shavers was having trouble with his right eye and appeared both clumsy and inaccurate with his punches.

"One of those jabs landed with the thumb of his glove in my eye and my vision went blurry," Shavers explained afterwards. "I saw three Larrys and ended up swinging at the wrong one."

In the 4th round his right eye began to bleed and by the 5th there was a small cut alongside his left eye too.

Knowing that he was so far behind Shavers stepped up his work rate noticeably in the 7th round and as he threw punch after punch he seemed to edge closer to Holmes. With just 30 seconds remaining the champion dropped his gloves for a split second and Shavers finally saw his chance.

Conjuring up seemingly all his pent up frustration and strength, he dropped Holmes with the perfect righthand cross shot. Holmes dropped to the canvas with a loud thud as if he had just been shot by a sniper in the crowd. It seemed improbable that he could recover from this but, midway through the count delivered by referee Davey Pearl, he rose somewhat gingerly to his feet.

"I was the champion of the world," Shavers lamented afterwards. "All my troubles were over. It was the greatest feeling I'd ever had. And it lasted for five whole seconds."

He tried everything to finish Holmes off in those remaining few seconds but the wily champion survived through a combination of retreating and clinching.

There was widespread disbelief in the crowd, first because they almost saw the dominant champion lose, and then because he somehow survived one of the biggest shots ever witnessed in a boxing ring.

The break between the 7th and 8th rounds was all Holmes needed, though, coupled with an ammonia capsule broken underneath his nose by trainer Richie Giachetti. Holmes returned to his powerful jabs and Shavers, who had blown himself out throwing everything he had in the previous round, became an exhausted and increasingly battered target.

At the start of the 11th round, with Holmes pleading for the fight to be stopped, the referee stepped in and threw his arms around a shattered Shavers. The beaten challenger was taken to hospital where 27 stitches were sewn above his right eye and, a fortnight later, a detached retina removed after surgery. He would never fight for a world title again.

Holmes, recognizing the moment, leaned over the ropes and issued this order to the watching press.

"No more Ali, please," he demanded. "I'm the only champion now."

And he would remain for quite some time to come.

"EARNIE HIT ME HARDER THAN ANY OTHER FIGHTER, INCLUDING MIKE TYSON. BEING HIT BY EARNIE SHAVERS WAS LIKE BEING HIT BY A MACK TRUCK."

LARRY HOLMES

18 SEPTEMBER 1998

DE LA HOYA
VS CHÁVEZ II

WORLD WELTERWEIGHT CHAMPIONSHIP
THOMAS & MACK CENTER, LAS VEGAS, NEVADA, U.S.A.

TALE OF THE TAPE

OSCAR DE LA HOYA	NAME	JULIO CÉSAR CHÁVEZ
GOLDEN BOY	NICKNAME	THE GREAT MEXICAN CHAMPION
MONTEBELLO, CALIFORNIA, USA	BIRTHPLACE	SONORA, MEXICO
25	AGE	36
28—0—0	PRE-FIGHT RECORD	100—2—2
23	KO'S	83
5'11"	HEIGHT	5'7.5"
146.5 LBS	WEIGHT	144.5 LBS
73"	REACH	68"
ORTHODOX	STANCE	ORTHODOX

ULTIMATE REVENGE

IT WAS THE BEGINNING OF THE END FOR THE GREAT OLD MEXICAN CHAMPION IN CHÁVEZ AS HE HANDED THE BATON OVER TO THE YOUNG, SUPERSTAR IN THE MAKING.

It was billed 'Ultimate Revenge' after De La Hoya had taken Chávez's WBC world title and inflicted only a second defeat in 99 bouts in the legendary Mexican fighter's long, star-studded career two years previously.

Back then a deep gash above Chávez's eye inflicted in the very first round saw the fight stopped in the fourth. A proud Chávez put the loss down to his lack of vision and insisted on a rematch, but he would have to wait until De La Hoya beat Miguel Angel Gonzalez in his first, mandatory defense, then Pernell Whitaker to take his fellow American's world welterweight title, and then three further defenses of his new title. Even after the rematch was announced it was subject to both fighters winning their tune-up bouts against Patrick Charpentier and Ken Sigurani respectively. With this final challenge met both could finally focus on each other.

De La Hoya had admitted that Chávez had been his idol and would later name him as the greatest Mexican fighter of all time. But their dynamics had changed since De La Hoya had crushed Chávez first time round.

Now De La Hoya, the new star in the sport, was the champion and Chávez the increasingly aging legend. When they took to the ring the latter, at 36, was 11 years older than the man who had beaten him.

Yet this time the fight was far more competitive as Chávez arrived in better shape, both mentally and physically. Two years earlier and injured early on he was unable to keep up with the younger, fitter man facing him. Two years on and he made a much better account of himself.

For the first two rounds they traded blows to delight the sell-out crowd in Las Vegas of 18,500. In the third round Chávez landed a blow so low that it had the young champion angrily gesticulating to both the challenger and referee.

As the fight went on neither were prepared to take a backward step, with Chávez connecting with his left hooks and De La Hoya responding with hard, left uppercuts. Yet it was De La Hoya who began to first edge and then canter away.

By the start of the eighth round Chávez was sporting a cut in the same spot as his savage injury two years previously and all three judges had the champion comfortably ahead on points.

It would all come to a brutal end three minutes later. Both fighters decided to drop any pretense to defend and went for each other. Between them they threw a combined total of 173 punches, with De La Hoya landing 45 of them and a rapidly-declining Chávez 38.

As he returned to his corner the legendary Mexican knew he had just been on the end of another brutal beating. So did his corner men. When the bell sounded for round nine Chávez stayed put and quit on his stool.

De La Hoya responded by jumping in the air with both arms aloft before then crashing down to the canvas and kissing his gloves.

His advisor, the respected trainer Gil Clancy, placed some perspective into this win. "That's the best Chávez has been in five years," he said. "This was the old Chávez."

The old Chávez, considerably older after this beating, was more magnanimous second time round. "I said that the first fight wasn't a fight," the Mexican insisted. "This time he beat me right. So I give him my respect. I wanted to continue the fight. My corner is the one who stopped the fight."

The champion later admitted Chávez had hurt him more than he knew. "He hit me with a hard right hander right on the button. My legs turned to jelly. I was out. But he just let me go because I was just so focused. This guy had a good right hand. I was even more satisfied that he quit on me."

Chávez would fight another ten times before hanging up his gloves on a remarkable career. He would never be world champion again.

For De La Hoya, however, it would prove to be one of the most significant victories in a career that would go on to claim 11 world titles in six different weight categories.

"I HIT HIM WITH SOME GOOD SHOTS AND HE STILL WOULDN'T GO DOWN. HE HAD ONE OF THE BEST CHINS IN THE WORLD. VERY RESILIENT. HE STILL IS MY HERO..."

OSCAR DE LA HOYA

12 SEPTEMBER 1992

CHÁVEZ vs
CAMACHO

WORLD LIGHT WELTERWEIGHT CHAMPIONSHIP
THOMAS & MACK CENTER, LAS VEGAS, NEVADA, U.S.A.

TALE OF THE TAPE

JULIO CÉSAR CHÁVEZ	NAME	HECTOR CAMACHO
THE GREAT MEXICAN CHAMPION	NICKNAME	MACHO
SONORA, MEXICO	BIRTHPLACE	BAYAMÓN, PUERTO RICO
30	AGE	30
81—0—0	PRE-FIGHT RECORD	41—1—0
67	KO'S	18
5'7.5"	HEIGHT	5'6.5"
140 LBS	WEIGHT	140 LBS
66.5"	REACH	69"
ORTHODOX	STANCE	ORTHODOX

ULTIMATE GLORY

IT WAS A FIGHT THE BOXING WORLD WANTED TO SEE. BUT, IN THE END, ONLY BLOODY-MINDEDNESS AND BRAVERY PREVENTED ANOTHER STOPPAGE FOR THE LION OF CULIACÁN.

This fight between two superstars had been a long time in the making. So much had anticipation been elevated that by the time Chávez, the legendary scrapper from Mexico, and Camacho, the flamboyant number one celebrity in Puerto Rico, finally "got it on" it had become the biggest non-heavyweight fight since Hagler vs Leonard.

The two fighters had been reasonably amicable acquaintances beforehand but as the fight drew closer any bonhomie disappeared. "I've finally got my chance to shut his mouth," Chávez said of his southpaw opponent. "Camacho is the fight I have wanted for years and it's the fight Mexico wants. I could never go back to Mexico if I lost to him. My fans don't want me just to win. They are begging me to give him a bad beating".

The Puerto Rican, a former champion in three weight classes, knew he faced a stiff challenge against a man who had claimed five world titles in 12 years and sported an intimidating record of 81 and 0.

"In the past I would take to the streets and party for three months", said the man nicknamed 'Macho'. When it was time to get back in shape I'd never be at my best. For Chávez, though, I started training six months ago."

Despite this he was outwardly confident. "I don't think he can handle my hand and foot speed," Camacho continued. "I have everything to beat this guy and all I have to do is execute."

Despite his confidence he entered the ring as the underdog in front of a sell out crowd largely supporting Chávez. Las Vegas had seemingly been overran by Mexican fans intent on ending a four day celebration of Mexican Independence Day by seeing their man beat a man who had 'mooned' them during a previous night when both fighters fought on the same card.

At first it all seemed to go to plan for Camacho. In a first round he clearly won, the Puerto Rican's jab repeatedly broke through Chávez's pressing tactics and his speed of legs created problems for the man they called the Lion of Culiacan.

But in the second round it was all change. It was as if Chávez had simply been sizing his foe up, seeing what he had in his armory before unleashing his own full set of weapons. A series of right hand leads caught Camacho at will. Left hooks added to the barrage and punches crashed into the side of the body. By the fourth Camacho had thrown away his own strategy and tried to stand and fight, toe-to-toe, man to man. This would prove to be punishing.

In the seventh round Camacho's left eye began to close. In the ninth a hook slashed open a cut in the corner of his right eye. He was taking everything Chávez could throw at him but had little left to counter with.

At the end of this round a small commotion took place in Camacho's corner. One of his team had quite clearly advised to throw the towel in. With his left eye now closed, his nose bloodied, the cut worsening above his other eye and his body battered by body blows, Camacho refused and rose to his feet.

His victory was to last the twelve rounds. It was an extraordinary show of bravery, pride and courage. But he was badly beaten by Chávez and he knew it.

"I couldn't keep him off me," Camacho admitted afterwards. "The pressure was amazing. I never fought anyone with courage like he has. I fought a courageous fight but there is no doubt that he won."

Chávez was more complimentary after than he was before. "He was a better fighter than I expected," he admitted. "He took a lot of punches."

He had said beforehand that he could never set foot in Mexico if he had lost. Instead the Mexican President, Carlos Salinas de Gortari, laid on his special car normally reserved for the Pope to collect Chávez from the airport and deliver him to the President's house.

Both fighters would continue to enjoy long careers after they met in the ring, with Chávez retiring after his 115th professional fight and Camacho fighting 88 times up to 2010. Two years later he died from gunshot wounds after being shot in his home town of Bayamon.

It was a sad ending for a man remembered for his world titles in victory, and his bravery in defeat against the irrepressible Julio César Chávez.

"IT WAS ONE OF THE BIGGEST FIGHTS OF MY CAREER. ALTHOUGH PEOPLE SAY I BEAT HIM EASY, IT WASN'T. HE WAS A VERY FAST FIGHTER AND IT WAS VERY DIFFICULT."

JULIO CÉSAR CHÁVEZ

24 FEBRUARY 1989

BARKLEY
VS DURÁN

WORLD MIDDLEWEIGHT CHAMPIONSHIP
TRUMP PLAZA, ATLANTIC CITY, NEW JERSEY, U.S.A.

TALE OF THE TAPE

IRAN BARKLEY	NAME	ROBERTO DURÁN
THE BLADE	NICKNAME	MANOS DE PIEDRA (HANDS OF STONE)
THE BRONX, NEW YORK, U.S.A.	BIRTHPLACE	EL CHORRILLO, PANAMA, CENTRAL AMERICA
29	AGE	37
25—4—0	PRE-FIGHT RECORD	84—7—0
16	KO'S	61
6'1"	HEIGHT	5'7"
159 LBS	WEIGHT	156 LBS
74"	REACH	66"
ORTHODOX	STANCE	ORTHODOX

STEEL VS STONE

SUPPOSEDLY WASHED UP AND FINISHED THIS PROVED TO BE ONE OF THE GREATEST NIGHTS IN ROBERTO DURÁN'S LONG, LONG CAREER WHERE, ONCE AGAIN, HIS INDOMITABLE HEART AND GUTS PROVED INSURMOUNTABLE.

All the facts suggested that Iran Barkley would prove to be a step too far for the once indomitable Roberto Durán. Barkley, much younger and bigger, was making the first defense of his newly-acquired WBC World Middleweight crown after demolishing the great Thomas Hearns in just three rounds in his previous fight, a result that won *The Ring* magazine's 'Upset of the Year' for 1988. Durán, five years previously, had in turn been wiped out by Hearns inside two rounds and, despite having previously held three world titles in three different weights, had not fought for a world crown since.

The boxing world believed that the great Panamanian was, in effect, washed up, but Durán, a man never to be written off, had other ideas. Often he would blow up in weight between bouts and sometimes would not be in perfect shape when he entered the ring. This was different. Durán, who had already twice retired only to make a comeback, trained fastidiously for four months in Miami recognizing this might be the last chance to become a world champion in a fourth weight.

With a six inch height advantage and seven inch reach advantage Barkley, known as "The Blade," was the 2.5-1 favorite to win and, on a night when outside the wintry conditions were frozen, inside the Convention Hall the action was red hot from the start.

For the first few rounds Barkley took the fight to Durán. Although he found his smaller, slippery target on occasions, most of the time the challenger evaded the American's jabs. Barkley started to aim for Durán's supposedly softer belly but found little change from this, either.

The pace quickened in rounds five and six and whilst it remained highly competitive Barkley held the edge over the older man. In the seventh Durán troubled Barkley with a number of right handers, but this seemed only to prompt the champion into a hard response with left hooks at the end of the round and, indeed, in the eighth, the latter punch wobbling the Panamanian.

It was all to change in the ninth. Durán had found Barkley's head with a series of right handers and it soon became clear, as the American's left eye started to close up, that he was running out of gas.

In the tenth Durán grinned at the champion after Barkley had missed with five punches in a row. The challenger's response was to fire off a crunching left hook. In the space of two rounds Barkley had seen his lead disintegrate and suddenly found himself in trouble.

With 30 seconds remaining in the penultimate round the standout moment of the fight took place. Durán unleashed five combinations that ended with two crunching right handers that dropped Barkley to the canvas. Although the American rose on the count of six he wandered around the ring seemingly lost before finally finding his corner.

Barkley survived the final round as Durán, knowing victory was his, did enough to win without endangering his lead. The only surprise was that the points win was not unanimous, with the split decision going his way 118-112, 116-112 and 113-116.

Durán was unbothered. A staggering 22 years after he turned pro he had just claimed a fourth world title, the first Latin fighter to do so.

Ring Magazine judged this to be the fight of the year and many boxing afficionados saw this is one of Durán's finest achievements.

"I am like a bottle of wine," Durán declared afterwards. "The older I get the better."

A stunned Barkley accepted that he had just been beaten by a force of nature.

"It was his heart," the now former champion admitted. "It just wouldn't let go."

"IT WAS DURÁN'S HEART, IT JUST WOULDN'T GO... DURÁN IS A GREAT FIGHTER."

IRAN BARKLEY

25 NOVEMBER 1980

LEONARD
VS DURÁN II

WORLD WELTERWEIGHT CHAMPIONSHIP
LOUISIANA SUPERDOME, NEW ORLEANS, LOUISIANA, U.S.A.

TALE OF THE TAPE

RAY LEONARD	NAME	ROBERTO DURÁN
SUGAR	NICKNAME	HANOS DE PIEDRA (HANDS OF STONE)
WILMINGTON, NORTH CAROLINA, U.S.A.	BIRTHPLACE	EL CHORRILLO, PANAMA
24	AGE	29
27–1–0	PRE-FIGHT RECORD	72–1–0
17	KO'S	55
5'10"	HEIGHT	5'7"
146 LBS	WEIGHT	146 LBS
70.5"	REACH	66"
ORTHODOX	STANCE	ORTHODOX

THE NO MÁS FIGHT

IT BECAME KNOWN AS THE 'NO MAS' FIGHT ON A NIGHT WHEN ONE MAN NOT ONLY GAINED REVENGE FOR A PREVIOUS DEFEAT BUT SO HUMILIATED HIS OPPONENT THAT, AT THE SORRY END, THE CHAMPION WOULD LOSE NOT ONLY HIS TITLE BUT HIS PRIDE.

This was billed as 'The Super Fight' and the second of a trilogy between these two all-time boxing greats. At the end it went down as one of the most talked-about and controversial clashes in the history of boxing.

Five months earlier Durán had stunned the world welterweight champion in Montreal with a points win after Leonard had decided to go toe-to-toe with the Panamanian.

He would not be making that mistake again having persuaded Durán to defend his newly-acquired title just 158 days later, this time in New Orleans.

That proved to be Leonard's first masterstroke. He knew Durán had a penchant for ballooning in weight in between fights partying and wanted to give the champion as little time as possible to get back into match shape.

Sugar Ray's second trick was to completely change tactics against the man dubbed "Hands of Stone." This time the American used his superior speed and ring movement to outbox and confuse his opponent, never falling into the first encounter trap of turning it into a slugfest.

"The whole fight I was moving," Leonard said later. "And Voom! I snapped his head back with a jab. He'd try to get me against the ropes but I'd spin off and "Pow!" I'd come back with a punch."

Up to the start of the seventh round the scores on the three judges' cards saw the two star names evenly-matched but Durán appeared to grow

"AT THE END OF THE FIFTH ROUND, I GOT CRAMPS IN MY STOMACH AND IT KEPT GETTING WORSE AND WORSE. I FELT WEAKER AND WEAKER IN MY BODY AND ARMS."

ROBERTO DURÁN

more and more frustrated with his inability to land the kind of punches that saw him win in Canada.

It came to a head during the 7th round when Leonard wound his right hand, motioning as if he was about to launch a haymaker, only to then catch his smaller foe full in the face with a fierce, left jab.

"I heard the crowd laughing," he recalled. "Then I looked at his face. He didn't know what the hell was going on."

In the dying seconds came the moment that has gone down in boxing folklore and been discussed and debated ever since. Following a clinch between the two fighters Durán suddenly turned his back on Leonard, waved his glove in the air and was reported to have said to referee Octavio Meyran: "No mas," which means 'No more' in Spanish.

The history books tell you that Leonard won by TKO after 2 minutes and 44 seconds of the eighth round, but this was by no means the end of it all.

Durán insisted stomach cramps that had come on since the fifth round after he lost too much weight too quickly was the reason why he had to stop, blaming the American commentator, Howard Cossell, for claiming he had uttered these words. The Panamanian's version was that he told Meyran "I'm not carrying on."

His own manager, Carlos Eleta, begged to differ. "Durán didn't quit because of stomach camps," he said. "He quit because he was embarrassed."

Durán's actions were met with shock and anger back home. He was instantly removed from all commercials he was involved in and his shame was not lifted until he knocked out Davey Moore in 1983 to become world junior middleweight champion.

The fight would become known simply as the 'No Mas' fight, as recognized today as it was forty years ago. And Leonard would go on to cement himself in boxing immortality with a series of impressive wins over Tommy Hearns and Marvin Hagler, as well as a second win in his third bout against Durán ten years later.

"To make a man quit, to make Roberto Durán quit, is better than knocking him out," is how he put it at the time." Durán, unhappily, would have agreed with this.

"HE WAS FRUSTRATED AND CONFUSED. I DID EVERYTHING TO MAKE HIM GO OFF LIKE A CLOCK WOUND UP TOO TIGHT. HE GOT WOUND UP SO TIGHT, HE BLEW A SPRING. TO MAKE A ROBERTO DURÁN QUIT, WAS BETTER THAN KNOCKING HIM OUT."

SUGAR RAY LEONARD

THE TRILOGY — PART I

1 DECEMBER 2018

WILDER
VS FURY

WORLD HEAVYWEIGHT CHAMPIONSHIP
STAPLES CENTER, LOS ANGELES, CALIFORNIA, U.S.A.

TALE OF THE TAPE

DEONTAY WILDER	NAME	TYSON FURY
BRONZE BOMBER	NICKNAME	GYPSY KING
TUSCALOOSA, ALABAMA, U.S.A.	BIRTHPLACE	MANCHESTER, ENGLAND, U.K.
33	AGE	30
40—0—0	PRE-FIGHT RECORD	27—0—0
39	KO'S	19
6'7"	HEIGHT	6'9"
212.5 LBS	WEIGHT	256.5 LBS
83"	REACH	85"
ORTHODOX	STANCE	ORTHODOX

BACK FROM THE DEAD

IT WAS A FIGHT THAT SAW THE CHALLENGER COME BACK FROM THE DEAD NOT ONCE, FROM A DEEP AND DARK PHYSICAL AND MENTAL PLACE JUST TWO YEARS BEFORE, BUT TWICE, WHEN HE ROSE FROM THE CANVAS WITH THE FIGHT SEEMINGLY OVER TO PULL OFF A DRAW NOBODY HAD PREDICTED.

It was a minor miracle that this fight ever took place at all, such was the deep, dark place Tyson Fury had found himself in. Having become world champion in all the belts bar the WBC version after his shock win over Wladimir Klitschko, the British fighter descended into depression, alcohol and weight gain. At one point he had ballooned to 390 lbs (196 kg) and there were concerns over his life, let alone his boxing career. To think he would be going toe-to-toe to Wilder, the WBC Champion, under three years later, was unthinkable.

With Fury's boxing license stripped Wilder turned his attentions on trying to organize a match-up with Anthony Joshua, who had taken over Fury's belts, but talks kept breaking down and when Fury returned to the ring the American was able to seal a deal. The pair faced off inside the ring in Belfast, Northern Ireland, after Fury had won on the undercard of Carl Frampton's world title defense, and the date was set for an end of year showdown in LA.

At the weigh-in Fury recorded 256 lbs, an incredible loss of weight and show of desire to reclaim his world champion status. He continued this into the opening rounds, his awkward and unorthodox stance that bamboozled Klitschko again proving too problematic for his opponent. Wilder kept throwing bombs and missing and the challenger took an early lead, bloodying the defending champion's nose in the 4th with a straight jab. In the 6th round Fury switched to a southpaw stance, backing Wilder on to the ropes and, in the next round, he got the better of a toe-to-toe session.

Against all the odds Fury had carved out a handsome lead but he was facing a proud American heavyweight in his home country possessing what some in boxing argued to be the most dangerous punch in the history of the sport. In the 9th Fury discovered this for himself, going down after being on the end of a short left hook followed a split-second later by an overhand right. Beating the count with ease, and seeing how fatigued Wilder was after his efforts, Fury countered to win both the 10th and 11th rounds landing many more blows.

Yet it was the 12th and final round that will stick in the memory. Fury was clearly ahead, despite his 9th round knockdown, and Wilder knew he had to produce something special. A right-left combination seemed to have done the trick. Fury went crashing down to the canvas and lay on his back almost motionless. If ever a boxer looked out for the count it was Fury at this moment but, to everyone's surprise, he suddenly sprung to his feet just as referee Jack Reiss counted to nine. Wilder, who had been blowing kisses to his wife at ringside, looked on in disbelief. He failed to land another telling blow and Fury finished much the stronger.

The three judges were undecided, with one giving Wilder the spoils, 115-111, the other going for Fury, 114-112, and the third declaring it a draw.

The two knockdowns undoubtedly saved Wilder because landing 71 out of 430 punches thrown compared unfavorably to Fury landing 84 from 327.

Predictably both claimed victory afterwards. "With the two knockdowns I definitely won the fight," Wilder insisted. "I came out slow and rushed my punches. I wanted to get him out of there and give the fans what they wanted to see."

Fury was having none of it. "I was on away soil and got knocked down twice but still believe I won the fight," he responded. "The whole world knows I won. I hope I did you all proud after nearly three years out of the ring."

The only way to settle this was a rematch and when it took place, in February 2020, more boxing history would be made.

"HOW DID I GET UP FROM THE KNOCKDOWNS? I DON'T KNOW. I HAD A HOLY HAND UPON ME TONIGHT AND IT BROUGHT ME BACK."

TYSON FURY

THE TRILOGY — PART II

22 FEBRUARY 2020

WILDER
VS FURY II

WORLD HEAVYWEIGHT CHAMPIONSHIP
MGM GRAND GARDEN ARENA, LAS VEGAS, NEVADA, U.S.A.

TALE OF THE TAPE

DEONTAY WILDER	NAME	TYSON FURY
BRONZE BOMBER	NICKNAME	GYPSY KING
TUSCALOOSA, ALABAMA, U.S.A.	BIRTHPLACE	MANCHESTER, ENGLAND, U.K.
34	AGE	31
42—0—1	PRE-FIGHT RECORD	29—0—1
41	KO'S	20
6'7"	HEIGHT	6'9"
231 LBS	WEIGHT	273 LBS
83"	REACH	85"
ORTHODOX	STANCE	ORTHODOX

UNFINISHED BUSINESS

AFTER THE INTENSE DRAMA OF WILDER-FURY I EVERYONE EXPECTED ANOTHER CLOSE, BRUTAL ENCOUNTER BETWEEN TWO UNBEATEN HEAVYWEIGHT CHAMPIONS. INSTEAD A MASTERCLASS WAS DELIVERED BY ONE OF THEM THAT HAS ALREADY GONE DOWN AS ONE OF THE GREATEST PERFORMANCES EVER WITNESSED IN THE RING.

After the incredible drama of their first meeting and the controversy that most draws tend to create, a rematch was always going to happen between two heavyweights still, by virtue of ending up evens in December, 2018, unbeaten during their stellar professional careers.

Both had causes for optimism, too. Deontay Wilder had twice knocked Tyson Fury down, but Fury knew that he was not in the shape he wanted to be for their first encounter, and that most ringside observers, despite him hitting the canvas on two occasions, had the British star as the winner.

First they both needed to get through two interim fights, with Wilder dismissing Dominic Breazeale and Luis Ortiz and Fury breezing past Tom Schwarz and Otto Wallin.

The stage was thus set for a rematch just 14 months after their first encounter billed as 'Unfinished Business'. On the evidence of the first fight, few predicted the utter dominance that would prevail.

Indeed Wilder entered the ring, complete with a 40 lbs suit and a mask to denote 'Black History Month', as the slight favorite with the bookmakers. Fury, whose own entrance involved a throne for the 'Gypsy King', had other ideas.

This was a man who, five years previously, had ended Wladimir Klitschko's long reign with a performance few saw coming. The Ukrainian simply had no answer to the challenger's clever and awkward tactics. In doing so he had claimed every world heavyweight

"I KNOCKED HIM OUT THE FIRST TIME WE FOUGHT. I TOLD HIM TWO YEARS AGO I WAS GOING TO BAPTIZE HIM. RISING UP IS PART OF THE BAPTISM. BUT THIS A DIFFERENT STORY. THIS IS UNFINISHED BUSINESS."

DEONTAY WILDER

title apart from the WBC crown, the crown that Wilder still held, albeit by the slimmest of margins.

Since his triumph over Klitschko, of course, Fury had spiraled so alarmingly down, caught in the grip of depression, alcohol and obesity, that few, if any, gave him any chance of returning to the ring, let alone becoming world champion again.

To produce the performance he did against Wilder first time round from the lowest depths he found himself in previously, was astonishing given the circumstances. Now he was about to perform another miracle, a display so close to perfection that many inside the noble sport of boxing put it up there with one of the greatest comebacks ever witnessed in any sport.

At weigh-in Wilder, all 6ft 7in of him, stood at 231 lbs, by far the heaviest he had ever been for a fight. But this was dwarfed by the larger man facing him. Fury, two inches taller than Wilder, hit the scales at 273 lbs, 17 lbs more than when he drew with the WBC champion. Three years previously he weighed considerably more but this time his weight gain was down to training and muscle. He explained before the fight that the extra weight was designed to create extra size and power to knock Wilder out, possibly as early as the 2nd round.

He made his intentions clear right from the first bell. Marching to the center of the ring Fury set up camp and started hammering Wilder with hard jabs whilst largely evading any swinging responses from the American. Short of a knockdown it was as an emphatic a statement as the former world champion could have made. Although Wilder made a fight of it in the second round, landing a couple of fierce blows that an unbothered Fury seemed to shake off, it all started to go horribly wrong in the third for the hitherto supremely confident man from Alabama.

Fury found Wilder exactly where he wanted him, on the ropes and in severe danger as the bigger man moved in. A left hook shook the American, but the follow up shot, a fierce right hander from Fury over the top that landed flush on his opponent's temple, saw Wilder crashing to the canvas. Although he got to his feet the defending world champion was clearly in trouble. He hit the deck for a second time only for the referee, Kenny Bayliss, to judge it to be a slip but, as he eventually made it back to his own corner, Wilder appeared disorientated.

From this point onwards Fury was in total control. He tried to finish it in the fourth but Wilder somehow clung on. It was still the Briton's round, however, as a combination of thunderous jabs and oxygen-depriving clinches sapped vital energy out of Wilder.

It got a whole lot worse for the American in the fifth when, for the second occasion on the night, he was sent down to the canvas, this time after a hard body blow. To his credit he rose to his feet for a second time and was then subjected to an all-out barrage from Fury, fighting as well as anyone could ever remember. With just 40 seconds left Wilder was sent stumbling onto the ropes. As Fury moved in for the kill, and with Wilder's back now turned, he managed to entwine his arm with the American's and was promptly, and somewhat controversially, deducted a point by Bayliss for excessive holding.

On another night it might have been a result-deciding decision that would have been talked about for many years.

But not on this night. The previously unbeatable, indomitable, hard-punching Wilder was being made to look like mincemeat served up on a plate for the hungry British star. Fury bossed the sixth round from start to finish, smothering his opponent and connecting with both left and right handers.

Still Wilder refused to buckle. As he rose to his feet from his stool for the seventh round he knew only a knockout punch could win the night, and the chances of that happening were as slim as - well - Tyson Fury recovering to become world champion after it all looked over for him just three years previously.

In other words anything could still happen, especially in a heavyweight division noted for its many upsets over the years due to one, fight-ending punch.

If Wilder had any false hopes at this stage a combination of Fury and the champion's own corner would shortly end them. A crunching left hander sent Wilder back towards his own corner. His team bore witness from close up as Fury then launched a barrage of shots against their man trying in vain to defend himself.

At this point, almost exactly midway through the round, his corner had seen enough and the night ended as a white towel sailed through the air and into the ring.

"WHAT'S GOING TO HAPPEN IN THIS FIGHT IS THAT I'M GOING TO GET WHAT I RIGHTFULLY WON LAST TIME. I'M GOING TO GET THE GREEN BELT AND KEEP MY LINEAL TITLE. IF HE WANTS TO REMATCH ME AFTER, I'LL BEAT HIM AGAIN."

TYSON FURY

"THIS BELT IS THE ONE THAT'S EVADED ME OVER THE YEARS AND I'VE NOW FINISHED OFF MY COLLECTION, A BIG COLLECTION OF EVERY BELT IN BOXING... THE WORLD WAS WATCHING AND GOT TO SEE TWO UNDEFEATED HEAVYWEIGHT CHAMPIONS IN THEIR PRIME DO BATTLE."

TYSON FURY

At this stage Fury held a comfortable lead with all three ringside judges, borne out by the fight statistics. The winner had landed 82 of his 267 punches, and 58 out of 160 power punches. In contrast the loser landed just 34 out of 161 punches, and only 18 out of 55 power punches.

For once there was no dispute and no controversy. Fury's performance was immediately anointed as one of the greatest in the history of boxing, as was his comeback from the depths of physical and mental decline.

Wilder, tasting defeat for the first time in his professional career, was unhappy with his corner team's actions, but was nonetheless magnanimous. "The best man won tonight," he declared. "But my corner threw in the towel and I was ready to go out on my shield. I make no excuses tonight. He had a great performance and we will be back stronger. Even the greatest have lost and come back. That's just part of it all. This is what big-time boxing is all about. The best must fight the best."

A delighted Fury reflected on the journey he had just traveled. "Last fight I was underweight and over-trained," he admitted. "Deontay is a hell of a performer, dynamite in his fists and he will always be dangerous. People look at my fat belly and my bald head and they think I cannot fight.

"I had my mental problems and issues and I was out of the ring for three years. But he was fighting the real Gypsy King this time. And the Gypsy King has returned to his throne."

Indeed he had. And it was unlikely anyone would ever doubt the

THE TRILOGY — PART III

09 OCTOBER 2021

FURY
VS WILDER III

WORLD HEAVYWEIGHT CHAMPIONSHIP
T-MOBILE ARENA, LAS VEGAS, NEVADA, U.S.A.

TALE OF THE TAPE

TYSON FURY	NAME	DEONTAY WILDER
GYPSY KING	NICKNAME	THE BRONZE BOMBER
MANCHESTER, ENGLAND, U.K.	BIRTHPLACE	TUSCALOOSA, ALABAMA, U.S.A.
33	AGE	35
30—0—1	PRE-FIGHT RECORD	42—1—1
21	KO'S	41
6'9"	HEIGHT	6'7"
277 LBS	WEIGHT	238 LBS
85"	REACH	83"
ORTHODOX	STANCE	ORTHODOX

ONCE AND FOR ALL

AFTER TWO FAMOUS PREVIOUS BOUTS THIS WAS THE BEST OF THE LOT IN A TRILOGY THAT WILL GO DOWN AS ONE OF THE VERY BEST IN THE HISTORY OF HEAVYWEIGHT BOXING. BOTH FIGHTERS HAD CAUSE TO LEAVE THE RING AS PROUD WARRIORS, BUT THERE WOULD BE ONLY ONE WINNER WHOSE VICTORY WAS ACHIEVED IN CRUSHING STYLE.

It had been quite some story just to get to the point where these two giants of men clambered into the ring to face each other for a third time. The first meeting ended in a controversial draw in December, 2018, with both camps believing they had done enough to win. In that bout Fury, the 'Gypsy King', who recovered incredibly after a long bout of depression, drinking, drugs and huge weight gain, was undoubtedly leading until Wilder dropped him late in the fight with a punch that would have knocked out a lesser fighter.

The second clash saw a more clinical response from Fury in February 2018, winning via a technical knockout in the seventh round to take the WBC and *The Ring* titles off Wilder. It was an imperious performance. Talks were then set in place for Fury to fight Anthony Joshua, a fellow British heavyweight who held the other world title belts, but these fell through after a court of arbitration ruled that Fury and Wilder had to get it on one more time.

The fight, initially due for July, 2021, was postponed after Fury contracted the Covid-19 virus, and reset for October. Both fighters entered the ring weighing at their heaviest in their long and successful careers, following an acrimonious build up and weigh in where Wilder repeatedly accused Fury, without any clear grounds, of cheating his way to previous victory.

What was to follow goes down in boxing folklore. Wilder started the better, winning the first round with a series of right handers to

"I DID MY BEST, BUT IT WASN'T GOOD ENOUGH."

DEONTAY WILDER

Fury's chest and stomach. Fury responded in the second round as he began to trouble his American opponent, pushing him back and getting into his groove.

This continued into the third round where, late on, Fury landed a right hook flush on to Wilder's temple. The American tried to gain his senses in a clinch but was caught by a fierce right upper cut which sent him crashing to the canvas. Wilder rose to his feet and managed to survive the obvious onslaught as Fury attempted to finish the fight.

The fourth round will go down as one of the most remarkable rounds in heavyweight boxing, certainly in recent times. Fury looked to press home his advantage but Wilder, possessing one of the most lethal punches in boxing, was a dangerous animal knowing that attack could be his most powerful defensive weapon. As the defending champion advanced towards the challenger, he was rocked by a fierce jab and then a straight right-hander to his temple. Just as he did in the first clash between these two Fury went down.

The fact that both men had now hit the floor inside the first four rounds showed what a full-on encounter this had already been. There had been no real sizing up, no cautiousness. Both men were going for it.

Now Wilder appeared to have the advantage, a fact he hammered home when he sent Fury back down to the canvass for the second time in the round after a short, right hook to the side of the British fighter's head. Normally the sight of a boxer being floored twice in the same round spelled the end.

But Fury had already proved his powers of recovery in the first, drawn fight back in 2018 when he was sent crashing to the floor with a punch so powerful from Wilder that it seemed impossible to recover in time from. The American was already celebrating his victory as Fury lay flat on his back, seemingly out for the count. Instead, he rose dramatically late into the count to see out the fight.

Once again, the champion regathered his senses, clambered to his feet and managed to survive the remaining few seconds of the round.

That was as good as it got for Wilder. He attempted to finish Fury off in the fifth round, launching huge bombs that might have ended the issue if any of them had landed. But Fury was a slippery opponent, with quick feet for such a huge man and even quicker senses, and he managed to keep out of any further trouble.

As the fight continued so Wilder tired and Fury began to take control, winning rounds six, seven, eight and nine, striking his opponent more and more and causing him to wobble on more than one occasion.

The tenth round would begin the final denouement of the fight. Fury landed a heavy right hander that sent Wilder crashing back down on to the canvas. To his credit he rose from the floor for the second time in the bout and managed to see out the rest of the round.

The American showed incredible heart and courage against the bigger champion, but it was clear that he was now a beaten man and it was just a matter of time before Fury finished the job.

It came in the next and penultimate round of the fight. Fury began it on the attack, finding his target at will. Just inside the first minute another huge eight hander landed on Wilder's temple and the big American fell for a third and final time. Referee Russell Mora immediately waved his arms to denote the end of the fight and Fury, producing his best display in the trilogy, had won by a knockout to retain his world titles.

"It was a great fight tonight," a delighted Fury declared afterwards. "It was worthy of the best of trilogies. We were both down a few times and it was edge of the seat stuff. It could have swung either way. We fought like two warriors in there. But when the chips are down I've delivered 33 times now."

The veteran promoter, Bob Arum, added: "I have never seen a heavyweight fight as magnificent as this."

Deontay Wilder should take a great deal of credit for his brave performance but in Fury he found a man too big, too strong and too clever. The American had knocked out 41 of his opponents but not even his best could finish off Fury.

The British world champion had ended any lingering doubts about his status in world boxing. He was now, quite clearly, the best in the world after one of the best heavyweight fights in history.

"I'm the best fighter in my era," Fury added. He had just proved it beyond any doubt.

"HOPEFULLY, WE PROVED THAT NO MATTER HOW HARD YOU GET HIT WITH TRIALS AND TRIBULATIONS YOU CAN ALWAYS PICK YOURSELF UP TO LIVE AND FIGHT AGAIN FOR WHAT YOU BELIEVE IN."

DEONTAY WILDER

"WITHOUT SOUNDING TOO SHARP AND CLEVER, I PLACE MYSELF RIGHT ON TOP OF THE PILE. I BELIEVE THAT I CAN BEAT ANYONE IN THE HISTORY, ANY MAN BORN. BUT, LIKE I SAID, I CAN ONLY BE THE BEST IN MY ERA, AND I'M DEFINITELY THAT."

TYSON FURY

8 DECEMBER 2007

MAYWEATHER
VS HATTON

WORLD WELTERWEIGHT CHAMPIONSHIP
MGM GRAND GARDEN ARENA, LAS VEGAS, NEVADA, U.S.A.

TALE OF THE TAPE

FLOYD MAYWEATHER	NAME	RICKY HATTON
MONEY / PRETTY BOY	NICKNAME	THE HITMAN
GRAND RAPIDS, MICHIGAN, U.S.A.	BIRTHPLACE	STOCKPORT, ENGLAND, U.K.
30	AGE	28
38—0—0	PRE-FIGHT RECORD	43—0—0
30	KO'S	29
5'8"	HEIGHT	5'7"
147 LBS	WEIGHT	145 LBS
72"	REACH	65"
ORTHODOX	STANCE	ORTHODOX

UNDEFEATED

SOMETHING HAD TO GIVE IN THIS HUGELY-ANTICIPATED CLASH
OF UNBEATEN FIGHTERS BUT IN THE END A GREAT BOXER WAS
WELL-BEATEN BY ARGUABLY THE BEST OF ALL TIME.

It was billed simply as 'Undefeated,' a long-awaited clash between two fighters who had never tasted defeat in their professional careers. Such was the anticipation that many saw it as the biggest clash between two unbeaten welterweights since Oscar De La Hoya faced up to Felix Trinidad in 1999.

In fact it was De La Hoya who Mayweather had beaten in his last outing to take the WBC's light-middleweight title, such was the versatility of a man who was already dubbing himself as the greatest fighter of all time. He had then announced he was about to retire but performed a U-turn to take on the Mancunian seven months later.

It was another sizzling occasion in Vegas on a night when something had to give. Such was the interest that the likes of Denzel Washington, Bruce Willis, Sylvester Stallone, Brad Pitt and David Beckham were all at ringside.

Unusually for Mayweather, especially in his hometown, he faced an audience not entirely on his side. Hatton was known for his loyal following from Manchester, England, and they came in their thousands to cheer him on for what always looked to be the toughest fight of his career.

And so it proved to be. It started well enough for the Briton, whose initial tactics of harrying and pressure seemed to unnerve Mayweather. Indeed a left jab from Hatton even knocked the American off balance.

But that was as good as it would get for the popular visitor. In the third round a hard right from Mayweather left a cut above Hatton's right eye. From that point his pace and movement seemed to slow.

In the sixth round came the moment of controversy that Hatton insisted made him lose his calm and played a significant part in his ultimate defeat. Referee Joe Cortez decided to deduct a point from Hatton after he threw punches at Mayweather's head as the American found himself ducked under the top rope. His anger and frustration was clear to see as he first turned his back and then shook his bottom at his opponent.

At this point Hatton started to tire. He had been chasing the elusive Mayweather around the ring for six rounds but now Mayweather was not only avoiding Hatton's punches but countering with damaging blows.

By the tenth round the American held a commanding lead. This lengthened considerably when a crisp left hook sent Hatton crashing down to the canvas. The challenger did well to rise to his feet although it was clear he was in big trouble.

Referee Cortez decided to continue the fight and Mayweather moved in for the brutal denouement. Almost instantly he flew a flurry of quick punches including another left hook that sent Hatton first back and then down again.

Even as Cortez was waving the fight to be over a towel was thrown into the ring from Hatton's corner.

The scorecards on all three judges showed that Mayweather was way ahead on points at the time of the stoppage but he still paid tribute to his defeated foe by stating that he had been one of his toughest opponents.

It was hard to take for Hatton. Suffering from his first defeat he was left angered by the point deduction and maintained for many years afterwards that he felt all the odds were against him in the ring that night in Vegas fighting a man like Mayweather.

He returned to his more natural light-welterweight division but lost heavily to Manny Pacquiao 18 months later to end an illustrious career.

In contrast Mayweather would fight, off and on, for the next ten years, and in all that time he would never taste the bitter sense of defeat.

16 JULY 2005

HOPKINS
VS TAYLOR

WORLD MIDDLEWEIGHT CHAMPIONSHIP
MGM GRAND GARDEN ARENA, LAS VEGAS, NEVADA, U.S.A.

TALE OF THE TAPE

BERNARD HOPKINS	NAME	JERMAIN TAYLOR
THE EXECUTIONER	NICKNAME	BAD INTENTIONS
PHILADELPHIA, PENNSYLVANIA, U.S.A.	BIRTHPLACE	LITTLE ROCK, ARKANSAS, U.S.A.
40	AGE	26
46—2—1	PRE-FIGHT RECORD	23—0—0
32	KO'S	17
6'1"	HEIGHT	6'1"
168 LBS	WEIGHT	171 LBS
75"	REACH	78"
ORTHODOX	STANCE	ORTHODOX

NEXT IN LINE

IT WAS CLOSE, SO DESPERATELY CLOSE, BUT IN THE END THE YOUNGER CHALLENGER WOULD EDGE IT AND BRING TO AN END ONE OF THE GREAT REIGNS IN BOXING HISTORY.

Bernard Hopkins had ruled the middleweight roost for the best part of a dozen years. The American last lost a fight back in 1993 against the great Roy Jones Jr. Since then he had embarked on an impressive unbeaten run that also saw him defend his world middleweight title on twenty occasions. It was boxing's longest active title reign. By July, 2005, he had turned 40 but remained in magnificent shape.

Facing him was an unbeaten challenger, fellow American and 2000 Olympic bronze medalist who, at 26 years of age, held a 14 year advantage over the great champion. Jermain Taylor may not have tasted defeat, and he was fighting a man who, by rights, was close to the boxing retirement home, but it was the wily old champion who started round one as the firm favorite to continue his dominance of the middleweight division.

He had an obvious game plan, too. For much of the first half of the fight he did very little, counting on the less experienced challenger to run out of steam in the latter rounds. This was a ploy Hopkins had previously used to great effect, his superior fitness proving crucial as fights lurched towards the end to pick off his tired opponent.

Still, most ringside observers were surprised by just how little Hopkins worked for the first few rounds, and how big a lead he allowed Taylor to gain. In the second, for example, a stiff left jab followed by a hard right hander saw Hopkins staggering back and, although the champion made some impact in the fourth round, especially in the clinches, Taylor built up a steady if undramatic advantage.

This was despite the fact that a swelling underneath Taylor's left eye began to appear from the fifth round and that he was the victim of an accidental clash of heads that saw a large gash appear on the top of his head resulting in blood streaming down his face.

Good work from the cuts man in the corner evaded a major problem for Taylor just in time before he faced another major problem - the Hopkins comeback.

There was little doubt that the veteran won the second half of the fight. In the tenth he rocked his young challenger with two solid rights to the head and in the 11th hurt Taylor again with a combination.

Had he done enough to retain his title? It was clearly desperately close but, interestingly, it was Hopkins who raised his hands at the sound of the final bell in expected history, and Taylor and his camp who looked downcast.

The stats hardly cleared the debate up, either. Taylor threw more punches but Hopkins landed more, 96 to 86. Taylor threw many more jabs and landed more as well, 36 to 18. But it was Hopkins who threw and landed more power punches, 78 to 50.

The judges did not quite see it this way, however, and awarded the fight to the new, undisputed middleweight world champion, Taylor, two to one, with the scorecards reading 116-112 Hopkins, 115-113 and 115-113 Taylor.

"It was an unbelievable fight," an ecstatic Taylor declared afterwards. "I have never experienced anything like it. I learned so much in this fight. Bernard Hopkins is a great champion and I will respect this man until the day I die. He came out and took his time. He came on late but I feel like I won."

Hopkins, unsurprisingly, did not agree. "I can hold my head up high," he reasoned. "When I fought Roy Jones in 1993 I knew I'd lost and I prepared myself to never feel that experience again. I believe I put in a great performance. If you saw Jermain Taylor and his people after the fight their body language speaks a lot when you win and when you lose. They obviously thought they lost."

The rematch would take place less than five months later and after an almost identical pattern of strategy Hopkins would lose again, this time unanimously, but again by the slimmest of margins.

Taylor would eventually lose his hard-fought titles to Kelly Pavlik three years later but Hopkins would reinvent himself one more time to become the world light-heavyweight champion and cement his name in the annals of the all-time greats.

12 APRIL 1997

WHITAKER VS DE LA HOYA

WORLD WELTERWEIGHT CHAMPIONSHIP
THOMAS & MACK CENTER, LAS VEGAS, NEVADA, U.S.A.

TALE OF THE TAPE

PERNELL WHITAKER	**NAME**	OSCAR DE LA HOYA
SWEET PEA	**NICKNAME**	GOLDEN BOY
NORFOLK, VIRGINIA, U.S.A.	**BIRTHPLACE**	MONTEBELLO, CALIFORNIA, U.S.A.
33	**AGE**	24
40–1–1	**PRE-FIGHT RECORD**	23–0–0
17	**KO'S**	20
5'6"	**HEIGHT**	5'10"
146.5 LBS	**WEIGHT**	146.5 LBS
69"	**REACH**	73"
SOUTHPAW	**STANCE**	ORTHODOX

POUND FOR POUND

A MUCH-ANTICIPATED CLASH BETWEEN TWO OF THE BEST BOXERS IN THE WORLD THAT WOULD TAKE THE WINNER'S CAREER INTO THE STRATOSPHERE.

This mega-fight was called 'Pound for Pound' and for good reason, too. It featured the 33 year old Whitaker, also known as 'Sweet Pea,' who had been the WBC's welterweight champion for four years, a world champion in four different weight divisions and a man who had featured as one of the top pound for pound fighters in the world for the past eight years.

Opposing him was the new superstar of boxing. De La Hoya, the 'Golden Boy' of the sport, was undefeated, a three division world champion already at the age of 24 and the WBC's super-lightweight champion after delivering a crushing defeat on the Mexican legend, Julio César Chávez.

They were currently ranked numbers two and three in the pound for pound boxers in the world behind Roy Jones Jr and although the younger man was seen by the bookmakers as the slight favorite, this was a much-anticipated fight few could call.

Both former Olympic champions had to get past mandatory challenges before they could meet in the ring. De La Hoya passed his test comfortably against the formerly undefeated Miguel Angel Gonzales, but Whitaker had a huge scare against the also undefeated Diosbelys Hurtado, twice being knocked down before rallying in the penultimate round to gain a stoppage.

This, therefore, would be Whitaker's ninth title defense while De La Hoya, with a four inch height and reach advantage over the champion, would be fighting for the first time at 147 lbs after jumping up from super lightweight.

The fight took place in front of 12,000 baying fans mainly on the side of the popular Latino from East LA. It would go the distance and have observers debating the result to this day.

Whitaker was deducted a point after an accidental headbutt in the 3rd round resulted in a small cut under 'Golden Boy's' right eye, but in return he scored the fight's only knockdown in the ninth when De La Hoya was caught off balance with a left hook and his glove hit the canvas. The American of Mexican descent rose immediately as if to suggest it was nothing more than a slip but referee Mills Lane judged it to be a knockdown and gave De La Hoya a standing count.

As the fight continued Whitaker's left eye swelled up from the repeated left jabs from his challenger landing on his face. Up to this point Whitaker, a Virginian, had been the more aggressive of the two, throwing many more punches, but it was De La Hoya who landed the bigger bombs.

After a final two rounds of caution led by jabs the bell sounded and both believed they had won. The judges saw it differently, deciding unanimously that De La Hoya had done enough to become the new WBC welterweight champion.

It would prove to be one of the more contentious outcomes in boxing over the past 25 years. Whitaker had out-punched De La Hoya by 232 to 191, landing 160 to just 45. But, crucially, the challenger gained a huge advantage in the power punches, outscoring Whitaker by 146 to 72.

A poll of boxing writers later would record 14 going with Whitaker, 11 with De La Hoya and one draw.

Whitaker, who would only fight three more times afterwards, was incredulous afterwards. "I couldn't have fought any better," he insisted.

De La Hoya, in contrast, was full of respect for the man years later after a stellar career that would last another 11 years. "In terms of defensive ability and ring generalship I never fought anyone better than Whitaker."

15 MAY 2004

JONES JR vs
TARVER II

WORLD LIGHT HEAVYWEIGHT CHAMPIONSHIP
MANDALAY BAY RESORT & CASINO, LAS VEGAS, NEVADA, U.S.A.

TALE OF THE TAPE

ROY JONES JR	NAME	ANTONIO TARVER
JUNIOR	NICKNAME	MAGIC MAN
PENSACOLA, FLORIDA, U.S.A.	BIRTHPLACE	ORLANDO, FLORIDA, U.S.A.
35	AGE	35
49−1−0	PRE-FIGHT RECORD	21−2−0
38	KO'S	17
5'11"	HEIGHT	6'2"
174 LBS	WEIGHT	175 LBS
74"	REACH	75"
ORTHODOX	STANCE	SOUTHPAW

MORE THAN PERSONAL

IT WAS A FIGHT THAT PRODUCED ONE OF THE GREATEST SHOCKS IN RECENT BOXING HISTORY AND ALL BUT ENDED ONE OF THE GREAT AURAS OF INVINCIBILITY.

Roy Jones Jr had enjoyed a ten year reign of being recognized as the best pound for pound boxer in the world but in his previous fight against Antonio Tarver he had gone the distance before winning, somewhat controversially, by a majority decision. In his defense he had needed to lose 24 lbs in order to make the weight having moved up to heavyweight to win the world title from John Ruiz. As a result he appeared slower and weakened by the dramatic weight loss which fellow Floridian Tarver almost took advantage of. He may have won but the night ended for Jones with a swollen eye, a bloodied nose and some rare doubts.

Initially Jones was not interested in the rematch. He had plans for a return to the heavyweight division and a super fight against Mike Tyson, but when this failed to materialize he agreed to face Tarver for a second time.

Dubbed 'More than Personal,' Jones was in better shape for this second meeting 17 months later and determined to deliver a more convincing performance. It was not by coincidence that he had lost just once in 50 professional fights, a disqualification against Montell Griffin that he avenged quickly and brutally in the immediate rematch. No wonder he was 4-1 favorite.

When the pair met in the ring for a final face off before the sound of the bell it was Tarver who appeared the aggressor. Asked by referee Jay Nady if there were any questions from either of the fighters, Tarver replied: "I got a question. You got any excuses tonight, Roy?"

Yet it was Jones who won the first round comfortably showing all his hallmarks. Aggressive, quick, powerful, it suggested it could be a long night for the challenger.

All this was to change, however, with a passage of play that left the boxing world stunned. For the first half of the second round Tarver appeared to hold back, happy to absorb Jones and wait for an opportunity. It came just after the midway point.

Jones launched a right hander that missed Tarver and opened himself up. The boxer they called "The Magic Man" took full and brutal advantage, hitting his target with an overhand left that dropped Jones to the canvas for only the second time in his professional career.

Initially Jones lay on his back close to Tarver's corner, his head the wrong side of the lower rope. After six seconds he turned over on to all fours and rose groggily to his feet on the count of nine. It was clear for all to see that his legs had gone and his eyes glazed. Referee Nady had seen enough and waved his arms in the air to denote a stunning and shock defeat for the champion as Tarver went wild in celebration.

To put into context how brutal this was, Jones had landed 12 of his 42 punches thus far, Tarver just 7 of 54. But it was his seventh that won the night and ended Jones' reign of invincibility.

The punch was awarded the "'Knockout of the Year,' by *The Ring* magazine, denoting the first time Jones had ever been knocked out in his long and stellar career. And the win was seen by most in boxing as the biggest upset since Buster Douglas had demolished Tyson back in 1990.

"It was beautiful," Tarver said later. "This fight will go down as one of the great ones in boxing history. It is Hagler-Hearns all over again."

Jones had no choice but to be philosophical after he had recovered himself from the unique experience of being knocked out. "I probably got bored with this guy," he reasoned. "I am a warrior. I don't feel good about this. He got me with a good shot. It can happen to the best of them."

The loss, however, proved not to be a one-off. Jones would lose his next fight against Glen Johnson, also by a knockout, and when he and Tarver met for a third time a year later as a decider in an absorbing trilogy, it was Tarver who came through after 12 rounds with an unanimous decision.

Despite his initial plans to retire Jones would continue for another 13 years with a mixed record, and Tarver a further ten.

But it was this stunning defeat by Tarver that ended the Roy Jones Jr era as the best fighter in the world.

17 DECEMBER 2011

WARD vs FROCH

WORLD MIDDLEWEIGHT CHAMPIONSHIP
BOARDWALK HALL, ATLANTIC CITY, NEW JERSEY, U.S.A.

TALE OF THE TAPE

ANDRE WARD	NAME	CARL FROCH
S.O.G. (SON OF GOD)	NICKNAME	THE COBRA
OAKLAND, CALIFORNIA, U.S.A.	BIRTHPLACE	NOTTINGHAM, ENGLAND, U.K.
27	AGE	34
24—0—0	PRE-FIGHT RECORD	28—1—0
13	KO'S	20
6'0"	HEIGHT	6'1"
168 LBS	WEIGHT	167.5 LBS
.71"	REACH	75"
ORTHODOX	STANCE	ORTHODOX

THE SUPER SIX FINAL

THIS WAS A SHOWDOWN BETWEEN A VERY FINE FIGHTER AND A GREAT ONE, AND THE GREAT WOULD PREVAIL WITH A BOXING MASTERCLASS AGAINST A MAN WHOSE ENORMOUS HEART WOULD NOT PROVIDE A BIG ENOUGH ANSWER.

This was the culmination of a tournament known as the 'Super 6 World Boxing Classic' that had raged for over two years. Whilst the undefeated Andre Ward came through the rounds and the semi-final against the tricky Arthur Abraham, his opponent in the final lost to Mikkel Kessler in the group stages. This was the Briton's first professional defeat and followed Ward beating Kessler in the previous tournament fight. The Dane took Froch's world title and immediately vacated it after leaving the tournament early. This gave the man they called 'The Cobra' the chance to regain it against Abraham in the next group fight. He then beat Glen Johnson in the semi-final to set up the final showdown against the much younger Ward.

A notoriously slow starter Froch found himself immediately under the pump against the American who planted himself in the center of the ring and showed off his superior speed to the punch almost from the very start. Froch was on the receiving end of numerous jabs and a snap left hook as he struggled to come to terms with his opponent's sheer quickness of feet and hands.

It was more of the same in the second round and, although Froch found some purchase with blows to Ward's body, it was the American who took the round yet again.

Ward peppered Froch with left hooks in both the fourth and sixth rounds after easing off a little in the fifth, and then got the better of the man from Nottingham in the close exchanges that dominated the seventh.

By now it was clear Froch would need a stoppage to avoid a second defeat in his career. Referee Steve Smoger needed to speak to him after he threw a shot at Ward after the bell denoting the end of the eighth round and, during the ninth, he glanced dejectedly across at his corner seeking some kind of inspiration.

At this point Ward had consistently out-foxed, out-worked and out-muscled his opponent and, although he slowed up in the final two rounds showing some fatigue he had more than done enough to win the tournament and add the WBC and The Ring super middleweight titles to his haul.

All three judges had Ward down as the comfortable winner by 115-113, 115-113 and a more realistic 118-110. It catapulted Ward into the top echelons in boxing - many now saw him behind just Floyd Mayweather and Manny Pacquiao in the pound for pound list - but Froch also took credit for the way he lasted the twelve rounds against an evidently superior boxer. It was a trademark of Froch that his enormous heart and will had seen him home against more skilled opponents but in Ward this was a journey too far.

"I couldn't get anything going," Froch admitted afterwards. "He was just too slippery. He's very clever up close. It was very frustrating for me tonight. Fair play to him, though."

Ward, perhaps, was not quite so generous. "I was surprised how slow Froch was," he said, after consistently beating the Briton to the punch. "You don't get points for leaving the chin open. You can't fight like that and not expect to get hit."

Ward would fight seven more times, moving up to light heavyweight in the process, and remain unbeaten when he retired at just 33.

Froch would fight just five more times but, in doing so, regained his pride by winning first the IBF world title after beating Lucien Bute and then the WBA with an avenging win over Kessler before ending his career with a winning double header against fellow Briton George Groves.

6

1 OCTOBER 1975

ALI vs FRAZIER

WORLD HEAVYWEIGHT CHAMPIONSHIP
ARANETA COLISEUM IN CUBAO, QUEZON CITY, PHILIPPINES

TALE OF THE TAPE

MUHAMMAD ALI	NAME	JOE FRAZIER
THE GREATEST	NICKNAME	SMOKIN'
LOUISVILLE, KENTUCKY, U.S.A.	BIRTHPLACE	BEAUFORT, SOUTH CAROLINA, U.S.A.
33	AGE	31
48—2—0	PRE-FIGHT RECORD	32—2—0
34	KO'S	27
6'3"	HEIGHT	5'11.5"
224 LBS	WEIGHT	215 LBS
78"	REACH	73"
ORTHODOX	STANCE	ORTHODOX

THE THRILLA IN MANILA

THEY FOUGHT THEMSELVES TO A STANDSTILL IN WHICH THE CHAMPION WOULD PREVAIL, JUST, AFTER ONE OF THE MOST TALKED-ABOUT DENOUEMENTS TO ONE OF THE MOST BRUTAL OF FIGHTS.

It is one of the most famous fights of all time, with one of the most famous names and one widely considered to be one of the best and most savage as well.

Muhammad Ali v Joe Frazier in the Philippines was the third and final bout between these two great champions and many consider it to be the best.

That is saying something because in their first meeting, the 'Fight of the Century' as it was billed, world champion Joe Frazier won a unanimous decision and thus inflicted Ali's first ever defeat after another contender for the greatest ever fight. In the second, with neither now world champion after defeats to George Foreman and Ken Norton respectively, Ali avenged his loss by coming out on top after twelve rounds, although many felt this was marred by his repeated holding tactics to prevent Frazier from unleashing his bombs.

By the time of the finale Ali had regained his heavyweight title and was intent on getting under Frazier's skin. The fight became known as the 'Thrilla in Manila' because Ali famously taunted 'Smokin' Joe' by chanting: "It's gonna be a killa and a thrilla and a chilla when I get that gorilla in Manila."

Frazier was not amused. He had stood up for Ali when he had his world title taken away from him for refusing to fight in Vietnam, even giving him money to help him out, only to be then mocked and taunted. He would defeat Ali but he would not forgive. This was made

"THEY WANT ME TO LOVE HIM, BUT I'LL OPEN UP THE GRAVEYARD AND BURY HIS ASS."

JOE FRAZIER

worse by then losing second time round to questionable holding tactics. And now Ali was at it again, the champion belittling a proud warrior, although Ali insisted later it was all designed to sell the fights.

The fight would take place at 10.45am local time to fit in with a worldwide TV audience of one billion. This may have been good for viewers but not for the fighters. The ring temperature was recorded at 49 degrees Celsius (120 F) and after the fight Ali had lost 5 lbs due to dehydration.

As referee Carlos Padilla Jr brought the pair together for final instructions in the ring Ali took the chance to throw one more verbal grenade at his shorter opponent. "You don't have it, Joe, you don't have it," he said. "I'm going to put you away."

As Frazier turned his back and headed for his corner he replied:"We'll see."

He was a notoriously slow starter and so it was of little surprise that Ali won the first two rounds, wobbling the challenger in the second after a series of straight right handers. In the third he goaded Frazier again. "Come on, you ugly gorilla," he shouted. "Hit me."

The problem for Ali was that this is exactly what Frazier started to do, encouraged by the champion's "rope-a-dope" tactics that made his body an easy target. These tactics – resting against the ropes to preserve energy whilst encouraging the opponent to run out of steam before launching a furious counter-attack – had served him well against Foreman, but not so well against Frazier.

By the fifth round Frazier was enjoying the better of it, landing two left hooks against the right side of Ali's head that would have put a lesser man down. He repeated it again in the sixth with two even harder punches that sent him back against the ropes.

Ali's famous trainer and cornerman, Angelo Dundee, disliked the rope-a-dope at the best of times and he was growing more agitated by the minute, screaming: "Get off those goddamn ropes."

At the start of the seventh round Ali whispered in Frazier's ear: "Joe, they told me you was washed up." Frazier responded: "They lied."

The seventh saw Frazier again on top at first, scoring heavily with a combination of numbing body shots, left hooks to the head and the occasional short right hander. Ali finally left the ropes and began to regain some equality in the fight again, bettering his stubborn rival in the eighth round after a toe-to-toe exchange of blows, although the round would end with Frazier launching a flurry of blows to Ali's bruised and battered body and head.

By the end of the ninth round Ali was visibly tired. He told his corner men: "Man, this is the closest I've been to dying." But Frazier was in trouble too.

His face was swelling up badly, a problem enhanced by the fact that his left eye had been nearly blinded by an accident ten years earlier. By the end of the 11th round he told his equally famous cornerman, Eddie Futch, that he could not see some of Ali's punches.

Futch's advice was to stand more upright in order to have a better chance of seeing the punches, rather than maintain his better-known bobbing and weaving style. It made sense in theory but, of course, it made Frazier an easier target and Ali took full advantage.

As both combatants rose from their stalls rather wearily for the start of the 13th round Frazier's face was so bloated and swollen that he was half blind. The stifling heat played its part once more because ice bags that could have aided the challenger simply melted before being applied to his bruised face.

Midway through the 13th an Ali right hander sent Frazier's mouthguard flying through the air and across the ring. For the rest of that round and indeed the 14th Ali, finding a new wave of motivation and energy as he saw his indomitable foe appearing hurt and bruised, punched him almost at will.

It was incredible how Frazier withstood the onslaught, just as it had been earlier when Ali had taken the best 'Smokin' Joe' could throw at him. Both fighters slumped onto their stools to contemplate one, final round.

At this stage one of the most famous episodes in boxing took place. Futch decided enough was enough and stopped the fight. Frazier was keen to continue. "I want him, boss," he said, despairingly.

Futch replied: "It's all over. No-one will forget what you have done here today."

Unbeknown to them Ali, equally exhausted, had asked his corner to cut and remove his gloves, to denote the end of the fight. Dundee refused.

When they realized Frazier could not continue Ali rose to his feet,

"HE COULD HAVE WHOOPED ANY FIGHTER IN THE WORLD, EXCEPT ME. HE IS GREAT, GREATER THAN I THOUGHT. HE IS ONE HELL OF A FIGHTER AND IT WAS ONE HELL OF A FIGHT."

MUHAMMAD ALI

raised his arm in the air in victory and promptly collapsed.

"Frazier quit just before I did," he was happy to admit immediately afterwards. "I didn't think I could fight anymore.

"Joe Frazier brings out the best in me. That's one helluva of a man and God bless him. He is the greatest fighter in the world next to me."

And thus ended an epic among epics between two of the greatest fighters in boxing.

Ali may have been the victor – Padilla had him comfortably ahead although ringside observers made it close – but both played their part in making sporting history.

10 NOVEMBER 1983

HAGLER
VS DURÁN

WORLD MIDDLEWEIGHT CHAMPIONSHIP
CAESARS PALACE, LAS VEGAS, NEVADA, U.S.A.

TALE OF THE TAPE

MARVIN HAGLER	NAME	ROBERTO DURÁN
MARVELOUS	NICKNAME	MANOS DE PIEDRA (HANDS OF STONE)
NEWARK, NEW JERSEY, U.S.A.	BIRTHPLACE	EL CHORRILLO, PANAMA
29	AGE	32
57–2–2	PRE-FIGHT RECORD	77–4–0
48	KO'S	58
5'9.5"	HEIGHT	5'7.5"
157.5 LBS	WEIGHT	156.5 LBS
75"	REACH	67"
SOUTHPAW	STANCE	ORTHODOX

SLIM MARGIN

IT PROVED TO BE A FIGHT OF CAT AND MOUSE TACTICS BUT EVEN THOUGH ONE WOULD COME BACK LATE TO PREVAIL THE OTHER WOULD ENJOY THE KUDOS EVEN IN DEFEAT.

Another epic between two of the "Four Kings" of the middle weights in world boxing during the 1980s, one that featured very differing tactics and a result that seemed to tarnish the winner whilst enhance the loser.

Such were the strange anomalies of the superstars who dominated the sport during this decade.

Hagler had been the world middleweight champion for three years and seven defenses, all ending with stoppages. Durán, the world light-middleweight champion, moved up a weight to face this intimidating opponent supposedly in the twilight of his career.

Moreover he had a two inch height disadvantage and a huge eight inch reach deficit to the defending champion.

Little wonder Hagler came into this fight as the 4-1 on favorite with the bookmakers.

As usual the build up of mutual disdain between the fighters only served to garner more interest and guarantee a crowd of almost 15,000 at the outside arena at Caesars Palace.

Once the bell rang to denote the start of the fight Durán adopted very different tactics than seen before. Very much a front foot fighter who was always the aggressor the Panamanian held back, moving sideways and downwards rather than forwards. Hagler had prepared for an immediate onslaught from his challenger. Instead he was facing a target who was suddenly, and unexpectedly, hard to hit.

Unbeknown to Hagler his opponent had damaged his right hand when he landed a punch on Hagler's rock solid forehead during the 5th round. For the rest of the fight Durán was in pain every time he threw a right hander.

It nearly ended in the 6th when Hagler momentarily came out of his shell to cause damage with shots repeatedly to Durán's body and head. Almost any other fighter would have succumbed to the sudden onslaught but few possessed Durán's will to win and Hagler knew, even when appearing on the verge of being beaten, Durán remained dangerous.

As a result he failed to move in for the kill and by the 7th round Durán was fully recovered and scoring points as he returned to being elusive in the ring.

By the 12th most had Durán ahead by a slim margin. During this round blood began to trickle from Hagler's left eye. Durán held out his chin and taunted the champion. "Hit me, hit me," he shouted. By the end of the round the largely Latino audience were chanting his name.

The fireworks began in earnest in the 13th. Hagler staggered Durán with a huge left to the face. Durán countered almost immediately, first to the body and then with two rights, a left and a further right to the head.

Hagler smiled back as the bell sounded but it was clear he needed to find another gear if he wished to remain the world champion. Both trainers knew it was still close enough for either fighter to win, even though the judges had Durán understandably ahead.

"You win the last two rounds, you win the fight," shouted Luis Spada, Durán's trainer.

Goody Petronelli, Hagler's trainer, was more or less barking the same order. "I want a strong 14th and 15th," he told his man. "You've got to win these last two rounds."

It was now, finally, that Hagler shed all his inhibitions and became the aggressor. Durán, the shorter, lighter man who had gone up a division to meet one of the greats, finally got caught and, this time, had little response. For two rounds Hagler battered his illustrious opponent.

Durán being Durán, it was not enough to knock him down or finish the fight, but it was enough to edge past the Panamanian. The judges were unanimously in agreement. Hagler had scraped home by the scores of 144-142, 144-141 and 146-145.

"Everybody is disappointed I didn't knock him out," said Hagler afterwards. "I felt that myself. It was hard to hit him with a solid punch. You don't barrel in on a guy like Durán. Why take unnecessary punishment unless you have to?"

Durán, who became the first man to last the distance in a world title fight with Hagler, did not hold back onhis feelings towards the way he had lost. "He came to tear my head off but when he saw that I could hit him hard he got scared and became a coward," he announced to the world's press. "Everyone was saying he was a destroyer but when he hit me it didn't do anything. His punches absolutely did no damage."

Both would have more fights against the other members of the "Four Kings" but this was the one fight where the loser would emerge in the better light.

"HE WASN'T THAT VULNERABLE TO A KNOCKOUT. IT WAS HARD TO HIT HIM WITH A SOLID PUNCH... YOU DON'T BARREL IN THERE ON A GUY LIKE ROBERTO DURÁN."

MARVIN HAGLER

15 JUNE 1984

HEARNS
vs DURÁN

**WORLD SUPER-WELTERWEIGHT CHAMPIONSHIP
CAESARS PALACE, LAS VEGAS, NEVADA, U.S.A.**

TALE OF THE TAPE

THOMAS HEARNS	NAME	ROBERTO DURÁN
THE HITMAN / MOTOR CITY COBRA	NICKNAME	MANOS DE PIEDRA (HANDS OF STONE)
MEMPHIS, TENNESSEE, U.S.A.	BIRTHPLACE	EL CHORRILLO, PANAMA
25	AGE	32
38–1–0	PRE-FIGHT RECORD	77–5–0
32	KO'S	58
6'1"	HEIGHT	5'7"
153 LBS	WEIGHT	154 LBS
78"	REACH	66"
ORTHODOX	STANCE	ORTHODOX

MALICE AT THE PALACE

IT WAS AN EXAMPLE OF TWO LEGENDS OF THE SPORT WHO WERE UNEVENLY MATCHED. A GOOD BIG ONE NORMALLY BEATS A GOOD SMALL ONE BUT FEW EXCEPT THE WINNER HIMSELF PREDICTED HOW.

This was a fight both wanted. Badly. It had been three years since Thomas Hearns had snatched defeat from the jaws of victory against Sugar Ray Leonard to lose his unbeaten streak and, although he had subsequently won the world light-middleweight title he had labored to numerous wins, was beset by injuries and seemed to have lost his 'Hit Man' reputation.

Durán had been buoyed, even in defeat in his last fight, where he became the first man to go the distance with Marvin Hagler in a championship fight despite making up a division to middleweight. With his standing seemingly enhanced despite this setback Durán relished the challenge Hearns would set him with the WBC title on the line.

And it certainly was a challenge for Durán because, despite his opponent's lack-luster form of late, Hearns was a staggering 5.5 inches taller than him and would enjoy an 11-inch reach advantage.

Despite the aura of his power and invincibility severely diluted of late, Hearns was confident enough to predict a second round knockout. It was a big call against a force such as Durán.

So keen was Durán for this fight that he refused to face the WBA's mandatory challenger, Mike McCallum, and thus forfeited his world title. It would prove to be a highly questionable decision.

Within moments of the first round beginning it became clear that the mismatch in terms of size would prove problematic for the courageous Panamanian.

Certain fighters are not necessarily better than others, but their styles suit or do not suit each other. Durán was on the small side of his weight in terms of height and reach, Hearns very much on the large side. This would prove to be a bridge too far.

Durán was at his most dangerous when he got inside his opponent. The issue here was that Hearns kept him at bay with his left jab. Durán did manage to find Hearns with a hard body shot but, in doing so, he left himself open to a counter left hook that cut his eye.

Thirty seconds later a hard right from Hearns dropped Durán. This was the first time the man they dubbed 'Hands of Stone' had been decked in 41 fights and ten years. It was a strange experience to be staring at the canvas.

He rose at six and received the mandatory count of eight. Hearns, knowing that Durán was never beaten, swarmed over him and, with just seconds remaining of the round, sent him down again with a fierce uppercut to the body.

Durán rose at three this time but was so dazed that as the bell sounded he wandered over to a neutral corner only to be led back to his own by one of his team.

"You have to keep your hands up," implored Durán's trainer, Luis Spada, sensing what was to come.

Hearns knew that he needed to finish the job and not allow the never-say-die Panamanian veteran back into the fight. He forced Durán onto the ropes and unleashed a furious flurry of punches.

Durán, naturally, tried to fight back in desperation but, in doing so, exposed himself. Hearns landed a massive right hander that landed flush on Durán's jaw and he crashed down facefirst on to the floor.

Referee Carlos Padilla stopped the fight immediately and in doing so confirmed the first knockout of Durán's long, long career.

The first words Durán uttered as he rose to his feet were: "What did I do wrong?" Later he acknowledged the severity of his experience. "It was like, suddenly, I was down and when I got up I was confused."

A jubilant Hearns explained how he had to fulfil his second round prediction. "You thought I was crazy saying I'd win in two," he said. "But I was deadly serious. I couldn't just win. I had to win big because I was fighting a legend. The 'Hit Man' was on vacation but now he's back."

Amazingly, the indefatigable Durán was not quite finished. He would go onto win the WBC's middleweight title later.

As for Hearns, a long career was still ahead of him and many more world titles, but this was his redemption fight that ended his post-Leonard depression.

"YOU THOUGHT I WAS CRAZY SAYING I'D WIN IN TWO, BUT I WAS DEADLY SERIOUS. I COULDN'T JUST WIN. I HAD TO WIN BIG BECAUSE I WAS FIGHTING A LEGEND. THE 'HIT MAN' WAS ON VACATION BUT NOW HE'S BACK."

THOMAS HEARNS

06 DECEMBER 2008

FROCH vs
PASCAL

WORLD SUPER MIDDLEWEIGHT CHAMPIONSHIP
TRENT FM ARENA, NOTTINGHAM, ENGLAND, U.K.

TALE OF THE TAPE

CARL FROCH	NAME	JEAN PASCAL
THE COBRA	NICKNAME	-
NOTTINGHAM, NOTTINGHAMSHIRE, U.K.	BIRTHPLACE	PORT-AU-PRINCE, HAITI
31	AGE	26
23—0—0	PRE-FIGHT RECORD	21—0—0
19	KO'S	14
6'1"	HEIGHT	6'10.5"
168 LBS	WEIGHT	168 LBS
75"	REACH	72"
ORTHODOX	STANCE	ORTHODOX

WORLD CLASS

SOMETHING HAD TO GIVE IN THIS WORLD TITLE FIGHT BETWEEN TWO UNBEATEN FOES, BUT IT WOULD BE THE FAMED SOLID CHIN AND GRANITE HEART OF THE ENGLISHMAN THAT WOULD PREVAIL.

They billed this clash between two unbeaten super middleweights as 'World Class' and the title proved to be more than accurate. When it was all over the 9,000 sell-out crowd inside the Nottingham Arena bellowed a roar of approval, not just for their hometown boy, Froch, but for his Haitian-Canadian opponent too. Both had fought to a standstill.

The WBC belt had become vacant after Joe Calzaghe moved up a weight to face Bernard Hopkins. Froch was due to meet Jermain Taylor but Taylor opted to fight his fellow American, Jeff Lacy.

Next in line was Pascal, a tough Canadian originally from Haiti who, like Froch, had not experienced defeat in his professional career.

Something had to give but Froch knew, at 30 years of age, that he badly needed to win his first ever shot at a world title.

Known for his hard chin and big heart 'The Cobra' would require both attributes in what proved to be a hard-fought slugfest.

Recognizing that this was his big chance Froch came out of the traps hungry for initial success. He would win the first round comfortably after a barrage of hooks found their target. There would be no sizing up of opponents, as Pascal reiterated when he responded in the second round landing a juddering jab and moving inside Froch's front foot to launch a hard left hook.

The next three rounds saw both trading blows, rocking each other as they found the target and it was not until the sixth round that Froch began to ease ahead. His renowned solid jaw had taken almost everything Pascal could throw at him and when he landed a hard, straight right Pascal was forced to hold for the first time in the bout.

In the next two rounds Froch was prepared to be caught on a few occasions by Pascal as he pressed home his growing advantage and his opponent's right eye began to be damaged.

Knowing the fight was slipping away from him Pascal rose from his stool for the ninth round like a man on a mission.

Sensing he had a chance when he saw a cut develop above Froch's left eyelid Pascal gave it everything but instead was wobbled by a one-two from the Briton. It was a brave effort from a man facing not just an opponent who refused to take a backward step but a wholly partisan crowd shouting out their approval for one of their own.

The final three rounds, and especially the 12th and last, became a frenzied brawl. Both missed as often as they hit each other but neither buckled despite all that had taken place before. In the final three minutes they went toe-to-toe, Froch wanting to finish it off and Pascal accepting that he needed a knockout to turn the tide.

As the bell went ringside observers believed it was one of the best world title fights seen on British soil for many a year. The judges felt the same but also believed that Froch had done more than enough to be crowned the new WBC World super Middleweight champion. In a unanimous decision the Briton would get the nod from all three judges with scores of 116-112, 117-111 and 118-110, all in his favor.

"I felt the fight was a little bit closer," said a magnanimous Pascal afterwards. "But the better guy won today."

Froch was full of respect for his beaten foe, too. "He came here to have a go," he said. "He didn't come here to lie down. I caught him with some really hard, accurate shots."

He would go on to win various world title belts at super middleweight whilst Pascal would go up a weight and become the WBC's world light-heavyweight champion.

Both would become firm friends in later years, united in the knowledge that they each gave their all and produced a fight to remember one night in Nottingham.

18 SEPTEMBER 1999

TRINIDAD vs
DE LA HOYA

WORLD WELTERWEIGHT CHAMPIONSHIP
MANDALAY BAY RESORT & CASINO, LAS VEGAS, NEVADA, U.S.A.

TALE OF THE TAPE

FELIX TRINIDAD	NAME	OSCAR DE LA HOYA
TITO	NICKNAME	GOLDEN BOY
CUPEY ALTO, PUERTO RICO	BIRTHPLACE	MONTEBELLO, CALIFORNIA, USA
26	AGE	26
35—0—0	PRE-FIGHT RECORD	31—0—0
30	KO'S	25
5'11"	HEIGHT	5'10.5"
147 LBS	WEIGHT	147 LBS
72.5"	REACH	73"
ORTHODOX	STANCE	ORTHODOX

FIGHT OF THE MILLENNIUM

*A CLASSIC PUGILIST AGAINST A PUNCHER WITH
A CONTROVERSIAL ENDING AND A RESULT THAT
HAS HAUNTED THE LOSER TO THIS DAY.*

It was one of the most-anticipated fights since Leonard took on Hearns twelve years earlier, a match between two unbeaten superstars of the ring, neither of whom had ever tasted defeat in the professional ranks. Billed 'The Fight of the Millennium' it would prove to be the last 'Superfight' of the 20th Century, pitting the ultimate 'boxer' against the 'fighter' to create a mouth-watering contrast in styles.

Nobody could predict with any confidence who would emerge the winner, which is why it would prove to be the most lucrative non-heavyweight fight in boxing history up to that point in time.

Oscar De La Hoya, the popular Mexican-American, had seen off the likes of Chávez, Camacho and Whitaker on his way to an unblemished professional record of 31 and 0. By the autumn of 1999 *The Ring* magazine had seen enough to name him the best, pound-for-pound boxer in the world.

Up for grabs this night in Las Vegas was his WBC title, a welterweight crown he had already defended eight times.

Facing him was a Puerto Rican with an even better record. Trinidad boasted a record of 35 and 0 and, as the IBF's world welterweight champion, had defended his title on no less than 14 occasions. He possessed a punch renowned for its ferocity. His challenge, though, was to find a target known for its movement and ability to score repeatedly with counters.

No wonder boxing stars such as Sugar Ray Leonard, Marvin Hagler and Mike Tyson were ringside. Film stars including Sylvester Stallone, Jack Nicholson and Cameron Diaz would join them.

Not surprisingly the fight failed to live up to its standing, so epic was the build-up and excitement prior to the first bell, but it would go the distance and have an ending shrouded in controversy.

For much of the fight De La Hoya appeared in charge. He did what he does best, moving, avoiding, connecting with combinations and keeping out of the way of Trinidad's dangerous responses. He won the first three rounds by keeping to the corners and forcing his opponent to travel around the ring. There was a trading of blows in the second round but De La Hoya kept mainly to his plan and in doing so built up his lead. By the end of the sixth Trinidad's eye was swollen and his nose bled.

After nine rounds De La Hoya led on the scorecards of two judges and, somewhat surprisingly, was drawing on the third. The problem was, though, that De La Hoya assumed he held a larger lead than he did and in the final three rounds he eased off and gave Trinidad his chance.

The end of fight stats suggest De La Hoya dominated the fight. He landed 263 punches to Trinidad's 166, and found the target with 143 jabs compared to 42 but, crucially, when it came to power punches landing Trinidad was ahead, just, by 124 to 120.

Much of this took place in those final rounds where the Puerto Rican, despite his left eye rapidly closing and his trunks splattered by his own blood, outpunched De La Hoya 64-33.

Still, as the final bell sounded the American raised his hands to the air in victory, convinced he had won. By being second best for those final three rounds, however, meant that he had lost not only his WBC belt but his first ever professional fight.

"That fight has haunted me every single day of my life," De La Hoya admitted twenty years later. "It's a tough one to talk about even now. A couple of days afterwards I'd watched the fight seven times and I just couldn't work out how he had won. Every day people tell me I won the fight. But still..."

Trinidad felt vindicated, however. "I was always said that I was the number one welterweight," he said. "I proved it."

20 JANUARY 2001

MAYWEATHER
VS CORRALES

WORLD SUPER FEATHERWEIGHT CHAMPIONSHIP
MGM GRAND GARDEN ARENA, LAS VEGAS, NEVADA, U.S.A.

TALE OF THE TAPE

FLOYD MAYWEATHER	NAME	DIEGO CORRALES
MONEY / PRETTY BOY	NICKNAME	CHICO
GRAND RAPIDS, MICHIGAN, U.S.A.	BIRTHPLACE	SACRAMENTO, CALIFORNIA, U.S.A.
23	AGE	23
24—0—0	PRE-FIGHT RECORD	33—0—0
18	KO'S	27
5'8"	HEIGHT	5'10.5"
130 LBS	WEIGHT	130 LBS
72"	REACH	70"
ORTHODOX	STANCE	ORTHODOX

RAGING RIVALS

THE SMALLER, FASTER MAN WOULD PREVAIL AGAINST A KNOCKOUT MACHINE AND MAKE THE WORLD SIT UP AND TAKE NOTICE OF A FIGHTER WHO WOULD BECOME ONE OF BOXING'S ALL-TIME GREATS.

Floyd Mayweather had built up a reputation as a fast-moving, fast-talking world champion who had dismissed all of his 24 previous opponents with consummate ease. 'Pretty Boy,' as he was then known as, had spent much of the build-up to this unification fight between two unbeaten champions trash talking his fellow American but many fight observers felt that, this time, he may have taken on too much.

Facing him was a man who had recorded 28 knockouts in his 33 professional victories, a boxer who was larger and whose size and power gave him what many felt was a significant advantage. It was time for Mayweather to put his money where his mouth was and this is precisely what he did.

For all his seemingly superior physical advantage Corrales probably weakened his cause by weighing in two pounds over the 130 lbs limit. It meant that he had to sweat out the excess two pounds during a 90-minute sauna session. It may have gone some way to explaining what would be a lethargic display against a man who dominated from start to finish.

The punching stats of the fight tell their own story. Mayweather landed 220 of his 414 punches. Corrales landed just 60 of his 205 punches. He just had no answer to a man whose fast hands and foot speed left the larger man grasping at air and in the whole ten rounds the fight would last he failed to hit the target with one, meaningful blow.

Mayweather picked off the more one-dimensional Corrales at will with deft jabs to the head and body and a series of short hooks that exposed an opponent, nicknamed "Chico," who was supposed to be providing the 'Pretty Boy' with his stiffest challenge to date.

Mayweather's father, Floyd Sr, could see the writing on the wall as early as the end of the first round. "Keep this up and we'll have him out of here in eight or nine rounds," he shouted from ringside. During the preceding three minutes his son had laid out how the fight would progress. Corrales could do nothing to counter Mayweather's hand speed and when he managed to move him into a corner and hone in on the smaller man, Mayweather evaded Corrales at ease by ducking and weaving out of trouble, landing a few jabs along the way.

By the seventh round Corrales had his strength severely drained by Mayweather's incessant attacks. The round would prove to be the worst dream for a proud man who had never been dropped in his career. Mayweather landed a lead left hook early in the round that caught Corrales by surprise. He dropped to his knee and took the count.

One minute later an almost exact shot resulted in the exact outcome, although this time a dazed and confused Corrales sat down. Again he rose to his feet but looked weary and in serious trouble. Mayweather cornered his bruised opponent and moved in for the kill.

Referee Richard Steele looked on the verge of stopping the fight when Corrales went down on his knee for a third time inside one round but when he rose once again he appeared clear-eyed and desperate to continue.

The bell probably saved him, but not for long. Corrales threw everything he had left at Mayweather in the eighth round but still lost it as most of his punches missed his evasive target.

It all came to a sorry end in the tenth. Mayweather knocked Corrales down for a fourth time with a short left hook. Showing immense pride and strength 'Chico' rose once more but was down on his knee again for a fifth time just a minute later.

At this point his stepfather/trainer, Ray Woods, was standing on the ring apron on the verge of throwing a towel into the ring. Corrales could see this and shouted "No, no, no" back at him but as he shouted out in angst referee Steele stopped the fight.

He was still angry and devastated afterwards. "A fighter likes to go out on his back," he explained. "I was coherent after each knockdown. My head was clear. I worked damn hard for this fight. There were only two more rounds. I wish he'd let me finish the fight."

Mayweather was in tears as he hugged his estranged father in a show of unity. "I used my defense the way my dad wanted me to," he said. "I wanted to show who is the best in the world."

Mayweather achieved that in spades. And although he would go on to record a perfect 50 and 0 professional record, many argue that this was his finest night.

"HE FOUGHT A SMART FIGHT, HE DID WHAT HE WAS SUPPOSED TO DO. I KEPT ON TRUCKING, I KEPT COMING FORWARD."

DIEGO CORRALES

5

15 APRIL 1985

HAGLER *vs* HEARNS

WORLD MIDDLEWEIGHT CHAMPIONSHIP
CAESARS PALACE, LAS VEGAS, NEVADA, U.S.A.

TALE OF THE TAPE

MARVIN HAGLER	NAME	THOMAS HEARNS
MARVELOUS	NICKNAME	HITMAN / MOTOR CITY COBRA
NEWARK, NEW JERSEY, U.S.A.	BIRTHPLACE	MEMPHIS, TENNESSEE, U.S.A.
30	AGE	26
60—2—2	PRE-FIGHT RECORD	40—1—0
50	KO'S	34
5'9.5"	HEIGHT	6'1"
159 LBS	WEIGHT	160 LBS
75"	REACH	78"
SOUTHPAW	STANCE	ORTHODOX

THE WAR

*UNDER EIGHT MINUTES OF UTTER MAYHEM, A FIGHT
SHORT IN TIME BUT ONE THAT HAS CONTINUED
LONG INTO THE NIGHT OF BOXING HISTORY.*

Beforehand they called it 'The Fight.' Afterwards, this would be changed to 'The War.' And that pretty much summed it up. The whole fight would last just 7 minutes and 52 seconds. But it was enough to make it one of the greatest fights of all time and, almost beyond debate, the greatest three rounds in boxing history.

Marvin Hagler and Thomas Hearns were part of the quartet of middleweight boxers known as 'The Four Kings,' a legendary foursome that also included Roberto Durán and Sugar Ray Leonard. Between 1980-89 they would between them hold 16 different world titles and face each other over nine memorable bouts. Few would disagree that this night in Vegas would serve up the best fight of the lot.

They nearly met three years earlier until a hand injury to Hearns cancelled the bout. Three years on and both had become that much more formidable in both reputation and in record.

Hagler had been the undisputed middleweight champion of the world for nearly five years. Known for his fitness and stamina, perhaps his most powerful weapon was his durability. In all his time he had been knocked down just once – and then he insisted it was a slip on his way to another victory. By the time he faced up to Hearns he had defended his world title ten times, knocking nine out along the way. The tenth? A points win over the durable Durán. Awkward, fearless and almost impossible to hurt, Hagler appeared almost unbeatable.

"HE GOES DOWN, AND I'M COUNTING. THOMAS HEARNS' HEART IS AS BIG AS HE IS. HE GETS UP AND COLLAPSES IN MY ARMS."

RICHARD STEELE

Hearns had moved up from welterweight to junior middleweight to now middleweight to take on the intimidating Hagler. Considered one of the hardest punchers of all time, Hearns also dispatched nearly all his opponents via a knockout. He, too, had seen off Durán. His only defeat was by Leonard, and that was another classic decided in the 14th round. Straight out of the famous Kronk gym in Detroit, run by his legendary trainer, Manny Steward, Hearns was predicting he would demolish Hagler in three rounds.

Well at least he got the three rounds correct.

The pre-fight assumptions were that Hearns would gain an early lead against the notoriously slow-starting champion. So relaxed was the challenger that he even had a pre-fight massage, something that infuriated Steward who felt it weakened his charge's legs.

Neither of them could have imagined how the first round would pan out from the moment the bell sounded. Hagler almost ran across the ring to launch an unrelenting assault on his taller foe, a tremendous gamble against such a feared puncher. Hearns was pinned back into his corner as a series of ferocious right handers found their target. Stunned into a response Hearns retaliated with equally numbing right handers of his own, one landing full on Hagler's chin to stun him temporarily.

Back came Hagler as if nothing had happened, catching Hearns with a fierce left hander. Hearns, otherwise known as 'The Hitman,' attempted to calm the frenzied pace down by boxing for a few seconds but before long, as Hagler continued to be the aggressor, this plan went out of the window.

It had turned into a high quality, bar-room brawl, with both now toe-to-toe trading punches. This would continue for the rest of the round, with neither caring much for defense nor any longer-term strategy.

Hearns' cornermen were shouting "Box him, Tommy," but the instruction fell on deaf ears. A concerned Steward then cupped his hands to his mouth and screamed "You've gotta stick and move." By then it was too late. The fight had turned into a slugfest.

By the end of this memorable first round Hagler had a huge cut above his right eye and blood was streaming down his face, but he had also hurt the dangerous challenger with a final flurry of punches.

Hearns would discover subsequently that he had broken his right hand during one of their exchanges.

Later this first round was named the greatest in boxing history by The Ring magazine and it would win the Round of the Year in their 1985 honors.

No wonder when you look at the stats. Hagler landed 50 from his 82 punches, Hearns 56 from 83. This remains a record number of punches landed in a round in middleweight history. Despite the stats slightly favoring Hearns the judges had Hagler ahead by two to one by way of his more effective bombs.

The first had clearly taken much more out of Hearns. He attempted to slow the pace in the second round and Hagler could see that his opponent's legs had been weakened by the previous three minutes.

'Marvelous' Marvin began to hunt a stumbling Hearns down. Wherever 'The Hitman' turned, with his thatch of curly hair, the menacing, bald champion was there. At one stage Hagler even experimented, switching from orthodox style before returning to his usual southpaw scoring points as he countered Hearns using his reach advantage with his jab. Yet again Hagler was deemed to have won the round in the eyes of two out of the three judges.

Round three started in the same way as its predecessor, with Hearns trying to calm things down. After a minute had passed the cut inflicted on Hagler in the first round opened up and blood began to pour down his face, forcing referee Richard Steele to pause the fight for the ringside doctor to take a look. When asked by the medic if he could see Hagler retorted: "I'm not missing him, am I?" Steele gestured for the fight to continue.

In truth, though, Hagler knew he needed to finish this fast because it was only a matter of time before the cut would force the fight to be stopped in Hearns' favor. Already the aggressor Hagler added desperation to his armory. It would prove to be the final ingredient required.

The defending champion's first round aggression reappeared instantly. A left to the head forced Hearns back on the ropes. He smiled at Hagler, a brave attempt to inform him he was not hurt. Moments later Tommy Hearns was not smiling.

A hard right hook landed high on Hearns' head. A searing right

"I TOLD YOU I WAS GONNA EAT HIM UP LIKE PAC-MAN, I FIGURED ONCE I GET THROUGH THE RIGHT HAND, THEN IT WAS ALL MINE. BECAUSE I THINK THE FIRST BIG ONE THAT HE TRIED, HE TRIED TO PUT ME AWAY OUT THERE. I WANTED TO SHOW THE WORLD I AM THE GREATEST."

MARVIN HAGLER

hand to the chin followed. 'The Hitman' started to fall forward as Hagler made sure by following up with two further uppercuts.

It was a miracle that Hearns got to his feet at all. He lay flat on his back and, for all the world, out for the count. Instead, he rose on the count of nine but, clearly in no shape to continue, fell into a cornerman's arms as referee Steele stopped the fight.

The 15,000 packed inside Caesars Palace could scarcely believe what they had seen and, at the end of it all, a blood-soaked Hagler was paraded around the ring in victory at the same time as a battered Hearns was helped back to his corner.

Both revealed mutual admiration afterwards.

"What can I say," said Hearns. "It happens to the best of us. It hurts. He came in, took my best shot and fought his ass off. The man showed his greatness tonight."

Hagler traded praise as much as he had earlier traded punches. "I want to give Tommy all the credit in the world," he insisted. "He came out the only way he could if he wanted to take something away from a champion. But I was so worked up I would have beaten an army."

In victory and defeat both champions have gone down in the annals of sporting history. And 'The War' as one of the all-time great fights.

17 JUNE 2000

DE LA HOYA
vs MOSLEY

WORLD WELTERWEIGHT CHAMPIONSHIP
STAPLES CENTER, LOS ANGELES, CALIFORNIA U.S.A.

TALE OF THE TAPE

OSCAR DE LA HOYA	NAME	SHANE MOSLEY
GOLDEN BOY	NICKNAME	SUGAR
MONTEBELLO, CALIFORNIA, U.S.A.	BIRTHPLACE	LYNWOOD, CALIFORNIA, U.S.A.
27	AGE	28
32—1—0	PRE-FIGHT RECORD	34—0—0
26	KO'S	32
5'10.5"	HEIGHT	5'8.5"
146.5 LBS	WEIGHT	147 LBS
73"	REACH	71"
ORTHODOX	STANCE	ORTHODOX

DESTINY

AN EPIC CONTEST BETWEEN TWO HUGE BOXING STARS THAT COULD HAVE GONE EITHER WAY. IN THE END IT WAS NOT THE FIGHTER WHO STARTED THE BEST, BUT THE ONE WHO ENDED THE BEST WHO WOULD PREVAIL.

It was billed as 'Destiny' between two Californian men who knew each other well and later would be seen as one of the all-time classics, especially in the 147 lbs division.

Many 'Superfights' fail to match their billing but this epic certainly did.

In one corner sat the superstar that was Oscar De La Hoya, back after his bitter defeat to Felix Trinidad, his first in his professional career, and a setback De La Hoya refused to recognize.

Facing him was a man whom he had fought over 60 rounds with during their amateur days, and whom had inflicted two of the five defeats De La Hoya had suffered as an amateur.

Since then De La Hoya's star had risen higher, not least after winning Olympic gold at the 1992 Barcelona Olympics. By the time he lost to Trinidad he was regarded as the best pound for pound boxer in the world.

Mosley had spent much of the previous two years as the IBF lightweight champion before he relinquished the title to move up to welterweight. By the time he faced De La Hoya he had fought just twice at 147 lbs. With a two-inch height disadvantage as well Mosley was seen as the 2-1 underdog.

The fight possessed similarities with De La Hoya's meeting with Trinidad. Although Mosley showed off his hand speed well in the first half of the fight it was De La Hoya's superior timing that prevailed.

He pressed from the first bell, hoping that his greater experience at this weight against a man who, for all his standing, was a novice at welterweight, would tell.

Mosley would win the first round but thereafter, despite both fighters not holding back, it was De La Hoya who would have the momentum in a tactical but fiercely contested bout.

Mosley's uncomfortable night up to this point grew worse, too, when his back stiffened up after five rounds which slowed him down. But, for all De La Hoya's energy and timing, he rarely troubled his opponent, even if he was edging ahead on the judges' scorecards.

As Mosley rose for the seventh round his father and trainer, Jack, shouted out: "Just relax. Use your rhythm." It was another slugfest of a round, with Mosley landing left hooks and hard, over the top rights. As he returned to his corner he raised his fist in a defiant message. He may have been behind on points but he was far from beaten.

Suddenly it was Mosley who looked more comfortable. De La Hoya still came after him - especially in an exhilarating ninth round - but he was missing more and losing the close-range and often furious exchanges.

In the tenth the momentum clearly swung. Mosley outpunched the 'Golden Boy' by 34 to 19 as his speed and superior jab dominated. Sensing his fighter's predicament De La Hoya's trainer, Robert Alcazar, bellowed a final instruction as the bell sounded for the final round. "We need this round."

It did not work out this way. All the points-scoring punches were coming from Mosley. Midway through the round he landed a right hook to the body and then caught his increasingly desperate opponent flush on the jaw with a hard right. By the end of the round he had landed 45 punches to De La Hoya's 18 as both went for each other right up to the bell.

The stats suggest that it was as close as the verdict. Mosley landed 284 punches to De La Hoya's 257, with 174 power punches to 165. Just as he did against Trinidad, De La Hoya led at the halfway stage only to lose it down the home straight.

Unlike against Trinidad, however, he kept going until the end giving his all. In a split decision two judges gave it to Mosley, 116-112 and 115-113, and one to De La Hoya, 113-115.

"I wanted it more from the beginning," Mosley declared afterwards. "I wanted to show the world that I am a true warrior."

De La Hoya was so disenchanted by a second defeat in his career that he considered retirement. Instead, despite another defeat to Mosley in the 2003 rematch, he would bounce back to strengthen his claim to be one of the all-time greats in the history of boxing.

"IT WAS THE BIGGEST FIGHT OF MY CAREER PROBABLY MY BEST WIN."

SHANE MOSLEY

13 FEBRUARY 1999

DE LA HOYA
VS QUARTEY

WORLD WELTERWEIGHT CHAMPIONSHIP
THOMAS & MACK CENTER, LAS VEGAS, NEVADA, U.S.A.

TALE OF THE TAPE

OSCAR DE LA HOYA	NAME	IKE QUARTEY
GOLDEN BOY	NICKNAME	BAZOOKA
MONTEBELLO, CALIFORNIA, U.S.A.	BIRTHPLACE	ACCRA, GHANA
27	AGE	29
29—0—0	PRE-FIGHT RECORD	34—0—0
24	KO'S	30
5'10.5"	HEIGHT	5'7.5"
147 LBS	WEIGHT	147 LBS
73"	REACH	71"
ORTHODOX	STANCE	ORTHODOX

THE CHALLENGE

IT WOULD PROVE TO BE TOO CLOSE FOR COMFORT AFTER A THOROUGH TEST OF ALL HIS CREDENTIALS TO BECOME ONE OF THE GREATS, BUT IT WAS ALSO ANOTHER STEP FORWARD IN A STELLAR CAREER.

Oscar De La Hoya may well have made a big name for himself but, for all the high profile wins up to this moment in his career, many viewed this fight against Ike Quartey as his most dangerous.

Pundits suggested that although the popular Latin-American had seen off some big names they had either been in the twilights of their careers, such as Julio César Chávez, or just too small for De La Hoya. In other words, all had suited the 'Golden Boy.'

Quartey, the youngest of no less than 27 children, had been the WBA's welterweight champion for four years until, following a lengthy absence from the ring due to personal, business and health reasons, he was stripped of the title in 1998.

By the time he stepped into the ring to face the celebrated De La Hoya the Ghanaian had not fought for 14 months but he was still unbeaten and, befitting a man who trained in the same gym as Azumah Nelson, packed a punch.

De La Hoya, for his part, knew a lot was riding on the outcome of this meeting. A week later Felix Trinidad and Pernell Whitaker would have it out, with the winner meeting the victor between De La Hoya and Quartey for both WBC and IBF belts.

It would not start well for the champion. Quartey, showing superior speed and power, took early control of the fight, perhaps exemplified by the two, crunching left hooks in the third round that rocked De La Hoya back onto his heels.

The challenger still led into the sixth round when De La Hoya found his range with a left hook to drop the man nicknamed 'Bazooka' to the floor. Ringside observers assumed that from this point onwards the 'Golden Boy' would take charge of affairs.

Instead Quartey regathered and, inside a minute of his own knockdown, gave as good as he got, sending De La Hoya crashing to the canvas with a copycat left hook. If the champion thought he might be in trouble as he rose to his feet, he knew by the end of the ninth he faced defeat after Quartey had taken the previous two rounds.

It was only in the tenth round that the proverbial tide finally turned. Quartey's impressive efforts had understandably tired him and as he slowed so De La Hoya upped his tempo. Although he would win rounds 10 and 11 he still knew, however, that only a big, final round would suffice.

As the bell sounded for the 12th De La Hoya sprang from his stool like a man possessed, landing a vicious left hook early into the round to send Quartey tumbling to the floor for the second time in the fight.

To the Ghanaian's credit he not only jumped to his feet but was able to withstand the inevitable onslaught to see the fight out. The big question amongst ringsiders was had De La Hoya done enough to come back from such a deficit?

The judges believed so, just, by two to one, scoring 116-112 and 116-113 in his favor, to one at 115-114 for Quartey.

Not surprisingly the challenger begged to differ. "Oscar didn't do anything for eight rounds," he said. "You saw the fight. I matched him for speed and power. He came to survive."

De La Hoya accepted he had got it wrong on the night. "I made it a tactical fight," he admitted. "It wasn't supposed to be like that. But it is still one fight closer to making history. I want to prove I'm the best."

For all his subsequent highs and occasional lows, however, Oscar De La Hoya would not forget the night he was so nearly the victim of a major upset at the hard hands of Ike Quartey.

"OSCAR DIDN'T DO ANYTHING FOR EIGHT ROUNDS... I MATCHED HIM FOR SPEED AND POWER. HE CAME TO SURVIVE."

IKE QUARTEY

11 DECEMBER 1982

CHACON vs
LIMÓN IV

WORLD FEATHERWEIGHT CHAMPIONSHIP
MEMORIAL AUDITORIUM, SACRAMENTO, CALIFORNIA, U.S.A.

TALE OF THE TAPE

BOBBY CHACON	**NAME**	RAFAEL LIMÓN
SCHOOLBOY	**NICKNAME**	BAZOOKA
SYLMAR, CALIFORNIA, U.S.A.	**BIRTHPLACE**	TLAXCO, TLAXCALA, MEXICO
31	**AGE**	28
50–6–1	**PRE-FIGHT RECORD**	50–11–2
43	**KO'S**	37
5'5"	**HEIGHT**	5'7.5"
130 LBS	**WEIGHT**	129.25 LBS
64.5"	**REACH**	66"
ORTHODOX	**STANCE**	SOUTHPAW

TRIUMPH AND TRAGEDY

IN THE END, AFTER FOUR FIGHTS WITH NOTHING BETWEEN THEM, IT CAME TO ONE PUNCH FOR REDEMPTION AND CLOSURE.

They may not have been quite so famous as some of the boxers embroiled in the great rivalries over the years in the sport, but few would disagree that the quartet of fights between Bobby Chacon and Rafael Limón demands that this pairing is right up there with the best.

And, unusually, it was the fourth and last meeting between the American-Mexican and the Mexican – their backgrounds alone added edge to the four fights – that served up the most compelling encounter of the lot. Indeed, it was the only time in their rivalry that the pair fought for a world title.

They first stared across a professional boxing ring at each other in 1975. After ten rounds Limón was awarded a close decision. The second fight took place four years later. This was an even bigger brawl than their first encounter. Chacon was leading when he unintentionally headbutted his rival. Limón was unable to continue and so the fight was judged to be a technical draw.

In 1980 Chacon avenged his defeat in fight one when winning a ten-round split decision. In all three fights there had been little between them. The rivalry simply increased, as did their mutual animosity. Two years later came the final chapter, by which stage both boxers' lives had changed dramatically.

Limón was by then the defending WBC super-featherweight champion. Chacon, in the twilight of his career, had suffered a personal tragedy when his wife, Valorie, had committed suicide, reportedly due in part to her husband's decision to continue boxing despite her pleas to stop. Despite this huge trauma Chacon drew strength and inspiration. "I can't lose, I can't lose," he was heard repeatedly in his dressing room pre-fight. The auditorium was packed with primarily his supporters.

It was Limón who dominated the early exchanges, though, his long reach and uppercuts to the body taking its toll on the older challenger. In the third round a straight left caused Chacon to lose balance enough for both gloves to touch the canvas. This prompted a standing count of eight.

Despite this Chacon came more and more into the fight, edging back to parity with his relentless pursuit of the champion. Then another setback. Limón dropped him to the floor in the tenth. The older man rose to his feet again without any difficulty, but he knew he needed an emphatic finish if he were to reclaim the world title for himself.

At the end of the 14th round most ringsiders could not split the boxers. It had been the case throughout all four fights spanning seven years. It was looking like another draw unless one of them could produce a decisive final moment.

It came from Chacon, bleeding from the bridge of his nose, with just ten seconds remaining of the fight. A hard right found Limón's chin and the champion finally hit the floor. He rose on the count of eight, but the fight was over two seconds later and there was no time for any response.

Chacon was awarded the fight with a unanimous verdict, the judges scoring reading 142-141, 141-140 and 143-141. Quite clearly that final punch won the fight.

The emotions appeared after redemption had been achieved. Chacon dedicated the win to his wife. "I finally broke down after the Limón fight," he said later. "I didn't like that guy to begin with and with everything that happened… I couldn't eat or sleep. I just kept thinking about Valorie and cried for days."

The Ring magazine would later make Chacon vs Limón IV their 'Fight of the Year.' Few fights, let alone rivalries, would prove to be quite so close, quite so bitter and, so it transpired, quite so emotionally charged as this final decider.

08 OCTOBER 2005

ARCE vs
HUSSEIN II

WORLD FLYWEIGHT CHAMPIONSHIP
THOMAS & MACK CENTER, LAS VEGAS, NEVADA, U.S.A.

TALE OF THE TAPE

JORGE ARCE	NAME	HUSSEIN HUSSEIN
TRAVIESO	NICKNAME	HUSSY
LOS MOCHIS, SINALOA, MEXICO	BIRTHPLACE	SYDNEY, NEW SOUTH WALES, AUSTRALIA
26	AGE	30
40–3–1	PRE-FIGHT RECORD	28–2–0
30	KO'S	21
5'4.5"	HEIGHT	5'6"
111 LBS	WEIGHT	112 LBS
66"	REACH	67"
ORTHODOX	STANCE	ORTHODOX

FRUSTRATION

THE SECOND MEETING BETWEEN THESE TWO DIMINUTIVE FIGHTERS AND A MORE BRUTAL ENDING AS ARCE UNDERLINED WHY HE WOULD BECAME ONE OF THE MOST CELEBRATED MEXICAN BOXERS OF ALL TIME.

This was the second meeting between these two diminutive fighters meeting for the WBC's Interim flyweight world title. Just seven months over Arce had prevailed at the MGM Grand with a Technical Knockout in the tenth round, but after such a slugfest a rematch was demanded and agreed and so it was that the pair squared each other up again, just along the Strip, at the Thomas & Mack Center.

Hussein, the Australian from Sydney, had suffered quite a beating at the hands of Arce last time round, but showed courage and resolve to withstand the aggressive Mexican until it came to an end.

Second time round it would not be the same.

Arce enjoyed huge popularity back home in Mexico and, increasingly, in Hispanic America. It was no surprise to see the auditorium packed full of Arce supporters.

It helped that he was quite a character. For example, he had appeared recently on reality TV back home. And when he entered the ring, he was always resplendent with a black cowboy hat on his head, whilst sucking a lollipop in his mouth.

Hussein had fallen into the showman's trap last time round. Instead of launching counter attacks he ended up trying to go toe-to-toe. This was a bad idea. By the tenth his trainer, the celebrated former world champion and fellow Australian, Jeff Fenech, had seen enough and threw in the towel. Hussein was clearly upset by the decision, as most boxers tend to be when they observe a flying towel.

Seven months on Hussein and Fenech expected a different approach. Arce, who ended that first bout with blood streaming down his face despite being dominant, made sure it never happened.

From the sound of the first bell Arce went to work. He did not care much for defense and barely took a backward step. Hussein found himself on the ropes, literally and metaphorically and, with two minutes gone, he was dropped by a right hook.

He rose quickly and was able to withstand the onslaught that followed but returned to his corner knowing he was in trouble.

Arce's work rate was staggering. It would have been interesting to see how long he could have kept it going for.

We will never know because, with ten seconds remaining of the second round, and after another relentless attack by Arce, Hussein went down for a second time following a crunching left hook.

He rose once more to his feet in good time but as he prepared to continue Fenech threw in the towel, much to the surprise of many at ringside.

He had been screaming to his charge to "get off the ropes" throughout the second round but when his fighter hit the canvas for a second time he had seen enough.

Hussein punched the corner in frustration and anguish. Once again, he believed he could have carried on.

Referee Kenny Bayless, who had no other option but to stop the fight, sympathized but saw it differently. "He was hurt more the second time," Bayless said. "I don't think he would have been able to recover."

A jubilant Arce was in no doubt. "I don't think he recuperated from the first fight," said the smiling Mexican. "I'm surprised he even got up. I was really motivated to show this guy what I could really do."

Jorge Arce would go on to become just the second Mexican to win world titles in four, separate weight divisions and continue the fine tradition of proud fighters from this country that failed to quite understand the meaning of defeat.

22 JUNE 2002

BARRERA vs
MORALES II

WORLD FEATHERWEIGHT CHAMPIONSHIP
MGM GRAND, LAS VEGAS, NEVADA, U.S.A.

TALE OF THE TAPE

MARCO ANTONIO BARRERA	**NAME**	ERIK MORALES
THE BABY-FACED ASSASSIN	**NICKNAME**	EL TERRIBLE
MEXICO CITY, DISTRITO FEDERAL, MEXICO	**BIRTHPLACE**	TIJUANA, BAJA CALIFORNIA, MEXICO
29	**AGE**	25
54—3—0	**PRE-FIGHT RECORD**	41—0—0
39	**KO'S**	31
5'6"	**HEIGHT**	5'8"
126 LBS	**WEIGHT**	126 LBS
70"	**REACH**	72"
ORTHODOX	**STANCE**	ORTHODOX

FOR HONOR AND PRIDE

A MORE TECHNICAL FIGHT, ANOTHER TIGHT CONTEST AND A SECOND CONTROVERSIAL VERDICT. ALL THE INGREDIENTS OF AN EPIC RIVALRY.

Marco Antonio Barrera could not wait to re-acquaint himself with Erik Morales. Despite being a three-division and lineal world featherweight champion his defeat against his compatriot - and many say controversial loss as well - had rankled with him ever since.

Morales had immediately quit the super bantamweight division and moved up to Featherweight, winning all five fights afterwards prior to the second meeting between the two Mexicans.

Barrera, who was handed back his WBO super bantamweight title once Morales had relinquished it, had also won his next five bouts.

After the toe-to-toe slugfest in the first match, and the wafer-thin verdict, the boxing public demanded a rematch and their wishes were duly granted.

It was dubbed 'Ultimate Feud' and with good reason. These two held a genuine dislike for each other that went far further than simply boosting ticket sales. In 2001 they even came to blows at a press conference in Houston, with Barrera landing a shot with his right hand.

Morales-Barrera part two of this epic trilogy was considered the most technical. Few could argue that Morales – 'El Terrible' – was in front at the midway stage, winning at least four of the first six rounds.

Barrera began cautiously, allowing his rival's greater reach to find its target.

Despite this it was Morales who suffered a cut on the bridge of his

251

nose in the second round and, later in the eighth, a cut and swelling under the right eye.

Moreover, Barrera appeared to have gone down in the sixth round when he was caught off-balance by a body shot and his gloves touched the canvas. The referee, Jay Nady, saw it differently and called it a slip.

If the first half went to Morales the second half was edged by Barrera, but was it enough to win the fight?

Morales was clearly tiring and the longer the fight went on, so Barrera was able to get up close and personal from where he was always the more dangerous.

It was probably in recognition of Barrera's rally that Morales found renewed energy to edge, in many ringsiders' eyes, rounds 10 and 11 which, coupled with his first half dominance, should have been enough to win the night and inflict a second consecutive defeat on his rival.

Even Barrera's corner team were concerned with one round to go. "You're losing," one shouted out. "You've gotta win the next round."

He edged the 12th with Morales' damaged eye all but closed. Morales was more aggressive, but Barrera landed more damaging shots.

As in the first fight when the bell rang there was little between them, as the stats back up. Barrera landed 207 of his 607 punches thrown. Morales 205 out of 599. Nothing between them. Again.

Certainly, Morales and his team felt they had done enough. As the final bell sounded he lofted his arms in the air in triumph before his team lifted him high and paraded him around the ring.

In contrast Barrera walked quietly to his corner before, somewhat belatedly, his team then raised him upwards and copied Morales.

The judges made it a close call but, unlike the first encounter, this was no split decision. Instead Barrera, much to the surprise of many, was awarded a unanimous verdict by 115-113, 115-113 and 116-112.

"I won the fight," Morales insisted afterwards. "He did nothing for the first six or seven rounds."

At one win each between these arch enemies, there was only one thing left to do.

Cue Morales vs Barrera, and the final denouement of one of the very best of boxing's trilogies.

"I WANT TO SAY TO ALL THE PEOPLE WHO WANT A THIRD MATCH BETWEEN ME AND ERIK MORALES, I AM READY."

MARCO ANTONIO BARRERA

30 NOVEMBER 1979

BENITEZ *vs*

LEONARD

WORLD WELTERWEIGHT CHAMPIONSHIP
CAESARS PALACE, SPORTS PAVILION, LAS VEGAS, NEVADA, U.S.A.

TALE OF THE TAPE

WILFRED BENITEZ	NAME	RAY LEONARD
EL RADAR / BIBLE OF BOXING	NICKNAME	SUGAR
BRONX, NEW YORK, U.S.A.	BIRTHPLACE	WILMINGTON, NORTH CAROLINA, U.S.A.
21	AGE	23
38—0—1	PRE-FIGHT RECORD	25—0—0
25	KO'S	16
5'10"	HEIGHT	5'10"
144.5 LBS	WEIGHT	146 LBS
70"	REACH	74"
ORTHODOX	STANCE	ORTHODOX

THE NEW KING OF BOXING

A CLASH BETWEEN TWO OF THE VERY BEST CRAFTSMEN IN THE FIGHT GAME. IT WAS AS IF IDENTICAL TWINS IN STYLE HAD MET IN THE RING. AND AT THE END OF IT ALL, THE LEGEND THAT WAS AND IS SUGAR RAY LEONARD WAS BORN.

Sugar Ray Leonard is best-known for his series of fights against the other three fighters who made up the 'Four Kings,' beating them all during a heady, few years in the 1980s, but it is sometimes forgotten that he also faced and overcame a number of other very fine boxers. One of them was Wilfred Benitez.

As Leonard was first to acknowledge, there was possibly no other boxer whose style more resembled Leonard's than the Puerto Rican. And while Leonard had won all 27 of his professional fights since striking gold at the 1976 Olympics, Benitez was, at the ripe old age of 21, already a two-division champion having won his first world title at a precocious 17 years of age – a record that stands to this day.

Despite this he would start the fight as the 3-1 underdog, an indication of how highly the world of boxing thought of the popular Leonard.

Benitez was known as "El Radar" because of his ability to dodge punches. Unlike many who simply used their legs to escape being hit, Benitez used his upper body, dodging and weaving and making himself a hard target to connect with.

Yet he had never faced anyone like Leonard before, a man possessed with extraordinary agility, mobility, reflexes and sheer power.

It promised to provide the perfect clash, with Benitez's famed right hander against Leonard's left.

No wonder the WBC's defending Welterweight champion took

home $1.2M and the challenger, $1M, a record amount for a non-heavyweight bout.

Just to add a little more spice to the occasion Benitez's own father, Gregorio, who doubled up as his trainer, wrote an article in The Ring magazine claiming that Leonard would win because his son had not trained hard enough. He would later insist he wrote it to motivate his son.

Once the fight began Leonard would start the stronger, a left jab in the third placing Benitez sitting on the canvas.

An accidental clash of heads in the sixth left the champion with a cut on his forehead but, after nine rounds, it was still sufficiently close enough for Leonard's legendary trainer, Angelo Dundee, to shout out orders to change tactics from the corner: "Go downstairs," he bellowed, believing that the elusive Benitez was easier to punch in the body than the head.

As Leonard became more aggressive so he drew away in the later rounds. In the 9th round he had Benitez pinned to the ropes and in the 11th round he stung him with a left hook.

As the Puerto Rican rose from his stool for the 15th and final round, he knew only a knockout would save his belt. Benitez threw everything at Leonard but to his surprise his opponent stood toe-to-toe with him, returning with interest anything that landed.

With just 30 seconds remaining of what had been an entertaining encounter a left uppercut sent Benitez down on his knees. Although he rose and smiled at Leonard it was a rather rueful smile. He knew the game was over.

Just to make sure Leonard landed two further punches and referee Carlos Padilla stopped the fight with just six seconds remaining for a Technical Knockout.

"It was as though I was looking in the mirror," a jubilant Leonard said immediately afterwards. "No one, I mean no one, can make me miss punches like that."

For his part Benitez was magnanimous in his first professional defeat."Sugar Ray is the best in the world now," he said. "He was a great challenger, and he will be a great champion."And so, the legend of Sugar Ray Leonard was born with this, his first world title. It would prove to be the first of many epic battles, and many more world belts.

"SUGAR RAY IS THE BEST IN THE WORLD NOW. I WAS HAPPY TO GET A FIGHT WITH HIM. HE WAS A GREAT CHALLENGER AND WILL PROVE TO BE A GOOD CHAMPION."

WILFRED BENITEZ

16 SEPTEMBER 1981

LEONARD
VS HEARNS

WORLD WELTERWEIGHT CHAMPIONSHIP
CAESARS PALACE, LAS VEGAS, NEVADA, U.S.A.

TALE OF THE TAPE

RAY LEONARD	NAME	THOMAS HEARNS
SUGAR	NICKNAME	HITMAN / MOTOR CITY COBRA
WILMINGTON, NORTH CAROLINA, U.S.A.	BIRTHPLACE	MEMPHIS, TENNESSEE, U.S.A.
25	AGE	22
30—1—0	PRE-FIGHT RECORD	32—0—0
21	KO'S	30
5'9"	HEIGHT	6'1"
146 LBS	WEIGHT	145 LBS
70.5"	REACH	78"
ORTHODOX	STANCE	ORTHODOX

THE SHOWDOWN

A BOXING CLASSIC BETWEEN TWO OF THE GREATS WOULD END WITH THE KIND OF COMEBACK ONLY THE GREATEST CAN AMASS.

This would prove to be another classic in the series of fights during the 1980s featuring the 'Four Kings,' as they would later be called. Marvin Hagler and Roberto Durán would make up the fabulous four, with the two others meeting each other twice during the decade. Their first encounter served up a spectacle that was in keeping with the legend created by the four.

Sugar Ray Leonard had experienced an interesting past couple of years. After winning the WBC world welterweight title he lost it to Durán before reclaiming it in the famous 'No Mas' fight against Durán. He then forayed into light-middleweight territory, becoming world champion in this division too.

Thomas Hearns, meanwhile, had bulldozed his way to the WBA welterweight title, knocking 30 of his 32 opponents out in an unblemished professional career. Something had to give, which is why this fight scheduled for 15 rounds was called 'The Showdown.'

Caesars Palace was packed to the rafters with every single seat of the near 24,000 capacity filled. A worldwide TV audience of 300 million would watch the fight as well. Nobody was left disappointed.

The early rounds went as expected. Leonard boxed from a distance, wary of Hearns' greater reach and powerful jab. Hearns played the part of the hunter and stalker whilst Leonard, rather like his hero Muhammad Ali, danced around the ring in his high white boxing boots, the red and white tassels bouncing in tune with his movements.

Nonetheless Hearns, the knockout specialist, managed to find his target to build up a healthy lead. By the fifth round Leonard was sporting a swelling under his eye and he knew, even a third of the way into the fight, that he was facing a second career defeat.

This spurred the 1976 Olympic champion into action and for much of the sixth and seventh rounds Leonard was in control, battering his taller opponent and, once, clearly hurting him with a left hook to the chin. Just for a moment it was Hearns, the taller but the lighter of the pair, who suddenly looked in trouble as he wobbled somewhat gingerly back to his corner. Few of his previous opponents had lasted even this long before in the ring with him. But Leonard was not like any opponent he had faced before. The WBC champion may have been behind, but he had not been hurt particularly by any of the bombs Hearns had thrown.

As denoting two great champions the pendulum would swing again in the eighth. Hearns conjured up a second wind and on the scorecards of all three judges won rounds nine through to twelve. During the 11th round Leonard's left eye was shutting fast as he swelled up. There was also a dark smudge appearing below it. In winning all four rounds Hearns had amassed a seemingly unassailable lead.

In between the 11th and 12th rounds the crowd started chanting 'Tommy' as they saw the man from Detroit was winning the fight. Hearns rose to his feet and acknowledged the crowd by waving his arms. A round later he realized he had still not finished the job.

Up to this point there had been a fair amount of psychology played out in the ring. Leonard would smile at Hearns from time to time as if to say none of his punches were making any impact. Hearns, in return, would stare menacingly at his opponent. But at the end of the 12th round this came to an end as both touched each other's gloves as the bell sounded. It was the first show of respect between these two legends and another stand out moment of the fight.

As Leonard sunk to his stool in his corner before the start of the 13th round his legendary trainer, Angelo Dundee, who had previously sat in Muhammad Ali's corner, uttered words that went down in boxing folklore. "You're blowing it, son. You're blowing it."

It seemed to have the desired effect. Galvanized by the Godfather of boxing trainers Leonard rose from to his feet knowing that only a knockdown or stoppage could save the night for him.

Appearing like a changed man he turned into the aggressor as he went for all out attack. The catalyst for what was about to unfold came from a thunderbolt of a right hook that shook Hearns to the core. It came out of nowhere and nobody was more surprised than the man ahead on points.

After a flurry of punches and pushes Hearns went down in between the ropes but referee Davey Pearl judged this to be more from a push than a punch. Moments later Hearns was down again and this time it counted. Pearl counted to nine before the "Hit Man" was ready to continue.

Now Leonard sensed his chance. The bell had saved Hearns at the end of the 13th but he was clearly not recovered in time for the 14th. Leonard rushed forward, pinned his rival to the ropes and unleashed a fierce and fast combination of punches. After 1 minute, 45 seconds of the penultimate round referee Pearl had seen enough and stopped the fight.

All three judges had Hearns ahead at this stage - 124-122, 125-122 and 125-121 - but it did not matter a jot.

The fight had been stopped and Leonard became the world unified welterweight champion.

"I knew I was ahead," a philosophical Hearns reacted later. "There was only one problem. I got hit with a good shot. I didn't think the fight should have been stopped. I wasn't hurt... but that's the breaks."

Leonard was understandably euphoric. "I've proved I'm the best welterweight in the world," he declared. "This fight surpasses all my previous accomplishments."

Cus D'Amato, who trained so many of the greats, summed it up perfectly even before the fight began. "This won't be decided by the better skill," he said. "It will be won by the one with the greater will to win."

That may seem a tad harsh on Hearns who, of course, also possessed an indomitable heart. Yet this fight showcased everything you needed to know about Sugar Ray Leonard. A magnificent fighter, with superb skills and athleticism. Most of all, though, Leonard would never recognize defeat until it was officially confirmed. Until that point, as he proved against Hearns, he was always in the game no matter how far behind he may have trailed. His will to win, as befitted all sporting greats, was the reason why he makes the top five, if not three, in the history of the sport.

They would meet one more time eight years later, a fight that ended in a draw, and would subsequently become friends. In between both would continue to cement their names in the top echelons of boxing history.

"*THEN AGAIN, WHEN I'D HIT HIM AND ROCK HIM, I BECAME REJUVENATED. I HAD THAT THING, THAT INTESTINAL FORTITUDE, THAT THING A LOT OF FIGHTERS HAVE - WE ALL HAVE IT, BUT THEY CAN'T ACTIVATE IT.*"

RAY LEONARD

14 SEPTEMBER 2013

MAYWEATHER
VS ÁLVAREZ

WORLD SUPER WELTERWEIGHT CHAMPIONSHIP
MGM GRAND GARDEN ARENA, LAS VEGAS, NEVADA, U.S.A.

TALE OF THE TAPE

FLOYD MAYWEATHER	NAME	SAÚL ÁLVAREZ
MONEY / PRETTY BOY	NICKNAME	CANELO
GRAND RAPIDS, MICHIGAN, U.S.A.	BIRTHPLACE	GUADALAJARA, JALISCO, MEXICO
36	AGE	23
44—0—0	PRE-FIGHT RECORD	42—0—1
26	KO'S	30
5'8"	HEIGHT	5'8"
151 LBS	WEIGHT	152 LBS
72"	REACH	70.5"
ORTHODOX	STANCE	ORTHODOX

THE ONE

IT WAS A BOXING MASTERCLASS DELIVERED BY THE KING OF DEFENSE AND COUNTER PUNCHING. NOT EVEN A MAN WHO WOULD BECOME ONE OF THE GREATS HAD ANY ANSWER TO FLOYD MAYWEATHER.

This was deemed a super fight between a man in his late thirties who had a perfect professional record after 44 fights and a young pretender, also unbeaten after 43 fights, with just one draw – early in his career - blotting an otherwise exemplary copy book.

Floyd Mayweather was criticized in his younger days when he beat much older and experienced opponents. Now the tables were turned and at 36 he was giving away 13 years against the extremely dangerous 'Canelo' Álvarez, the new darling of Mexican boxing. The five-weight world champion was aiming to add the WBC's light middleweight title to his vast collection and, on the face of it, he faced a stiff challenge against a hungry young man who knew nothing about defeat.

However, Álvarez had never fought anyone like Mayweather before. And it showed. It turned out to be a masterclass from the American that left the normally classy Álvarez flailing in the wind.

The first couple of rounds were a taste of things to come. 'Canelo', normally the aggressor, barely laid a glove on his elusive opponent. Mayweather was too quick, too agile and too slippery. The master of defense was moving around at such a speed that most of Álvarez's punches either struck Mayweather's arms or missed the intended target completely. Meanwhile the man with the longest streak of professional wins in boxing stIll plying his trade picked the Mexican off with counterpunches and jabs.

This was even more prevalent in the 4th round where Mayweather stepped it up and landed a number of unanswered blows on an already confused opponent. In the 6th round 'Canelo' tried to mix it up with Mayweather, just in the way that Ricky Hatton had attempted to do previously. The result was the same. Mayweather was more than equipped to deal with anything thrown at him. And in the 7th round Mayweather hurt Álvarez with a vicious uppercut that sent the Mexican back onto his heels. By now 'Money' Mayweather was so far ahead that the fight was all but won, save for a surprise knockout from his opponent. And Mayweather just did not know what the canvas felt like.

He had changed his nickname to 'Money' due to the vast amounts he was earning – he picked up a cool $41.5M for this fight alone – but it was also no wonder that his original nickname was 'Pretty Boy,' because his face showed few scars of battle. He just could not be hit, not even by a fighter as gifted as Álvarez.

He even had time to ease off and take a rest, allowing the Mexican to win rounds eight, nine and ten, before finishing off with a two round flourish to win the penultimate and final rounds. In the 11th round Álvarez launched a big punch at Mayweather, only to miss his target and land on the rope. This provoked Mayweather to stop, mid-fight, bend over and look in an exaggerated fashion at the rope as if he were watching 'Canelo's' punch disappear into the horizon.

In a fight in which Mayweather landed 46% of his punches and Álvarez 22% there was only one surprise. One of the judges called it a draw at 114-114. When this was announced there was stunned silence at the MGM Grand Arena. He would subsequently resign. The other two called it right, giving it to Mayweather by 116-112 and an even more dominant 117-111. "It is about skills," a nonchalant Mayweather announced later. "I came out and showed mine. I just listened to my corner and got the job done."

'Canelo' delivered an honest appraisal afterwards. "I didn't know how to hurt him," he admitted. "We tried to catch him but he's a great fighter. There was no solution for him." He would later admit, a little older and wiser, that being schooled by Mayweather provided a valuable lesson for him. 'Canelo' would go on to become one of the modern greats of the ring. And Mayweather. He has gone down in boxing history.

"I WANT TO COMMEND THIS YOUNG, STRONG LION BECAUSE HE WILL CARRY THE TORCH. TONIGHT, EXPERIENCE PLAYED A MAJOR KEY. 'CANELO' HAS EVERYTHING IT TAKES TO BE A LEGEND IN THE SPORT. TONIGHT WAS JUST MY NIGHT. WHAT ELSE CAN I SAY? WE DID IT AGAIN."

FLOYD MAYWEATHER

21 MAY 2011

PASCAL vs HOPKINS II

WORLD LIGHT HEAVYWEIGHT CHAMPIONSHIP
BELL CENTER, MONTREAL, QUEBEC, CANADA

TALE OF THE TAPE

JEAN PASCAL	NAME	BERNARD HOPKINS
-	NICKNAME	THE EXECUTIONER / THE ALIEN
PORT-AU-PRINCE, HAITI	BIRTHPLACE	PHILADELPHIA, PENNSYLVANIA, U.S.A.
28	AGE	46
28—1—1	PRE-FIGHT RECORD	51—5—2
18	KO'S	32
5'10.5"	HEIGHT	6'1"
175 LBS	WEIGHT	175 LBS
72"	REACH	75"
ORTHODOX	STANCE	ORTHODOX

DYNASTY II

*IT WAS A CASE OF A GOOD YOUNG ONE AGAINST
AN EXCEPTIONAL OLD ONE, AND THE OLD ONE
WOULD PREVAIL TO MAKE BOXING HISTORY.*

Bernard Hopkins had been one of the great names in global boxing for the past quarter of a century but, despite his credible draw against Jean Pascal the previous December, he came into this rematch as the underdog.

Five months on meant he was five months older and, at 46, nobody in the history of boxing had ever won a world title at such an age.

His draw in Quebec City had surprised the boxing world against the talented Haitian-Canadian but surely lightning could not strike twice? Pascal would be only the better for his first experience face to face with Hopkins.

Moreover, Pascal was settling in nicely as the WBC's and IBO's world light heavyweight champion. This would be his fifth defense of his title and he would not want to be losing to a comparatively old man.

This, however, was no ordinary old man. He may have been severely disadvantaged in terms of age but in every other sense – height, ringcraft, experience and the ability to overcome major challenges in the ring – Hopkins held the aces.

And so it came to prove once the fight began in Montreal. If the first two rounds were tentative Hopkins began to pull away after a big third round which included a huge right hander that stunned the champion.

Although Pascal had the better of it when they went toe-to-toe in the 4th Hopkins replied by winning the 5th and 6th rounds with his combination of pinpoint jabs and big right handers combined with his ability to avoid the Canadian's power punches.

At the start of the 7th Hopkins was enjoying a big enough lead to produce a piece of showboating. Before the bell rang, he got down onto the canvas and performed a series of press-ups.

This might have angered many opponents, but Pascal had little answer to Hopkins on the night. In the 9th his glove touched the canvas after an exchange but referee Ian John-Lewis judged it to have been a slip. In the 10th, after Hopkins had twice been warned for holding Pascal's head down, the champion's glove touched the deck again having been forced back and off balance following another big right hander from the challenger. Once again, and somewhat controversially, it was judged to have been a slip.

It would not matter in the end. In the penultimate round, despite his 18-year advantage, it was Pascal who was noticeably tiring. Aware that only a knockdown could save the day, he threw everything he had left in him at Hopkins for the final three minutes.

In doing so he clearly hurt the great American a couple of times but it was all too little, too late. He won the round but it was evident to everyone at ringside that he had lost the fight.

The judges confirmed this fact, unanimously, with scores of 116-112, 115-113 and 115-114. Bernard Hopkins thus became the new WBC and IBO light heavyweight champion of the world, surpassing George Foreman in the process in terms of age.

"Bernard fought a great fight," Pascal was happy to admit afterwards. "He has a great defense and a lot of tricks. I am a young fighter and I am green. These two fights with Bernard will help take me to the next level. I learnt a lot from his style."

The last word went to the new, and old world champion. "I didn't feel like I was 46 tonight," said Hopkins. "I felt like I was 36. I'm a great fighter. It was exciting. I think everyone enjoyed themselves."

Everyone except Jean Pascal.

"BEFORE I LEAVE THIS GAME, YOU'RE GOING TO SEE THE BEST FIGHTS OF BERNARD HOPKINS' CAREER."

BERNARD HOPKINS

5 MAY 2012

MAYWEATHER
VS COTTO

WORLD LIGHT MIDDLEWEIGHT CHAMPIONSHIP
MGM GRAND GARDEN ARENA, LAS VEGAS, NEVADA, U.S.A.

TALE OF THE TAPE

FLOYD MAYWEATHER	NAME	MIGUEL COTTO
MONEY / PRETTY BOY	NICKNAME	JUNITO
GRAND RAPIDS, MICHIGAN, U.S.A.	BIRTHPLACE	PROVIDENCE, RHODE ISLAND, U.S.A.
35	AGE	31
42−0−0	PRE-FIGHT RECORD	37−2−0
26	KO'S	31
5'8"	HEIGHT	5'7"
151 LBS	WEIGHT	154 LBS
72"	REACH	67"
ORTHODOX	STANCE	ORTHODOX

RING KINGS

IT WAS BUSINESS AS USUAL FOR THE UNBEATEN GLOBAL BOXING STAR BUT IN HIS TOUGH, PROUD OPPONENT, HE FOUND A MAN WHO WAS NOT QUITE PREPARED TO ABIDE BY THE SCRIPT.

The world was used to watching Floyd Mayweather bewilder and bamboozle his opponents in the ring. The unbeaten American superstar was so elusive and slippery his unmarked face bore little resemblance to any other bruised fighter.

Mayweather was at times impossible to hit. He may not have been the biggest puncher but he invariably wore his opponents down who used up all their energy attempting to find their target. In doing so, they opened themselves up to counterattacks until they ran out of juice.

This was the usual narrative, but not this time. Not against Miguel Cotto.

On the line was Cotto's WBA light middleweight world title and also the WBC's vacant diamond light middleweight title. Mayweather was the firm favorite but this was the first time he would be fighting at this heavier weight since he outpointed Oscar De La Hoya five years previously.

Moreover Cotto, the tough Puerto Rican, was known as a man who never knowingly took a backward step. No wonder the likes of De La Hoya, Sugar Ray Leonard, Thomas Hearns and Bernard Hopkins were all ringside to watch the drama unfold.

The facts suggest Mayweather won with consummate ease. He landed with 179 of his punches at a 26 % success rate compared to Cotto's 105 at 21%. And in terms of power punches Mayweather's 128

(34 %) far outweighed Cotto's 75 (23 %).

The judges' scores at the end also confirm that this was a comfortable win for Mayweather. But the American's face, complete with bloodied nose, suggested otherwise.

For once Mayweather was in a real fight. His speed and elusiveness meant that as the rounds went on his lead was stretching but in Cotto he had an opponent who refused to give up.

Although the fight began slowly it burst into life in the fourth round when Mayweather upped the tempo and adopted aggressive tactics, finding his target with a series of right handers. From then on, he decided to use the ropes as a springboard for more attacks and especially counterattacks.

For many this would spell danger but to the superfast Mayweather, this aided his fight plan. He was quicker with his punches and more accurate but whereas others before had almost given up by the halfway stage chasing shadows, Cotto just kept on coming.

In the eighth round he even gained some purchase. Mayweather's nose was bloodied after being caught by several punches – an almost unheard of feat – forcing the American to shake his head at his opponent and smile.

It was only in the 12th and final round that Cotto visibly tired, clearly hurt by a left upper cut but determined to last the distance.

The judges scored it 117-111, 117-111 and 118-110 but, despite the apparent comfort of Mayweather's win, the still unbeaten champion was full of respect for his beaten foe.

"You're a hell of a champion," he announced in the ring as he embraced Cotto. "You're the toughest guy I ever fought."

Later he would expand on this. "He's a tough competitor," he said. "He didn't just come to survive. I dug deep and fought him back."

Cotto was sanguine about the result. "The judges said I lost the fight," he said. "I can't do anything else. I'm happy with my fight and performance and so is my family. I can't ask for anything else."

He would go on to claim the WBC's middleweight title four fights later. And Mayweather? He had just taken another scalp on his way to his incredible 50 and out professional record.

"TONIGHT WE GAVE THE FANS WHAT THEY WANTED TO SEE. WE MATCHED THE BEST WITH THE BEST. COTTO WAS A VERY TOUGH COMPETITOR AND HE WON SOME ROUNDS. HE PUSHED ME TO THE LIMITS AND THIS IS WHAT IT'S ALL ABOUT."

FLOYD MAYWEATHER

6 DECEMBER 2008

DE LA HOYA
VS PACQUIAO

WORLD WELTERWEIGHT CHAMPIONSHIP
MGM GRAND GARDEN ARENA, LAS VEGAS, NEVADA, U.S.A.

TALE OF THE TAPE

OSCAR DE LA HOYA	NAME	MANNY PACQUIAO
GOLDEN BOY	NICKNAME	PAC MAN
LOS ANGELES, CALIFORNIA, U.S.A.	BIRTHPLACE	KIBAWE, BUKIDNON, PHILIPPINES
36	AGE	29
39—5—0	PRE-FIGHT RECORD	47—3—2
30	KO'S	35
5'11"	HEIGHT	5'5.5"
145 LBS	WEIGHT	142 LBS
73"	REACH	67"
ORTHODOX	STANCE	SOUTHPAW

THE DREAM MATCH

THIS DENOTED THE PASSING OF THE BATON FROM ONE OF THE GREATEST IN BOXING HISTORY TO ANOTHER. AS ALWAYS TIME FINALLY CAUGHT UP WITH THE OLDER FIGHTER.

This would prove to be Oscar De La Hoya's last fight to end what had been one of the most stellar careers in boxing history. His star had been on the wane, having lost three of his last six fights against the mighty trio of Shane Mosley, Bernard Hopkins and Floyd Mayweather, and he chose his final bout to be against another of the all-time greats.

Despite this sudden flurry of defeats and, at 35, being six years older than his worthy opponent, the popular, Mexican-American was deemed to be the favorite against Manny Pacquiao, due mainly to his massive height and reach advantage.

The Filipino had also never fought at this weight before, having to step up two divisions whilst De La Hoya needed to step down one for them both to meet the welterweight requirements.

The man who had won a staggering ten world titles in six different weight divisions wanted to bow out in style.

Pacquiao, of course, was an exceptional fighter. Ring Magazine had him down as the best pound for pound boxer in the world and his five world titles in five different weight divisions needed no further justification.

The fight was for no titles, no belts, just bragging rights and glory. And money. No wonder it was billed 'The Dream Match,' and generated $17M in gate receipts, the second largest ever after De La Hoya's defeat to Mayweather the year before.

To add some spice to the event Pacquiao's trainer, Freddie Roach, had been De La Hoya's for his defeat against Mayweather. De La Hoya was this time using the legendary Angelo Dundee.

Despite this it soon became clear that the boxing baton was being passed on from one great champion to another.

Pacquiao would dominate from virtually the start until the bitter end at the start of the ninth round.

Although the veteran tried to take it to his younger opponent his occasional punches that found the target were no answer to Pacquiao's flurries and combinations. After four rounds Pacquiao had barely broken sweat but De La Hoya's face was red and swollen.

After six 'Golden Boy's' legs were beginning to look unstable. The 'Pac-Man's' greater speed of punches were causing serious damage and De La Hoya had no answer to the tenacity of the smaller man who was getting inside him and landing blows.

Even when he did manage to succeed with a couple of telling punches it was clear that they made no impact and were returned with considerable interest.

It all led to a brutal eighth round in which Pacquiao forced De La Hoya into the corner and then went to work on him, pummelling the Mexican-American's body before launching a big left-hander that saw his opponent wobble.

It was looking decidedly bleak for De La Hoya as he trudged back to his corner. His team agreed, prompting coach Nacho Berstain to wave the white towel to denote retirement from his corner.

At this point two of the judges had Pacquiao winning every round, and one gave De La Hoya just the single, solitary round out of eight.

Before the bout Roach had declared that De La Hoya was too old for this. When it was all over De La Hoya walked over to Pacquiao's corner and told Roach: "You're right, Freddie. I don't have it anymore."

Later he would speak in glowing terms about his conqueror. "His determination, his speed, his skill, his power, his footwork makes him one of the fighters I have most appreciated."

De La Hoya duly retired to end a stunningly successful career. Pacquiao would go on to win twelve world titles and become the only eight division world champion in the history of boxing.

"I'LL NEVER FORGET WALKING TO THE RING THAT NIGHT... IT WAS LIKE WALKING INTO A SLAUGHTERHOUSE AND KNOWING THAT THIS IS IT. I'VE NEVER FELT THAT BEFORE IN MY LIFE... BUT I WAS A DEAD MAN WALKING WHEN I STEPPED INTO THE RING AGAINST PACQUIAO. I HAD NOTHING LEFT."

OSCAR DE LA HOYA

10 MARCH 1986

HAGLER vs MUGABI

WORLD MIDDLEWEIGHT CHAMPIONSHIP
CAESARS PALACE, OUTDOOR ARENA, LAS VEGAS, NEVADA, U.S.A.

TALE OF THE TAPE

MARVIN HAGLER	NAME	JOHN MUGABI
MARVELOUS	NICKNAME	THE BEAST
NEWARK, NEW JERSEY, U.S.A.	BIRTHPLACE	NSAMBYA, UGANDA
31	AGE	24
61—2—2	PRE-FIGHT RECORD	25—0—0
51	KO'S	25
5'9.5"	HEIGHT	5'8.5"
159 LBS	WEIGHT	157 LBS
75"	REACH	74"
SOUTHPAW	STANCE	ORTHODOX

THE FIGHTS!

THIS WAS NOT FOR THE FAINT-HEARTED AND MANY BELIEVED MUGABI WOULD POSE A SERIOUS THREAT TO THE EXPERIENCED, OLD CHAMPION, BUT IN THE END MARVIN HAGLER PROVED ONCE AGAIN WHY HE IS RECOGNIZED TO BE ONE OF THE GREATEST OF ALL TIME.

After Marvin Hagler had destroyed Thomas Hearns inside three of the most pulsating rounds ever witnessed at a world title fight he was the hottest ticket in town, even if after 65 fights he was clearly coming to the end.

Next up would be a tough Ugandan fighter who had won all 25 of his professional fights, all by a knockout.

There was no doubt that Hagler, with all his experience, was the favorite against a man who had to go up a weight to meet the American, but in Mugabi he also faced a dangerous opponent who did not seem fazed by the stature of the world champion.

On the line was Hagler's undisputed middleweight crown but Mugabi showed his lack of fear by punching a hole in the poster of Hagler publicly before the fight. Hagler, it should be said, took note.

Hearns, who was ringside and hoping Hagler would win so that he could avenge his defeat with a rematch, predicted a slugfest between these two offensive fighters, and he was not wrong.

It should have taken place in November, 1985, but a slipped disc in Hagler's back plus a broken nose meant it was postponed until March the following year.

By the time the fight finally came interest had reached a frenzy. Who would prevail between a man who had never been knocked out in his whole career, last lost ten years ago and had successfully defended his undisputed title 11 times, with ten knockouts, against a man with 25 knockouts to his name in his perfect professional record?

Initially an upset looked possible. Mugabi, the younger, quicker man, started the better of the two, delivering a barrage of blows at the end of the first round before raising his glove in triumph. He then rocked Hagler in the second.

But by the fourth Mugabi was already tiring and Hagler was beginning to hit harder, more accurate blows.

By the sixth round the tide had clearly turned. Mugabi liked to target the head, which is why Hagler moved in to fight at close quarters, confusing his opponent by switching from southpaw to orthodox and delivering a series of crunching blows to the body.

Although the champion relaxed a little during the next three rounds, he came back strong in the tenth, returning to his close body tactics that he knew made Mugabi uncomfortable. The Ugandan looked out on his feet and was visibly hurt by a bomb from the American late in the round.

As they returned to their respective corners both knew the end was nigh. Midway through the 11th round Hagler moved in to finish the job. He first rocked Mugabi with a combination, then jolted his head upwards with a left hook and finally sent him crashing to the floor with another combination.

Mugabi stayed sat on his backside as referee Mills Lane counted him out.

Although they did not know it at the time this fight affected both Hagler and Mugabi. The latter was never quite the same again after this harrowing first defeat whilst Hagler, hurt by Mugabi and indeed by Hearns in the fight before, would fight one last time and lose – to Sugar Ray Leonard.

30 JANUARY 1982

BENITEZ
VS DURÁN

WORLD SUPER WELTERWEIGHT CHAMPIONSHIP
CAESARS PALACE, LAS VEGAS, NEVADA, U.S.A.

TALE OF THE TAPE

WILFRED BENITEZ	NAME	ROBERTO DURÁN
EL RADAR / BIBLE OF BOXING	NICKNAME	MANOS DE PIEDRA / HANDS OF STONE
BRONX, NEW YORK, U.S.A.	BIRTHPLACE	EL CHORRILLO, PANAMA
23	AGE	30
43−1−1	PRE-FIGHT RECORD	74−2−0
28	KO'S	56
5'10"	HEIGHT	5'7"
152 LBS	WEIGHT	153 LBS
70"	REACH	66"
ORTHODOX	STANCE	ORTHODOX

THE NEW BEGINNING

IN THE END NEITHER FIGHTER WOULD LOSE THIS ONE. BENITEZ WOULD UNDERLINE HIS TALENT WITH THE WIN BUT DURÁN WOULD RESTORE HIS PRIDE AND HIS REPUTATION FIGHTING ABOVE HIS NATURAL WEIGHT. HE WOULD ULTIMATELY BENEFIT MORE.

It had been 18 months since Roberto Durán had famously quit in the ring against Sugar Ray Leonard. His words that night – "No mas, no mas" – had haunted him ever since and although he had fought twice since and won this match-up with the defending light middleweight world champion was his chance for redemption.

But Wilfred Benitez was a very skilled technician, a man who had lost only once in his 45 fights – also to Leonard – and that was three years previously. Since then he had grown from strength to strength and saw this encounter with the damaged Panamanian as his last fight at this weight before moving up to face, he hoped, the likes of Thomas Hearns and Marvin Hagler.

Benitez was the bookmakers' favorite to win his third defense of his world title at 9-5 but trained hard knowing that Durán, who had also returned to his mean persona both in training and in the days prior to the fight, would not be giving up for a second time.

It was all a bit fractious before the fight, with Benitez's father and trainer, Gregorio, taunting Durán about his Leonard surrender, Durán responding by announcing his father would fight Gregorio and Benitez Jr lunging at his opponent.

By the start of the first round, however, Benitez was far more relaxed, indeed relaxed to wink at Leonard who was ringside. He seemed to have everything under control.

He knew, for example, that a wounded Durán would come at him in the early rounds. With a two and a half inch height advantage and a defense renowned for its elusiveness, Benitez was ready. It was not long before Durán in frustration lunged with a jab and missed, opening up his body as an easy target for Benitez to find.

By the fourth round Durán was openly grimacing as Benitez continually hammered away at Durán's body. In keeping with his character – at least in every other fight save his second meeting with Leonard – Durán bounced back in the sixth round, winning it with three big punches to Benitez's head. The defending champion did not bat an eyelid.

Instead he responded by forcing a cut above Durán's left eyelid in the seventh round and followed this up with a stiff uppercut and then a flurry of toe-to-toe punches which Benitez won by three to one.

As the fight reached its last third Durán was evidently tiring. This was not surprising. He was the older man, was fighting some way above his most comfortable weight and had already fought 76 times as a professional, compared to Benitez's 45 fights.

Benitez was clearly tempted to end the fight with a slugfest but prudence got the better of him. He was not known as 'El Radar' for nothing. He held the lead and his defense made him hard to hit, so why risk it just to try and finish Durán off?

In the 13th round Benitez sported a small cut above his left eye. In the 13th Durán was so focused on staying the distance that he left his corner without his mouthpiece and saw out the round. In the final round he was so exhausted he could barely stand but still Durán searched for the telling blow.

It was not to be. The judges' verdict was unanimous. Benitez won with scores of 145-141, 144-141 and 143-142 to retain his world title.

The boxing world expected Durán to retire. Far from it. He would go on to fight for an incredible twenty years, finally ending after 119 professional fights, and more world titles to his name.

Benitez, the victor on the night, would ultimately end up the loser. In his next fight he was badly beaten by Hearns and never won another title again.

"I WANTED TO BEAT HIM AT HIS FIGHT, TO SHOW HIM I WAS THE CHAMPION."

WILFRED BENITEZ

3

17 MARCH 1990

CHÁVEZ
VS TAYLOR

WORLD LIGHT WELTERWEIGHT CHAMPIONSHIP
LAS VEGAS HILTON, LAS VEGAS, NEVADA, U.S.A.

TALE OF THE TAPE

JULIO CÉSAR CHÁVEZ	NAME	MELDRICK TAYLOR
THE GREAT MEXICAN CHAMPION	NICKNAME	TNT / THE KID
SONORA, MEXICO	BIRTHPLACE	PENNSYLVANIA, U.S.A.
27	AGE	23
68—0—0	PRE-FIGHT RECORD	24—0—1
55	KO'S	14
5'7.5"	HEIGHT	5'7.5"
139.5 LBS	WEIGHT	139.75 LBS
66.5"	REACH	66"
ORTHODOX	STANCE	ORTHODOX

THUNDER MEETS LIGHTNING

IT WAS DEEMED FIRST THE FIGHT OF THE YEAR AND THEN THE FIGHT OF THE DECADE, A COMPELLING CLASH BETWEEN POWER AND SPEED AND TWO ENORMOUS HEARTS WHICH WAS CONCLUDED WITH ONE OF THE MOST TALKED-ABOUT DECISIONS IN THE HISTORY OF THE SPORT.

This would prove to be the ultimate clash of styles and indeed personalities between two unbeaten champions, a fight that would go right down to the wire and enter boxing folklore for all the right and wrong reasons. Dubbed 'Thunder v Lightning' in reference to the power of Julio César Chávez and the frightening hand and footspeed of Meldrick Taylor, the fight created extra interest because Mike Tyson had recently lost to Buster Douglas, thus switching the focus away from the dominant heavyweight division.

Taylor, from Philadelphia, was very much the new kid on the block. Unbeaten in 25 fights, he emerged onto the boxing scene in double-quick time after winning Olympic gold in 1984 aged just 17. He was super confident, too.

"I see myself attacking him all the way with my hand-speed and strength," he predicted before the fight. "No-one's ever fought him the way I'm gonna fight him. I'm hurting him with combinations. And then I'm gone. He throws a punch and I'm not there."

It made sense in theory but in Chávez he would be coming up against the epitome of Mexican fighters, a man who rarely if ever took a backward step and, as his record confirmed, did not understand the meaning of defeat. As he walked to the ring at the Las Vegas Hilton Chávez held an astonishing record of 68 fights and 68 wins, including 55 knockouts. It was the longest winning streak in professional boxing for almost 80 years from a man who had no issues taking punishment

"I SEE MYSELF ATTACKING HIM ALL THE WAY WITH MY HAND SPEED AND STRENGTH, NO ONE'S EVER FOUGHT HIM THE WAY I'M GONNA FIGHT HIM."

MELDRICK TAYLOR

in order to deal it out.

It was little wonder he was a national hero back in Mexico, a man who rose from abject poverty to being recognized as the best boxer in the world at this time. He served as an emblem of hope and pride.

Chávez's usual style was to stalk his opponent, corner him, hit him with numbing body blows and then, as his opposite tired, finish him off with pounding right handers to the head, but Taylor's speed presented an altogether different challenge.

As the first few rounds went by it was the American who took an increasingly healthy lead, hitting Chávez with a series of super quick combinations before dancing out of the way to avoid any retribution. The Mexican might catch his rival once or twice, but that would be it.

Far from discouraged, however, and showing the mark of a great champion, Chávez simply picked up his relentless pursuit of Taylor and, in doing so, found his target more and more as the fight went on whenever the American moved in for some combinations.

It was clear to most after nine rounds of this clash that Taylor held a big advantage but by then he had also taken severe punishment in his pursuit of points as he began to tire.

The big question on everyone's minds ringside was whether Taylor could hold on against the incredibly strong and resolute Chávez and inflict the first ever defeat on the legendary Mexican, or would Chávez's iron will and determination create a devastating finish.

As the minutes ticked by so Taylor's lead decreased. Chávez was catching him more and more and the American was beginning to pay a heavy toll. At the end of the 11th round Taylor, now sporting a badly-swollen face, a broken eye socket and a badly-bleeding lip, was so disorientated that he initially made his way over to Chávez's corner before being re-directed by referee Richard Steele.

Despite this two of the judges still had him ahead on their scorecards, 107-102 and 108-101. These were big leads, even if the third judge had Chávez ahead by a point, and it was clear that all Taylor needed to do was survive the round. Chávez, in contrast, required a knockout to maintain his unbeaten record and hold onto his WBC crown.

Strangely, Taylor's trainer, Lou Duva, barked out contradictory orders as the bell sounded, telling his young champion he needed to win the final round.

As a result the American declined to stay away from Chávez but instead traded blows with the stronger, more powerful Mexican. By now it was clear Taylor was close to exhaustion. Indeed he fell to the canvas after missing his opponent with a big, left hander.

The fight entered the final minute and Chávez knew time was fast running out, even though he had dominated the twelfth round. He launched a flurry of hard punches on Taylor who responded by feigning weakness in a last show of bravado.

The experienced champion did not buy it. He had been in the ring enough times to know when an opponent was tired or not. In the case of Taylor he had all but run out of gas.

Chávez moved in for the denouement. With 25 seconds remaining of this epic clash a hard right forced Taylor to stagger towards the corner. The American looked up and realized he had nowhere to go. Chávez had maneuvered himself into a position where there was no escape from the ropes for his opponent. Another series of power punches followed before a big right hander finally dropped Taylor to the deck.

He rose from the floor, using the ropes to pull himself up. Referee Steele issued the mandatory eight count. When over he asked Taylor if he could continue fighting. He asked the American for a second time. When no answer was forthcoming Steele waved his arms to signal the end of the fight and a technical knockout for Chávez.

There were two seconds of the fight remaining on the clock. Cue pandemonium and a decision that has been debated ever since.

There is little doubt Taylor held a big enough lead to have won the fight if two more seconds had been allowed to pass, even if it was a split decision. Some, including Taylor's camp, also argued that he nodded his head in answer to Steele's question.

Others, though, simply point to the state of Taylor by this stage. Disorientated, fatigued and badly beaten up, he would need an extended stay in hospital afterwards which included blood transfusions to recuperate from his injuries and sheer exhaustion.

Chávez was both honest and magnanimous after snatching victory from the jaws of defeat, as well as the IBF light-welterweight world title to add to the WBC belt he already owned. "He was faster than me, he was stronger than me," he admitted, moments after claiming the most dramatic win of his career. "I was surprised by his hand speed.

"HE WAS HITTING HARDER, HE WAS FASTER, I WAS VERY TIRED, BUT I HAD MORE HEART THAN HIM. MELDRICK IS A GREAT FIGHTER, A VERY SMART BOXER. FOR EVERY PUNCH I GAVE, HE CAME BACK WITH THREE. HE'S THE HARDEST BOXER I HAVE FACED, AND HE DESERVES A REMATCH."

JULIO CÉSAR CHÁVEZ

Meldrick Taylor deserves a rematch."

Although Taylor recovered to later win a different world title for a short period of time, he was never quite the same again after this physically and mentally shattering loss.

The two adversaries would meet again in 1994 but there was no repeat of their first clash. Chávez would win with a TKO in the eighth round and this time there were no complaints, no debates.

Regardless of the rights and wrongs of the final round decision to stop the fight the Mexican legend proved once again an adage prevalent in all of sport. It isn't over until it is over.

Staring at defeat he somehow came up with an answer against a superior opponent on the night.

Taylor found himself just two seconds away from glory. But even two seconds is a long time in boxing, especially if the man facing you is Julio César Chávez.

22 OCTOBER 1966

ORTIZ vs RAMOS

WORLD LIGHTWEIGHT CHAMPIONSHIP
EL TOREO DE CUATRO CAMINOS
MEXICO CITY, DISTRITO FEDERAL, MEXICO

TALE OF THE TAPE

CARLOS ORTIZ	NAME	ULTIMINIO RAMOS
-	NICKNAME	SUGAR
PONCE, PUERTO RICO	BIRTHPLACE	MATANZAS, CUBA
30	AGE	24
47—5—1	PRE-FIGHT RECORD	50—2—3
18	KO'S	36
5'7"	HEIGHT	5'4.5"
135 LBS	WEIGHT	135 LBS
70"	REACH	68"
ORTHODOX	STANCE	ORTHODOX

STOPPAGE AND BLOOD

*A CONTROVERSIAL END DESPITE SOME
MAJOR DAMAGE CAUSED RESULTED IN A
SECOND FIGHT AND ARGUMENTS SETTLED.*

The first meeting between Carlos Ortiz and Ultiminio Ramos proved to be one of the more controversial world title fights in boxing history.

Ortiz, the pride of Puerto Rico, was mounting a second defense of his WBC and WBA world lightweight title. Highly experienced at 30, with 54 fights under his belt, he enjoyed a major height and reach advantage over his plucky opponent from Mexico.

Ramos, known throughout boxing as 'Sugar,' was Cuban-born but fought out of Mexico after fleeing the island following Fidel Castro's takeover. The Mexican people had taken the former world featherweight champion to heart, and when he challenged Ortiz it would be in front of 35,000 home fans in the Mexican capital.

At first it was all going very well for the man looking to wrestle the crown off Ortiz. The Puerto Rican was floored in the second round by a lead right and although he rose after the mandatory count of eight the Ramos camp would later argue referee Billy Conn had taken five seconds longer.

This became more controversial when Ramos suffered a cut above his left eye later in the round. Despite this it was a fairly even contest until the fight came to an abrupt end in the fifth. It had been an absorbing round with both fighters not taking a backward step. The Ring magazine later named it the round of the year.

But midway through it referee Conn stepped in and stopped the fight, awarding it to Ortiz. By this stage blood was pouring out of

Ramos' gashed eye and the referee felt he had no other option but to halt proceedings.

Later the referee and the ringside physician had different verdicts, with Conn insisting the physician had told him to stop the fight and the physician, no doubt mindful of 35,000 enraged Mexicans venting their displeasure inside the venue, suggesting the opposite.

Conn felt vindicated by the fact that Ramos required 28 stitches in his wound and later needed surgery on the damaged eye.

Nonetheless, it created a messy scenario which forced the WBC President, Luis Spota, to declare the title vacant and order a rematch. This took place nine months later in San Juan, the Puerto Rican capital.

If there were question marks concerning the first fight, there were none concerning the second.

Although Ramos landed a huge punch in the third round it seemed to have no effect on Ortiz.

Instead, in the early seconds of the next round, Ortiz put Ramos down. The Mexican stayed on all fours on the deck until he rose on the count of eight. From that point Ortiz pummelled 'Sugar' at will until referee Zach Clayton had seen enough and stopped the fight after 1 minute, 18 seconds.

This time there would be no arguments. Ortiz regained his WBC title that many felt he should never had been forced to give up, but then lost it two fights later. Despite winning his next ten successive fights Ortiz retired when he then lost.

Ramos, meanwhile, would never fight for a world title again.

16 MARCH 1980

ANTUOFERMO
VS MINTER

WORLD MIDDLEWEIGHT CHAMPIONSHIP
CAESARS PALACE, LAS VEGAS, NEVADA, U.S.A.

TALE OF THE TAPE

VITO ANTUOFERMO	NAME	ALAN MINTER
-	NICKNAME	BOOM BOOM
PALO DEL COLLE, PUGLIA, ITALY	BIRTHPLACE	CRAWLEY, SUSSEX, U.K.
27	AGE	28
45—3—2	PRE-FIGHT RECORD	36—6—0
19	KO'S	22
5'7.5"	HEIGHT	5'9"
158 LBS	WEIGHT	160 LBS
68"	REACH	71"
ORTHODOX	STANCE	SOUTHPAW

BLOOD, GUTS AND PRIDE

ANOTHER CONTROVERSIAL FIGHT FULL OF BLOOD THAT
WENT THE DISTANCE. IT WOULD GO DOWN AS ONE OF
THE GREAT NIGHTS IN BRITISH BOXING HISTORY.

On the face of it, Vito Antuofermo was the strong favorite to retain his world middleweight title against a tough, British opponent in Alan Minter.

Minter was the British and European middleweight champion, but this seemed a significant step up against a man who had claimed the world title two fights previously and then defended it with a credible draw against the mighty Marvin Hagler.

Hagler was not recognized as a great of the sport just at that time – his greatness would follow soon afterwards – but in hindsight anyone who Hagler failed to beat should be considered with the utmost respect.

Antuofermo also had the home crowd on his side at Caesars Palace, the same venue where he managed in the previous fight, to hold his own against Hagler. He was expected to see off a man known for his bravery but also ability to bleed heavily.

As is often the way in boxing, it did not quite work out this way. Minter, a former Olympic bronze medallist, was a classical boxer, using his jab as his main weapon to keep his distance from the adopted American born in Italy.

The defending champion, in contrast, did not care for such niceties, and tended to lower his head as he rushed into Minter, opening himself up for some damage caused by the British jab.

The fight would ebb and flow, with both fighters having their moments and taking rounds, without ever gaining obvious supremacy. To many it seemed to be decided in the penultimate round when a hard right from Antuofermo found Minter's body and put the British fighter down. He insisted it was a slip but he had to take the mandatory eight count nonetheless.

When the final bell sounded both believed they had won the fight. The surprise was not so much in the result – Minter was awarded the fight and thus became the new WBC and WBA middleweight champion – but the huge discrepancy in the scoring. One judge had it 145-143 to Antuofermo, one gave it to Minter, 144-141, and the third, from Britain, saw Minter winning by an astonishing 149-137. In other words, Minter won 13 of the 15 rounds.

Afterwards both boxers saw it differently. "When they said split decision and then 'Minter,' it was unbelievable," said the new world champion. "If they had said 'Antuofermo' I might have had a heart attack."

The defeated ex-champion begged to differ. "I thought for sure I won," he insisted. "This fight, they gave it to him. I was right, your judge was wrong. They should suspend both judges who gave it to him."

In the obvious rematch that needed to take place three months later Minter this time had the advantage of a home crowd at Wembley Arena in London. This time there was no debate. Minter retained his title with a Technical Knockout of Antuofermo in the eighth round. The American was badly cut and all three judges had the British fighter ahead when the bout was stopped.

Minter's world title was short-lived. In his next fight he was battered by Hagler in three rounds and would retire from boxing three fights later. Antuofermo fared little better. He had his chance to reclaim his world title lost to Minter but it was against the new world champion, Hagler, who was in mood for another draw.

Second time round Hagler did a job on Antuofermo, who had to retire in the fourth round. He, too, would never fight for a title again.

19 APRIL 2008

HOPKINS vs
CALZAGHE

WORLD LIGHT HEAVYWEIGHT CHAMPIONSHIP
THOMAS & MACK CENTER, LAS VEGAS, NEVADA, U.S.A.

TALE OF THE TAPE

BERNARD HOPKINS	NAME	JOE CALZAGHE
THE EXECUTIONER / THE ALIEN	NICKNAME	PRIDE OF WALES / ITALIAN DRAGON
PHILADELPHIA, PENNSYLVANIA, U.S.A.	BIRTHPLACE	HAMMERSMITH, LONDON, U.K.
43	AGE	36
48−4−1	PRE-FIGHT RECORD	44−0−0
32	KO'S	32
6'1"	HEIGHT	5'11"
173 LBS	WEIGHT	173 LBS
75"	REACH	73"
ORTHODOX	STANCE	SOUTHPAW

BATTLE OF THE PLANET

A CLOSE AND AT TIMES DIRTY FIGHT BETWEEN TWO STELLAR NAMES IN WHICH THE YOUNGER MAN CAME THROUGH - JUST - TO MAINTAIN HIS PERFECT RECORD.

They billed it as the 'Battle of the Planet' and the world of boxing was fascinated to see whether Bernard Hopkins, at 43, still had what it took, and whether Joe Calzaghe could step up a weight and come through in a first ever fight away from Europe.

Hopkins, who had enjoyed a stellar career, had lost his long reign as middleweight world champion but had answered back by claiming The Ring's light-heavyweight title. Calzaghe, meanwhile, had staged 21 successful defenses of his world super-middleweight title and was still unbeaten after 44 professional bouts.

He was the younger man by seven years, but he was on 'away' territory, fighting at a heavier weight and against a man more experienced and successful than any before.

The Thomas & Mack Center had 14,000 boxing fans inside the arena, half of them having traveled over from Calzaghe's native Wales.

They were silenced as early as the first round when Hopkins knocked the Welshman down with a short right hander. Calzaghe rose without difficulty but sported a small cut on the bridge of his nose.

It was a sign of things to come, at least initially. Calzaghe could not get going with his speed because Hopkins smothered him and hit him repeatedly in the process. Moreover, the fight took a dirty turn that lasted for the fruition of their meeting.

In the second round, for example, the busy referee, Joe Cortez, warned first Calzaghe for landing a low blow, then both boxers for hitting behind the head.

In the fourth Cortez called a timeout to lecture both in the middle of the ring after more fouls were committed.

By the tenth Hopkins' advantage was fast slipping away as he tired. This was not aided by another Calzaghe low blow that sent him crashing to the canvas. Cortez awarded him a five-minute break to gather himself whilst Calzaghe whipped up the Welsh element of the crowd who jeered at what they believed to be play-acting by Hopkins. "It was a low blow," Hopkins reiterated later. "That's why Joe gave me five minutes."

In the 11th and penultimate round Hopkins complained about yet another low blow but this time Cortez waved for the fight to continue. The now angry but fatigued American responded by launching attacks on his opponent for the remainder of the round and the final three minutes, but Calzaghe answered back with interest.

As the bell sounded both fighters believed they had won. The judges confirmed it had been close, with a split decision – 116-111, 115-112 and 113-114 – going to Calzaghe.

Hopkins was far from happy. "I feel like I took the guy to school," he said afterwards. "I made him fight my fight, not his. I wanted him to run into my shots. I reckon I made it look pretty easy. I controlled the pace and I controlled the fight."

Calzaghe was unconcerned by such complaints. He had come through his biggest test. "I knew it wouldn't look pretty tonight," he explained. "He gave me some good shots. It was the toughest fight of my career. It wasn't my best performance but I won the fight.

"To win a world title in a second division and away in America is just the icing on the cake for my career."

25 APRIL 2009

FROCH *vs* TAYLOR

WORLD WELTERWEIGHT CHAMPIONSHIP
FOXWOODS RESORT CASINO, LEDYARD, CONNECTICUT, U.S.A.

TALE OF THE TAPE

CARL FROCH	NAME	JERMAIN TAYLOR
THE COBRA	NICKNAME	BAD INTENTIONS
NOTTINGHAM, NOTTINGHAMSHIRE, U.K.	BIRTHPLACE	LITTLE ROCK, ARKANSAS, U.S.A.
31	AGE	30
24—0—0	PRE-FIGHT RECORD	28—2—1
19	KO'S	17
6'1"	HEIGHT	5'11"
167 LBS	WEIGHT	166 LBS
75"	REACH	74.5"
ORTHODOX	STANCE	ORTHODOX

CONTINENTS COLLIDE

ARGUABLY CARL FROCH'S FINEST MOMENT WHEN HE PROVED HIS HUGE HEART AND BELIEF WOULD COME THROUGH EVEN WHEN THE ODDS WERE SO HEAVILY STACKED AGAINST HIM.

This would prove to be Carl Froch's greatest fight, featuring a comeback against all odds and a dramatic finish right up there with almost anything boxing has served.

The Nottingham-born fighter had only become world super-middleweight champion four months previously when he had beaten Jean Pascal for the vacant title. He would be making his first defense on only his second trip to America where he would be facing an extremely dangerous opponent.

Jermain Taylor had previously been the undisputed world middleweight champion, with Bernard Hopkins one of his notable scalps, and had now stepped up a division to face Froch.

In a title eliminator he had defeated Jeff Lacy, too, no mean feat, but he was in a heavier division now facing a bigger, stronger and undefeated opponent. They called the fight 'Continents Collide' and something had to give from this collision.

For much of the fight it appeared that it would be Froch. The man they called the "Cobra" started slowly and struggled against Taylor's superior speed and movement. In the third round he was sent crashing to the floor, as well, for the first time in his professional career after being on the receiving end of a stiff, right hander from Taylor.

As the fight entered the later stages Taylor slowed down, the heavier weight he needed to put on against the heavier man beginning to tell. If two thirds of the fight saw the American eluding many of Froch's attacks and countering, the final third turned into a war, with both now landing blows as Froch, belatedly, found his range.

By the start of the 12th and final round two of the judges had Taylor still ahead by a clear margin. The other, surprisingly, saw it differently. No matter. It was clear that the only way Froch could retain his title was by knocking his rival out.

"You have to do something special now," shouted his trainer, Rob McCracken, from the corner, as the bell sounded. And that's exactly what the big-hearted Froch did.

He unleashed 34 punches while Taylor could respond with only three back. Eventually Taylor went down after being caught flush on the head by a fierce right hander.

Taylor remained down in a neutral corner before rising on nine clearly dazed with 29 seconds remaining.

Now Froch moved in for the kill. He battered Taylor with nine more unanswered blows, leaving referee Mike Ortega no other choice but to stop the fight. There were just 14 seconds remaining and Froch had snatched victory from the jaws of defeat.

It was reminiscent of Julio César Chávez winning from a losing position after having Meldrick Taylor stopped with just two seconds remaining.

"He's a great fighter," Jermain Taylor conceded afterwards. "I give him all the respect. I just couldn't finish off the fight."

Froch was understandably delighted and relieved. "I didn't start quickly enough," he admitted. "I was hoping my intuition was right and Jermain would get tired. In the final rounds I wanted to put pressure on him. Jermain is an unbelievable fighter, but the ref did the right thing in stopping it when he did. Somebody could have got hurt."

"THIS WAS MY FIRST BIG FIGHT IN AMERICA AND BEFORE THE LAST ROUND MY TRAINER TOLD ME I NEEDED TO HAVE A BIG ROUND. EVERYBODY SAW WHAT HAPPENED."

CARL FROCH

28 JUNE 1991

FENECH
VS NELSON

WORLD SUPER FEATHERWEIGHT CHAMPIONSHIP
MIRAGE HOTEL & CASINO, LAS VEGAS, NEVADA, U.S.A.

TALE OF THE TAPE

JEFF FENECH	NAME	AZUMAH NELSON
MARRICKVILLE MAULER	NICKNAME	THE PROFESSOR
ST PETERS, NEW SOUTH WALES, AUSTRALIA	BIRTHPLACE	ACCRA, GHANA
27	AGE	32
25—0—0	PRE-FIGHT RECORD	33—2—0
19	KO'S	24
5'7.5"	HEIGHT	5'5"
129 LBS	WEIGHT	130 LBS
67"	REACH	68"
ORTHODOX	STANCE	ORTHODOX

FRUSTRATING DECISION

THIS WOULD BE ONE OF THE MORE CONTROVERSIAL OUTCOMES IN MODERN HISTORY WHEN IT APPEARED AS IF THE FIGHT HAD A CLEAR WINNER AND HISTORY-MAKER.

This was a fight between the two greatest fighters in boxing history from their respected continents.

In one corner stood the three-weight world champion from Australia, Jeff Fenech. He was seeking to become the first boxer in the history of the sport to win world titles at four different weights.

In the other stood the Ghanaian, Azumah Nelson, widely regarded to be the best boxer ever out of Africa. It was for his WBC super featherweight crown that the two squared up against each other for on a warm, sunny day outdoors at the Mirage in Las Vegas.

The fight was on the undercard of the Mike Tyson vs Donovan Ruddock heavyweight rematch. This was much to the annoyance of Fenech who felt his standing in world boxing, and the potential of history being made if he won against a superb world champion from another division, deserved greater attention and respect.

Moreover, Fenech had a perfect professional record up to this point whilst the Tyson-Ruddock encounter was not for any title.

Still, the diminutive pair met and, despite Fenech needing to go up a weight to face the world champion, it was the Australian who started much the better against the strangely lethargic Nelson.

Fenech focused a lot of his early work on Nelson's ribcage, beating him to the punch time and time again. The Ghanaian would later reveal he had just recovered from a bout of malaria which went some way to explaining his apparent slowness to respond.

He remained competitive for eight rounds of this world title fight but was, according to ringsiders, trailing as the fight entered its final third.

Fenech, on a mission to make history, then swarmed all over Nelson as the fight veered towards its ending.

A combination of damaging attacks and a dogged perseverance seemed to wear the super featherweight champion down and as the fight entered the 12th and final round Nelson did not possess any weapon except his durability.

A lesser boxer might have been down and out in that last round as Fenech honed-in for what he believed was one of his greatest victories.

The 12th was all one way. Nelson should be lauded for simply lasting the round.

As the bell sounded Fenech raised his arms in expected victory. His mood was changed moments later when ring announcer Jimmy Lennon Jr revealed the verdicts. With the judges scoring 115-113 to Fenech, 116-112 to Nelson and 114-114, the fight was declared a draw.

Fenech was furious and let his anger be known inside the ring. The vast majority of ringsider observers understood his frustration.

Not only had he failed to claim the super featherweight world title and thus create history with his fourth title in a fourth weight, but his perfect professional record had been blemished.

More importantly he clearly felt he had done more than enough to have won the fight. It has gone down as one of the most controversial decisions in the past thirty years.

Nelson seemed ambivalent to all the reaction afterwards. "I didn't feel his punches," he insisted, even though he appeared very unsteady in that final round. "He's tough, though. I want to give him another chance. And I want to prove I'm the best."

Fenech had spent the first few minutes after the announcement shouting: "No way, no way."

By the time he was interviewed his anger had been replaced by tears. "I'll do another 12 rounds right now," he said. "I threw punches from start to finish. That's how I fight. I felt I'd done enough. I won it."

It was not to be and when the pair met up again for the rematch it would be a very different story.

"I WAS THE FIRST GUY TO BE A THREE-WEIGHT UNDEFEATED CHAMPION. THAT WOULD HAVE BEEN MY FOURTH WEIGHT - UNDEFEATED. IT HAD NEVER BEEN DONE BUT BECAUSE OF, LET'S CALL THEM STUPID DUMB JUDGES BECAUSE THEY ARE, IT DOESN'T HAPPEN."

JEFF FENECH

2

27 JUNE 1988

TYSON vs SPINKS

WORLD HEAVYWEIGHT CHAMPIONSHIP
TRUMP PLAZA, ATLANTIC CITY, NEW JERSEY, U.S.A.

TALE OF THE TAPE

MIKE TYSON	NAME	MICHAEL SPINKS
IRON MIKE	NICKNAME	JINX
BROOKLYN, NEW YORK, U.S.A.	BIRTHPLACE	ST. LOUIS, MISSOURI, U.S.A.
21	AGE	31
34—0—0	PRE-FIGHT RECORD	31—0—0
30	KO'S	21
5'10"	HEIGHT	6'2.5"
218.25 LBS	WEIGHT	212.25 LBS
71"	REACH	76"
ORTHODOX	STANCE	ORTHODOX

ONCE AND FOR ALL

IT WAS SUPPOSED TO BE A MEETING BETWEEN THE TWO BEST HEAVYWEIGHTS ON THE PLANET BUT, IN REALITY, IT WAS THE DESTRUCTION OF ONE, AND THE CONFIRMATION OF THE OTHER IN THE MOST BRUTAL FASHION.

It is unusual for a fight that would last for such a short amount of time to stand out quite as much as this does, but it would prove to be the pinnacle of Mike Tyson's career at just 21 years of age, a fight that confirmed him as the most talked-about heavyweight since Muhammad Ali and the self-styled 'baddest man on the planet'.

Promoted as 'Once And For All,' this heavyweight showdown was designed to unify the division and produce an undisputed champion. It was the culmination of a series of HBO-backed fights that saw Tyson and Spinks emerge for the final bout after seeing off the likes of James Smith, Trevor Berbick and Tony Tucker on Tyson's side of the draw, and Larry Holmes and Steffen Tangstad on Spinks' side.

As they prepared to face each other Tyson held all three world titles from the major sanctioning organizations – the WBC, WBA and IBF – while Spinks was considered as the unofficial 'People's Champion' with his *The Ring* magazine and lineal titles.

His rise to this position followed an Olympic gold medal as a middleweight in 1976. At first he was more focused on helping his older brother, Leon, become world heavyweight champion, but then he rose up the world's light-heavyweight rankings, became champion and dominated the division until deciding to move up to heavyweight where he defeated the IBF, Ring and Lineal champion, Larry Holmes, to take the world title. He would subsequently be stripped of the IBF title for opting to take a more lucrative fight against Gerry Cooney

"FEAR WAS KNOCKING AT MY DOOR BIG TIME."

MICHAEL SPINKS

rather than the top ranked Tucker.

Tyson had forced his way to the top with sheer brutal power and ferocity. At just 20 years and 145 days of age he became the youngest ever world heavyweight champion when he demolished Berbick. He followed that up by seeing off Smith and then Tucker to claim the WBA and IBF versions as well.

It was not simply his age or his record of wins. It was the destructive way in which he swatted almost all before him in the ring.

With both fighters unbeaten in their careers, it was little wonder their clash became the richest fight in boxing history at the time, grossing over $70M, with Tyson pocketing a record purse at the time of $22M and Spinks a further $13.5M. Donald Trump thought little of making a bid for a record venue fee of $11M to stage it at the Convention Hall next to his own Trump Plaza in Atlantic City.

Neither was it any surprise that the build up was high profile. Both appeared on the covers of TIME, People and Sports Illustrated magazines whilst, ringside on the night, celebrities such as Jack Nicholson, Sylvester Stallone, Madonna and Oprah Winfrey were all present.

Most expert pundits went for Tyson, including Holmes, who had fought them both in recent times.

James Smith said of Spinks winning: "He'd need me to be in the ring with him." Surprisingly, for a 4-1, outsider Spinks received some support from Ali, Sugar Ray Leonard, Floyd Patterson and Archie Moore, all believing the former light heavyweight stood a chance.

Their respective moods pre-fight were telling. A rage had been building inside Tyson for a few weeks leading up to the fight, partly from the death of his trusted friend and mentor, Jim Jacobs, but also due to false claims about abuse published in the media and a published, unauthorized, warts and all biography written by his ex-confidante Jose Torres. At the final press conference Tyson said of Spinks: "I want to take his manhood. I want to rip out his heart and show it to him."

All Spinks could mutter in response was: "A little terror in your life is good."

Moments before the two fighters were due to leave their dressing rooms a commotion broke out inside Tyson's. Butch Lewis, Spinks' manager, noticed a bump in Tyson's gloves and demanded his hands be re-wrapped. "Hold it," he shouted. "Get rid of that or we don't fight." It took Eddie Futch, Spinks' trainer, to be called in and approve the gloves as they had been found. Lewis admitted later it was in part "to put a little psyche on Tyson."

It was a big mistake. An already fired-up Tyson was incandescent with anger. "You know," he whispered into his trainer, Kevin Rooney's ear, "I'm gonna hurt this guy."

Tyson's ring walk would have placed the fear of God in most opponents. There were no robes. No gowns. Just a glowering Tyson in his black shorts, boots and gloves. He marched through the 22,000 inside the venue without a hint of emotion.

No wonder Spinks refused to look him in the eye when the pair faced each other in the center of the ring for the pre-fight formalities.

Tyson went on the attack from the opening bell. Inside the first ten seconds he landed a solid left hook forcing Spinks to cover himself up and retreat to the ropes. A raised elbow from the shorter Tyson provoked a verbal recrimination from referee Frank Cappuccino. "Mike, knock it off," he shouted at the aggressor. "Knock it off." Undeterred Tyson almost ran at Spinks. A left upper cut followed a split second by a right hand forced Spinks down on to his knee, only the second time in his professional career. "That punch paralyzed me," Spinks would admit later. "He hit me in a good spot."

He rose after a count of four and attempted to land a right hander. Tyson dodged the punch and delivered a left-right combination of such force that Spinks hit the deck again.

This time there was no way back. Spinks was counted out and Tyson, whose face remained impassive as he walked back to his corner with his arms outstretched and his palms facing upwards, became undisputed world heavyweight champion after a unification world title fight that lasted just 91 seconds. It was the sixth shortest world heavyweight title fight in the history of boxing.

In total ten punches were thrown – eight from Tyson and two from Spinks – but it was enough for the round to be voted round of the year by The Ring magazine.

Spinks was philosophical afterwards. "I came to fight him like I said I would," he said. "I came up short."

Tyson confirmed what the rest of the world could see almost

"MY TRAINER TOLD ME BEFORE THE FIGHT THAT HE BET BOTH OUR PURSES THAT I WOULD KNOCK HIM OUT IN THE FIRST ROUND. SO I WENT OUT AND KNOCKED HIM OUT IN THE FIRST ROUND."

MIKE TYSON

immediately once the fight began. "The first punch I threw he wobbled a bit," he explained afterwards. "I knew right then that I had him."

This would prove to be Spinks' final fight. He announced his retirement shortly afterwards safe in the knowledge that a distinguished career would never be on the end of such a fearful beating again.

In a sense this was the beginning of the end for Tyson, too. He would win emphatically again, then lose, regain titles before sinking both in and out of the ring but the general consensus remains that this was his greatest performance.

21 AUGUST 1981

SANCHEZ
VS GOMEZ

WORLD FEATHERWEIGHT CHAMPIONSHIP
CAESARS PALACE, SPORTS PAVILION, LAS VEGAS, NEVADA, U.S.A.

TALE OF THE TAPE

SALVADOR SANCHEZ	NAME	WILFREDO GOMEZ
CHAVA	NICKNAME	BAZOOKA
TIANGUISTENCO, MÉXICO, MEXICO	BIRTHPLACE	SANTURCE, PUERTO RICO
22	AGE	24
40—1—1	PRE-FIGHT RECORD	32—0—1
30	KO'S	32
5'6"	HEIGHT	5'5.5"
126 LBS	WEIGHT	126 LBS
68"	REACH	66.5"
ORTHODOX	STANCE	ORTHODOX

BATTLE OF THE LITTLE GIANTS

IT WAS A FIGHT TO LAST THE SANDS OF TIME WITH AN UPSET THAT FEW SAW COMING, BUT ULTIMATELY IT WOULD BE THE LOSER THAT WOULD ENJOY THE BENEFITS OF HIS SPORT AND LIFE.

It was dubbed the 'Battle of the Little Giants' but, in truth, Wilfredo Gomez was the overwhelming favorite to win this bout and add the WBC's featherweight title to his already earned junior featherweight crown.

This was because the fearful Puerto Rican had knocked out all 32 opponents in his 32 wins, with just one draw the only blemish in a near perfect career.

He faced the lesser-known Salvador Sanchez, despite being a world champion in the division above Gomez and having a record almost as good. Sanchez may have been bigger and taller but there was a reason why Gomez was nicknamed 'Bazooka' and he had already predicted a knockout by the third round.

He could not have been more wrong. Sanchez dropped him after just forty seconds into the fight. Gomez looked stunned by this setback as he clambered to his feet. The partisan Mexican crowd inside Caesars Palace roared with their approval.

Sanchez saw a chance to finish it there and then. He moved in for an early finish, battering Gomez and almost sending him back down to the canvas with an overhand right close to his own corner.

Somehow "Bazooka" survived and by the third round had sufficiently recovered to be back in the fight. Over the next three rounds he would regularly score points with his powerful combinations, but in the process his right eye swelled up and then began to close.

By the seventh round the eye was almost closed and his left eye was now also damaged. Despite this Gomez enjoyed his best round, landing a huge left on to Sanchez's chin that saw the Mexican momentarily be lifted off his feet.

Any hopes back in Puerto Rico with the watching fans praying for their hero were dashed in the eighth and what proved to be the final round.

Gomez was almost boxing blind by now. He was badly hurt by a straight right hander from Sanchez that sent him hurtling towards the ropes. Sensing this was his chance the Mexican set upon his injured prey, launching a furious barrage of unanswered blows that saw Gomez sent hanging through the ropes and almost out of the ring.

The extraordinarily brave Gomez, determined not to record a first ever professional defeat, somehow managed to beat the count again but, as Sanchez moved in for what would undoubtedly been a messy end, referee Carlos Padilla had seen enough. He waved his hands to stop the fight and Sanchez was declared the surprise winner by a technical knockout.

Sanchez became an overnight hero in his Mexican homeland, his victory over Gomez catapulting him into national fame. Gomez, in contrast, sunk into a year's depression before recovering and going on to win further world titles in three different divisions.

It would all, however, have a tragic ending. There was talk of a rematch but, just under a year after they fought each other, Sanchez would be killed in a car crash. He was 23 years old.

We will never know what Sanchez might have achieved, of course, but Gomez sent flowers to the funeral and subsequently became friends of the Sanchez family.

He went on to greater feats but he would never forget the night Sanchez delivered a boxing lesson.

08 MAY 2021

ÁLVAREZ VS SAUNDERS

WORLD SUPER MIDDLEWEIGHT CHAMPIONSHIP
AT&T STADIUM, ARLINGTON, TEXAS, U.S.A.

TALE OF THE TAPE

SAUL ÁLVAREZ	NAME	BILLY JOE SAUNDERS
'CANELO'	NICKNAME	SUPERB
GUADALAJARA, JALISCO, MEXICO	BIRTHPLACE	WELWYN GARDEN CITY, HERTFORDSHIRE, U.K.
30	AGE	31
55—1—2	PRE-FIGHT RECORD	30—0—0
37	KO'S	14
5'8"	HEIGHT	5'11"
168 LBS	WEIGHT	168 LBS
70.5"	REACH	71"
ORTHODOX	STANCE	SOUTHPAW

FACE THE FEARLESS

*FOR A WHILE IT WAS A COMPELLING CONTEST UNTIL
THE BEST POUND FOR POUND BOXER IN THE WORLD
PUT AN END TO IT ALL WITH ONE, CRUNCHING PUNCH.*

This would be the moment when the brash Billy Joe Saunders would find out if his fighting could match his talking.

The confident British fighter came to Texas with an unbeaten record and, taller and with a greater reach, he believed that he could be only the second man to beat Álvarez.

That first defeat was by Floyd Mayweather in 'Canelo's' earlier days but, since then, he was older, wiser and so much better that few argued against him being the best pound for pound boxer in the world.

The fight had taken some time to happen. It was due the year before in 2020 but the COVID-19 pandemic delayed it twelve months. In the interim period 'Canelo' had added Callum Smith and Avni Yildirim to his scalps. Now the WBC, WBA and The Ring super middleweight Champion was eyeing up Saunders' WBO crown.

The fight would make history by recording the largest indoor venue boxing crowd ever in America. The 73,126 crowd packed into the AT&T Stadium surpassed the previous mark set by Leon Spinks vs Muhammad Ali II.

The Mexican would start the better of the two, using his feints to create the chance to hammer his opponent hard with body shots. Saunders remained competitive, moving well around the ring and responding with flurries of punches.

Indeed, after falling behind, the unbeaten British fighter had mounted something of a comeback between rounds five and seven, landing 31 punches to 'Canelo's' 18 but, at no time did the Mexican seem unduly troubled.

As the two rose for the start of the eighth round 'Canelo' knew he needed to regain the momentum. What happened next underlined the sheer brutality of boxing and how a fighter's chances can disappear with one punch.

There was no doubt that Álvarez had upped the ante after the previous three rounds. By the end of the round, he had landed 12 of his 23 punches. It was one of these that ended the debate.

Saunders had launched a right hander at 'Canelo' who first evaded it and then responded with a huge right hander which crunched into his opponent's face. The British fighter recoiled in pain and from the force of the punch.

The Mexican knew immediately that Saunders was in trouble. He waved to the largely partisan Mexican crowd packed inside the arena, partly in celebration and partly to incite more cheers.

He moved in for the kill but Saunders, showing remarkable character in withstanding everything 'Canelo' could throw at him, survived until the bell. As he trudged back to his corner, his shoulders slumped and his face wracked in pain, his body language told its own story.

Trainer Mark Tibbs took one look at what turned out to be a fractured right eye socket and waved for the fight to be stopped. "He couldn't see and I didn't get the response I wanted from him," Tibbs explained later. "I had to pull out."

In truth the Mexican was ahead at this stage in any case, landing 73 of 203 punches (35.4 %) compared to 60 from 284 (21.1 %) from Saunders.

'Canelo' thumped his chest in joy. He had been riled by Saunders all week, even being forced to allow the British fighter a larger ring and, unusually, was provoked to predict a knockout between the 7th and 9th rounds. He was not far wrong.

"It was not as difficult as I expected," he insisted later. "I knew it would be the final round. I broke his cheek. He couldn't come out for the ninth."

And that was that. Álvarez added the WBO crown to his super middleweight haul and, in doing so, magnified his position in world boxing. Saunders, in contrast, was taken to hospital.

"IT'S HARD BECAUSE I SAW WHEN HE BROKE HIS CHEEKBONE AND I WENT BACK TO THE CORNER AND I TOLD EDDY THAT I DIDN'T THINK HE COULD CONTINUE, YOU CAN RISK YOUR LIFE AND CAN'T CONTINUE THAT WAY."

SAUL ÁLVAREZ

01 MARCH 1992

FENECH vs NELSON II

WORLD SUPER FEATHERWEIGHT CHAMPIONSHIP
PRINCES PARK FOOTBALL GROUND, MELBOURNE, VICTORIA, AUSTRALIA

TALE OF THE TAPE

JEFF FENECH	NAME	AZUMAH NELSON
MARRICKVILLE MAULER	NICKNAME	THE PROFESSOR
ST PETERS, NEW SOUTH WALES, AUSTRALIA	BIRTHPLACE	ACCRA, GHANA
27	AGE	33
26—0—1	PRE-FIGHT RECORD	33—2—1
19	KO'S	24
5'7.5"	HEIGHT	5'5"
129 LBS	WEIGHT	129 LBS
67"	REACH	68"
ORTHODOX	STANCE	ORTHODOX

PAINFUL LESSON

AFTER A HOTLY-DISPUTED DRAW LAST TIME ROUND THERE WOULD BE NO ARGUMENTS WHEN THESE TWO WARRIORS MET FOR A MUCH-ANTICIPATED REMATCH WHICH ENDED UP BEING BRUTALLY ONE-SIDED.

Jeff Fenech had been on the verge of becoming a four-division world champion when he took on Azumah Nelson in 1991 in Las Vegas. Having ruled the world at bantamweight, super-bantamweight and featherweight he had stepped up to super featherweight to take on the WBC's champion on the undercard of Mike Tyson v Donovan Ruddock 2.

After a fierce twelve rounds, however, the judges declared the contest a draw, which meant Nelson retained the title and Fenech, whose perfect record had its first blemish on it, returned home frustrated and angry with the result.

Most ringside, including Tyson, believed the Australian had deserved the victory against the tough but strangely passive Ghanaian. Fenech was distraught and vowed to right this wrong when Nelson agreed to travel down under to Melbourne for the much-anticipated rematch.

This time it was no undercard fight, but the main event, and 30,000 baying Australians braved the rainstorms in the expectation that their man, desperate to make history against an opponent recovering from malaria, would take one step further from their first meeting.

It would not quite turn out like that.If Nelson was quiet in the first fight, he was quite the opposite in the second. Fenech had managed to keep Nelson pinned to the ropes in Las Vegas, negating his famed punching power by not allowing him the room.

In the first round of this encounter, however, Nelson flew out of his corner and was the aggressor from the off. A right hander caught Fenech by surprise and down the 'Thunder from Down Under' went on to the canvas.

It got worse in the second round. Fenech took another right hander, lost his balance and seemed to slip as he hit the deck. Referee Arthur Mercante saw it differently and counted Fenech until the Australian rose to his feet.

In the third round Fenech finally got Nelson where he wanted him, pinned to the ropes in a corner, but he failed to land a telling blow and then received a cut by his right eye in the fourth round.

Rounds five and six saw the two fighters go toe-to-toe. Fenech appeared to be gaining the upper hand towards the end of the sixth when Nelson suddenly countered and left the contender pleased to hear the ringing of the bell.

Ironically the seventh saw Fenech enjoy his best round. He failed to inflict any damage but undoubtedly won the round. He was behind on points but suggested a comeback was still more than possible.

Nelson, however, begged to differ and ended the debate abruptly in the eighth. Fenech hit the floor for a third time after receiving a left hook full in the face, a second left and then two right handers.

Fenech then made the mistake of rising too soon, as if to say he was not hurt. This was a mistake. Instead of allowing himself to regather his senses he was up but not ready for the inevitable onslaught as Nelson recognized the opportunity to finish it.

He moved in with a left hook, followed by an uppercut and finally a stiff, right hander. Mercante had seen enough and stopped the fight.

It was the plucky Fenech's first taste of defeat and sparked the beginning of the end for the Australian. Four fights later he would retire.

He would return for a fifth, against Nelson, and avenge this defeat. But it was 16 years later, in 2008, when both had long finished with boxing and returned after long, long lay-offs for this one-off third meeting between two men whose best days were long behind them.

"HE WAS FULL OF CONFIDENCE IN THE RING, SO HUMBLE OUTSIDE OF IT THAT HE'S FOREVER ENDEARED HIMSELF TO THE PEOPLE OF GHANA."

KENNETH BOUHAIRIE

29 MAY 2016

BELLEW vs MAKABU

WORLD CRUISERWEIGHT CHAMPIONSHIP
GOODISON PARK STADIUM, LIVERPOOL, MERSEYSIDE, U.K.

TALE OF THE TAPE

TONY BELLEW	NAME	ILUNGA MAKABU
BOMBER	NICKNAME	THE JUNIOR
LIVERPOOL, MERSEYSIDE, U.K.	BIRTHPLACE	KANANGA, DEMOCRATIC REPUBLIC OF THE CONGO
33	AGE	28
26–2–1	PRE-FIGHT RECORD	19–1–0
16	KO'S	18
6'3"	HEIGHT	6'0"
199 LBS	WEIGHT	196 LBS
74"	REACH	74"
ORTHODOX	STANCE	SOUTHPAW

THE RUMBLE IN THE JUNGLE II

AT THE THIRD ATTEMPT TONY BELLEW WOULD TRANSFORM HIS BOXING SUCCESS ON FILM INTO REALITY, WITH A BRUTAL ENDING TURNING AROUND A BRUTAL START.

After two attempts at a world title, at light-heavyweight, Tony Bellew finally had his chance to fulfil a lifelong dream at his preferred weight, and at his perfect venue.

The passionate Everton football fan had been granted his wish to fight for the world cruiserweight title at his beloved Goodison Park, the home stadium of the Liverpool-based club.

The year before he had co-starred in the movie, 'Creed,' as the world light-heavyweight champion, but that was just fantasy for the big screen.This was reality.

Standing in his way was the dangerous Ilunga Makabu. The Congolese fighter had knocked out 17 of his 18 victims, having lost his debut fight.

Makabu was due to meet Gregory Drozd for the WBC's cruiserweight title but the Russian pulled out after an injury and was stripped of his title. Bellew stepped in to fight for what was now the vacant WBC crown.

Unbeknown to everyone except for his own entourage, Bellew had endured a terrible training camp.

"It was a disaster of a training camp," he would reveal afterwards. "Six weeks ago I had a detached rib and a messed up left hand."

"Two weeks ago I was in a hyperbaric chamber trying to recover and getting some oxygen in. If it had been any other fight I would have pulled out and postponed it." But this was not any other fight.

It was a sign of his disruptive training camp that Bellew began the fight in the worst possible fashion.

Buoyed by the roar of 15,000 Bellew fans as he marched out to the same TV cop show theme that the Everton team always use, the home favorite was down on the canvas in the first round by a juddering punch from Makabu. Bellew rose and countered strongly as the first round came to an end.

"The fans were so loud they got me up off the floor," he explained later.

Bellew edged a tight second round and as the third started both did away with defense and went for each other. Makabu, in particular, was so confident with his impressive knockout record, that he threw caution to the wind and went all out against his opponent.

This would prove to be a big mistake. Bellew hit Makabu with some hard right handers before then landing a left-right combination that rocked the clearly hurt Congolese fighter back and onto the ropes. The Liverpudlian then finished his night's work with the perfect left hook that left his opponent knocked out on the floor.

There was concern at first as Makabu remained motionless for a minute until he finally came round.

Then all the emotion poured out of Bellew as he was awarded with the WBC's world champion belt and announced the winner.

"He broke my nose but I have a green and gold belt," Bellew said. "If you had to take my nose off my face for that belt, I'd take it."

"Nothing was going to stop me tonight. That's why I got up off the floor. I achieved the dream tonight. I am world champion."

13 NOVEMBER 1999

HOLYFIELD
VS LEWIS II

WORLD HEAVYWEIGHT CHAMPIONSHIP
THOMAS & MACK CENTER, LAS VEGAS, NEVADA, U.S.A.

TALE OF THE TAPE

EVANDER HOLYFIELD	NAME	LENNOX LEWIS
THE REAL DEAL	NICKNAME	THE LION
ATMORE, ALABAMA, U.S.A.	BIRTHPLACE	WEST HAM, LONDON, U.K.
37	AGE	34
36−3−1	PRE-FIGHT RECORD	34−1−1
25	KO'S	27
6'2.5"	HEIGHT	6'5"
217 LBS	WEIGHT	242 LBS
78"	REACH	84"
ORTHODOX	STANCE	ORTHODOX

THE SEARCH FOR THE TRUTH

THIS TIME THERE WOULD BE NO ARGUMENTS AS
ONE GREAT CHAMPION SAW OFF ANOTHER TO
UNIFY THE COVETED WORLD HEAVYWEIGHT TITLE.

The draw that was awarded after their first meeting was so controversial that all the sanctioning bodies involved accepted an immediate rematch needed to take place. Within a week of Holyfield–Lewis I - a fight virtually everyone felt Lewis had won - Holyfield–Lewis II had been confirmed for eight months later.

On the line was the unification of one of the most coveted titles in world sport - heavyweight champion.

Holyfield began the fight looking like a man who wanted to prove that he could beat an opponent towering over him. He started to use his jab but soon found himself smothered by the British fighter.

The judges gave the first two rounds to Lewis, especially after an uppercut caught Holyfield flush on the chin.

Despite two big right handers to Lewis' face Holyfield found himself behind even more after three rounds but then started to find his way on to the scorecards over the next four rounds.

In the fifth round Lewis sustained a cut over his right eye which he insisted had come from a clash of heads rather than a Holyfield punch.

And in the seventh the fight resorted into a slugfest with Holyfield emerging the better after numerous exchanges of punches. A couple of right handers from the American noticeably wobbled Lewis, too, but Holyfield failed to capitalize on the moment.

From this point, however, the taller man began to take more control. Most had Lewis winning rounds 8 to 11 even though he was tested again in the ninth when Holyfield landed a big right hander, a double jab and an uppercut.

Lewis hit back, though, rocking Holyfield with a big, right uppercut that clearly rocked the American and had him stumbling his way back to his corner.

Holyfield emerged from his corner for the last round like a man on a mission to knock out Lewis. He knew this was what he probably needed to do. But one of Lewis' many qualities was a granite-like chin. Holyfield managed to land one big right hander but the man looming over him barely moved.

As the final bell sounded their reactions told their own story. Lewis raised both arms aloft in celebration. Holyfield trudged back to his corner.

This time there would be no repeat draw nor negative reaction to the verdict. All three judges gave the fight to Lewis, 115-113, 116-112 and 117-111.

The stats backed this up, too. Lewis landed 195 out of 490 punches thrown at an impressive 40%. Holyfield was some way behind, with 137 punches landed from 416 punches thrown at 33 %.

Still, Holyfield had performed better in losing second time round than he had when he drew the first encounter.

Lewis had become the first unified heavyweight world champion in almost seven years.

"I couldn't let my fans or myself down," he explained afterwards. "This has been my dream. At times I was playing with him. I knew I had to unify the belts."

Holyfield was not overly happy with the result but was also philosophical. "Of course, I'm disappointed I didn't get the decision," he said. "I hit him with some great shots and I thought it would catch up with him. I didn't get hurt by his jab and I was able to counter his potshots, but when it falls into the judges' hands you have to live with their decision."

Lewis' reign as undisputed champion was short-lived. The WBA stripped him off his belt when he refused to fight their challenger, John Ruiz, in favor of Michael Grant. Holyfield then beat Ruiz to reclaim the WBA crown while Lewis beat Grant to keep the other belts.

"THAT REMATCH IS UNFORGETTABLE, AND IT WAS DEFINING. YOU'RE UP AGAINST ONE OF YOUR GREATEST PEERS AND YOU'RE ABLE TO SHOW THAT YOU'RE MORE EFFICIENT THAN HE IS. I GOT ALL THE BELTS. NOBODY ELSE COULD SAY THAT THEY WERE THE CHAMPION OF THE WORLD EXCEPT ME. I COULD SAY THAT I WAS THE BADDEST MAN ON THE PLANET."

LENNOX LEWIS

1

30 OCTOBER 1974

FOREMAN VS ALI

WORLD HEAVYWEIGHT CHAMPIONSHIP
STADE TATA RAPHAËL, KINSHASA, ZAIRE

TALE OF THE TAPE

GEORGE FOREMAN	NAME	MUHAMMAD ALI
BIG GEORGE	NICKNAME	THE GREATEST
MARSHALL, TEXAS, U.S.A.	BIRTHPLACE	LOUISVILLE, KENTUCKY, U.S.A.
25	AGE	32
40—0—0	PRE-FIGHT RECORD	44—2—0
37	KO'S	31
6'3.5"	HEIGHT	6'3"
220 LBS	WEIGHT	216 LBS
78.5"	REACH	80"
ORTHODOX	STANCE	ORTHODOX

THE RUMBLE IN THE JUNGLE

IT IS, QUITE SIMPLY, ONE OF THE MOST FAMOUS SPORTING EVENTS, NOT JUST BOXING, IN THE PAST ONE HUNDRED YEARS, A FIGHT WITH A NAME TO REMEMBER AND AN UNFORGETTABLE OUTCOME WHERE, AGAINST ALL THE ODDS, THE OLDER MAN DEFIED LOGIC AND STRATEGY TO CEMENT HIMSELF IN SPORTING FOLKLORE.

Some say this was not only the greatest boxing match of all time, but one of the greatest sporting occasions ever. It had everything. Music, politics, drama, comebacks, an overwhelming favorite against an aging underdog, surprise tactics bordering on the insane and a name used to describe this strategy spoken about to this day. It even had an Oscar-winning docufilm made about the events surrounding and indeed on the day of October 30th, 1974. And the name chosen for the fight, 'The Rumble in the Jungle,' resonates with anyone of a certain age as it approaches its 50th anniversary.

Muhammad Ali had been stripped of his world title after refusing the Vietnam draft. It was a brave stance that met with divided opinion at the time, but it cost him three and half years of his prime time in boxing. When he returned he lost a world title bid against Joe Frazier, in their first of an epic trilogy, and was then destined to fight other challengers and wait his turn. In his absence George Foreman, the 1968 Olympic Heavyweight Champion, had risen to the top, destroying all before him. This included Frazier, knocked down six times in two rounds, and Ken Norton, overwhelmed by Foreman's size, power and sheer intimidating ring persona inside the same distance.

Promoter Don King was the man ultimately responsible for getting this fight on, a meeting between the 25-year-old Foreman who had won his last eight heavyweight bouts inside two rounds, and the aging Ali at 32 considered, despite his enormous success in the sport, as cannon fodder by everyone, including Foreman's camp.

King's challenge was to find $10M to be divided equally between the two fighters, and to find a country to stage it as the size of the event and King's involvement was seen as too big a risk in the United States. His answer was eyebrow-raising. The Zaire (now DRC) dictator, Mobuto Sese Seko, was persuaded by his American advisor to stage the fight to raise positive international profile for his dictatorship, whilst the Libyan dictator, Muammar Gaddafi, provided the financial sponsorship.

Both fighters arrived in Zaire well in advance of the fight due initially on September 25th to train and acclimatise to the tropical conditions, but Foreman received a cut above the right eye and 11 subsequent stitches eight days before the fight from a stray elbow in sparring and the fight was put back a month. A concert as part of the whole event took place regardless on the designed dates featuring the likes of James Brown, BB King and Bill Withers, while Ali went to work on winning the popular vote, running along country lanes to the chant of "Ali Bomaye" from locals running alongside him which, translated meant "Ali, kill him."

The genuine fear, however, was that Foreman could kill Ali, so much so that the Foreman camp even prayed in their dressing room pre-fight to avoid such an outcome. The odds agreed. Ali was the 4-1 outsider. Foreman the 5-1 on favorite. What was unknown until afterwards was that Foreman's preparations were severely dented by the cut and delay.

The first bell sounded at 4am local time, 10pm US Eastern Standard time, in front of 60,000 packed into the open air "20th of May Stadium."

Ali would confound everyone from the start. He emerged from his stool intending to be the aggressor, attacking the champion with a series of disorientating right hand leads without ever setting up his left. Towards the end of the round Foreman began to find the measure of his famous opponent. His size and nous meant he was often able to cut the area of the ring down to his favor, cornering his opponent before striking with his fearsome haymakers. Inside the final minute he managed to catch Ali on a couple of occasions. It was looking good for Foreman but little did he know what was about to take place.

Just before the fight Ali had told his famous trainer, Angelo

"FLOAT LIKE A BUTTERFLY, STING LIKE A BEE. HIS HANDS CAN'T HIT WHAT HIS EYES CAN'T SEE. NOW YOU SEE ME, NOW YOU DON'T. GEORGE THINKS HE WILL, BUT I KNOW HE WON'T."

MUHAMMAD ALI

"MUHAMMAD AMAZED ME, I'LL ADMIT IT. HE OUT-THOUGHT ME, HE OUT-FOUGHT ME. THAT NIGHT, HE WAS JUST THE BETTER MAN IN THE RING."

GEORGE FOREMAN

Dundee, that he had a 'secret plan' for Foreman. It was about to unfold in the second round. As the bell rang he moved towards the ropes and promptly covered up his head with his arms. Foreman needed no second invitation and started to pound the challenger with heavy punch after punch, landing either on Ali's body or deflecting off his arms and elbows.

"Get away from the ropes," an exasperated Dundee shouted from the corner.

"I know what I'm doing," Ali responded.

This tactic remained constant over the next few rounds. Foreman was punching Ali like a punchbag in a gym, but it was proving largely ineffectual. Meanwhile Ali would occasionally counter with straight rights which would find their target and, by the fourth round, Foreman's face was beginning to puff up with bruising.

As the years have passed this fight has taken on almost mythological proportions. One myth is that Ali did nothing else but defend himself. This was not strictly true, except for most of the fifth round when he literally leant on the ropes and invited Foreman to unleash hell. Despite this he appeared unperturbed, at one point smiling and winking at an astonished Frazier watching from ringside. He also used other famous Ali tactics, such as leaning on Foreman in clinches to take all his weight and also taunting his rival. "They told me you could punch, George," he whispered in his ear. "That don't hurt. I thought you were supposed to be bad." This served to infuriate Foreman who responded in exactly the manner Ali wanted, with more, energy-sapping punches failing to score.

"I thought he was just another knockout victim," Foreman admitted later, "until the 7th round when I hit him hard to the jaw and he held me close and whispered in my ear: "That all you got, George?" I realized then that ain't what I thought it was."

In the eighth round Foreman looked a spent force, still trying to knock the challenger out but with much less power and conviction. He managed to manoeuvre Ali to the ropes once more but this time Ali responded, landing several right hooks over Foreman's jab. A five punch combination then followed. This telling attack culminated with a left hook and a hard right straight to the face, forcing Foreman to first stumble and then collapse to the canvas. Beginning to rise on eight he was counted out amid scenes of wild euphoria and astonishment.

For all Foreman's punches Ali's tactic had been proven right even before the final knockout, with all three judges having him ahead on points.

It was the most extraordinary outcome to the most extraordinary fight, and Muhammad Ali proved that night that he could not only take the hardest punch in boxing but also possess the awareness to change tactics and fighting style to counter whatever his dangerous opponent could throw at him. And, at the age of 32, he possessed an enormous heart and nerve to pull this off.

He was now the most famous man on the planet but fights such as this and, later, a third duel against Frazier, a loss of his title and a regain against Leon Spinks and, afterwards, ill-advised bouts against Larry Holmes and Trevor Berbick, would take a terrible toll.

Foreman was never quite the same again, retiring in 1977 before, astonishingly, returning to reclaim the world heavyweight title aged 45, defeating Michael Moorer in 1994 wearing the same, red shorts he wore in defeat to Ali in Kinshasa with Angelo Dundee this time in his corner.

He became great friends with Ali, too, in their later years. "I was asked in 1981 "what happened in Africa, George?"" Foreman admitted much later. "I said: "He beat me. I lost." Before that point I was bitter and only had revenge on my mind but after that I let it go. We then became the best of friends. Ali was the greatest man I have ever known. Not greatest boxer. That's too small for him. Everything America should be, Muhammad Ali is."

"I TOLD YOU ALL, ALL OF MY CRITICS, THAT I WAS THE GREATEST OF ALL TIME. NEVER MAKE ME THE UNDERDOG UNTIL I'M ABOUT 50 YEARS OLD."

CASSIUS CLAY

ABOUT THE AUTHOR

IAN STAFFORD

Ian Stafford is a multi award-winning sports journalist and author, broadcaster, speaker, interviewer and sporting entrepreneur. He has interviewed most of the world's greatest sporting personalities over the past 30 years either in written or spoken form for leading international publications, TV and Radio channels, as well as covered all of the planet's biggest sporting events. Ian is also the author of 25 published books and is the resident writer for Opus, including the F1 Opus, Maradona, Pele, Usain Bolt and, of course, the WBC's Greatest Fights Opus.

OPUS

WWW.THISISOPUS.COM/WBC

First published in Great Britain by OPUS, 2022

OPUS is an imprint of The Luxury Book
Company Limited

Copyright (c) OPUS, 2022

www.thisisopus.com

The authors and publishers have made all
reasonable efforts to contact copyright holders for
permission, and apologize for any commissions
or errors in the form of credits given.
Corrections maybe made to future printings

A CIP catalogue record for this book is available
for the British Library

Paperback ISBN 978-1-8383432-5-5

Printed and bound by Clays UKCIP